SPIRALGUIDE

AA Publishing

Contents

Written by Justin Henderson
Where to sections written by Marael Johnson
Revised and updated by Jane Egginton

Project Editor Laura Linder
Project Designer Alison Fenton
Series Editor Karen Rigden
Series Designer Catherine Murray

Published by AA Publishing, a trading name of AA Media Limited, whose registered office is Fanum House, Basing View, Basingstoke, Hampshire, RG21 4EA. Registered number 06112600.

ISBN: 978-0-7495-6244-1

The contents of this publication are believed correct at the time of printing. Nevertheless, AA Publishing accept no responsibility for errors, omissions or changes in the details given, or for the consequences of reader's reliance on this information. This does not affect your statutory rights. Assessments of attractions, hotels, restaurants and so forth are based on the author's own experience and contain subjective opinions that may not reflect the publisher's opinion or a reader's experience. We have tried to ensure accuracy in this guide, but things do change, so please let us know if you have any comments or corrections.

A CIP catalogue record for this book is available from the British Library.

New edition 2009

Cover design and binding style by permission of AA Publishing
Colour separation by Keenes, Andover
Printed and bound in China by Leo Paper Products

Find out more about AA Publishing and the wide range of travel publications and services the AA provides by visiting our website at www.theAA.com/bookshop

A03805
Maps in this title produced from map data

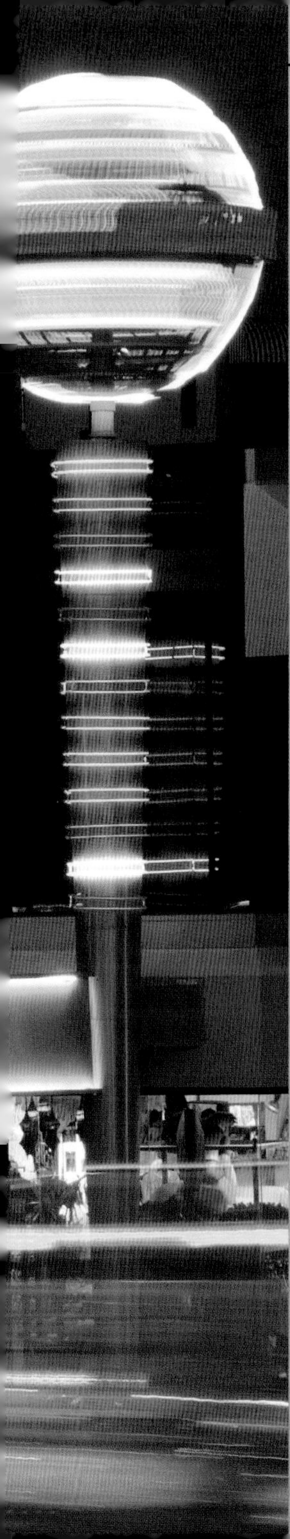

The Magazine

A great holiday is more than just lying on a beach or shopping till you drop – to really get the most from your trip you need to know what makes the place tick. The Magazine provides an entertaining overview to some of the social, cultural and natural elements that make up the unique character of this engaging city.

CRUISING SUNSET

It may be glitzy, brash and corny, but the sun has never really set on Sunset Boulevard. One of LA's longest streets, the "Strip" works as a starting point from where you can see the Hollywood that once was...and what it has become.

History in the Making

In the 1920s, a 12-block segment between Western and Gower avenues became the hub of the nascent movie industry, making it an easy ride from studio to opulent hillside mansion. The neon and billboard center of the world quickly became famous for its glamorous nightclubs, gangsters, luxury hotels and drug-overdosed young (and dead) stars. Through the first half of the 20th century, the major movie studios – 20th Century Fox, Warner Bros., Paramount and Columbia – were located here, just a stone's throw from those lesser studios that cranked out Grade-B Westerns.

Today, only Paramount remains; TV studios, corporate offices and movie museums have moved in. Tours and nostalgia rule here, but the Strip still has some of the most glamorous nightlife on the West Coast.

Hispanic History

East of El Pueblo – the historic heart of LA (➤ 147) – Sunset is dominated by LA's Hispanic culture. Weaving west past the Dodger Stadium, artsy Silver Lake and bohemian Los Feliz, the LA demographic becomes evident. Here the scene is primarily ethnic with Spanish street signs and other neighborhoods called "Little Armenia" and "Thai Town."

Old School

Shortly before Vermont Avenue, Sunset straightens out for its fabled run through Hollywood. To the right lies Barnsdall Art Park and Hollyhock House (➤ 126), designed by Frank Lloyd Wright. On your left is "Gower Gulch," an area that in the 1930s and '40s swarmed with extras from the Westerns shot nearby: Gower Gulch shopping mall stands opposite the old studio. Cruising west, look for the old Warner Bros. Studio at 5858 Sunset.

Crossroads of the World shopping mall is a Sunset Boulevard landmark

SUNSET BOULEVARD – THE MOVIE

By the mid-20th century much of the movie industry had left Sunset Boulevard and moved to "beautiful downtown Burbank." Here the major studios had more room, lower rents and better parking. As studios had also branched out to other cities for on-site locations Sunset Boulevard was showing its age, as did Gloria Swanson's pathological, aging movie star in Billy Wilder's 1950s film *Sunset Boulevard*. Wilder's brilliant black comedy/drama remains among the best films ever made about Hollywood; many movie buffs see the parallel between the out-of-date movie star, trying her best to re-create the tinsel myth of stardom, and the long-gone 1930s and '40s heyday of Sunset Boulevard.

The Hollywood Athletic Club at 6525 Sunset is where Charlie Chaplin and at least three Tarzans (Buster Crabbe, Johnny Weissmuller and Bruce Bennett) swam in the Olympic-size pool.

Global Crossroads

The Crossroads of the World at 6671 Sunset, a landmark 1936 building and one of LA's earliest shopping malls, remains a charming piece of Streamline Moderne architecture.

Fight traffic another few miles and you'll hit Sunset Strip, a 2-mile (3km) stretch of Sunset Boulevard that has been a clubber's paradise since the 1920s.

It's All Rock 'n' Roll

TV pretty much killed the old nightclubs, and so the resilient Strip reemerged as a birthplace of the rock 'n' roll era, with clubs like the

Roxy and Whisky-a-Go-Go (➤ 136) presenting the early gigs of Buffalo Springfield, Elton John and The Doors.

The Future's Bright

The still-thriving Comedy Store (➤ 135) was the scene of early success for Robin Williams, Jim Carrey, David Letterman and Jerry Seinfeld, among others. Comics, actors and musicians of all kinds still flock here, looking for that big chance. If you hit a club on a good night and dress the part of a Someone, you might even get into one of these places to see the future of rock or TV trying out his or her showbiz wings.

Green Scene

At Doheny you enter the greener precincts of Beverly Hills, followed by Bel Air, Brentwood and Pacific Palisades: mile after leafy mile of gently rising and falling Sunset Boulevard lined with exclusive residential enclaves.

The understated sign of the Beverly Hills Hotel (➤ 41) announces its legendary presence. In Bel Air, UCLA's verdant Westwood campus (➤ 85–87) butts up against Sunset, opposite the Bel Air gates. Richard Meier's stunning Getty Center (➤ 80–84) gleams on the hill to the right as you cross the 405 Freeway.

From the Beginning to the End

Farther west, in Pacific Palisades, Sunset glides through a sunny retail village shopping center for yet another suburb with real estate prices affordable by multimillionaires only. Near the end of the Strip you'll pass the Self-Realization Fellowship Lake Shrine (➤ 67), then the air turns salty, the sun starts to set and you find you've traveled from the beginnings of LA in El Pueblo to the western edge of the continent. Will Rogers State Historic Park and Beach (➤ 66–67) are on the left, Topanga Canyon (➤ 68) is up to the right and the wide Pacific Ocean in front of you.

MULHOLLAND DRIVE

Dancing along above Sunset on the rim of the Hollywood Hills, Mulholland Drive, named for the designer/architect of the Los Angeles Aqueduct, which in turn created the highly populated San Fernando Valley, offers some of the best views in LA, as well as some of the most exclusive real estate (Hollywood greats Marlon Brando and Jack Nicholson both have Mulholland addresses). Farther northwest it includes a 7-mile (11km) stretch of barely passable dirt track and snakes a scenic, curvaceous route all the way to the Pacific at the far end of Malibu, providing hours of intense driving and spectacular scenery. Pick it up off the 405 Freeway or from one of the canyon roads winding up from Sunset. And back in town, don't miss David Hockney's monumental view of Mulholland at LACMA, the Los Angeles County Museum of Art (➤ 108–112).

QUAKE, RATTLE and ROLL

Several hundred thousand earthquakes have rattled LA in the past decade. Most passed without comment, some shook the ground enough to be noticeable and only a few caused damage worth mentioning.

The "Big One"

This is not to say it isn't possible that you'll be here for a "Big One." Those in LA on January 17, 1994, got a rude awakening at 4am when King Kong himself picked up and shook every house in Santa Monica. This earthquake, rocketing out of an especially dangerous type of crack in the earth known as a blind thrust fault, hit an imposing 6.8 on the Richter scale, claiming 61 lives, leaving 20,000 people homeless and causing more than $40 billion in damage. At the same time a secondary epicenter slammed Santa Monica, collapsing every brick chimney in the area.

Tiny Tremors

Most quakes – fortunately– are detectable only by a seismograph. An inescapable geological truth is revealed on a seismic map of Los Angeles

Clearing up the damage following a 1941 quake

County: Fault lines are more plentiful than freeways. Southern California straddles the Pacific and North American tectonic plates, two major pieces of the Earth's crust engaged in a grinding slow dance, as the Pacific plate moves northwest 1.6 inches (4cm) per year. For much of the length of this boundary, most visible in the north–south slash of the San Andreas Fault, the plates run parallel; in Southern California, though, the San Andreas takes a turn to the west. This causes the plates to push more fiercely into each other, producing countless faults and near-constant earthquakes. An estimated 200 of these faults could produce a quake of 6 or higher on the Richter scale.

Queen Quake

The San Andreas Fault – perhaps the most famous in the world – is woven into Southern California's sun-baked skin. An 800-mile (1,290km) band of broken and crushed rock, the San Andreas comes onshore near Eureka in Northern California and extends south all the way into Mexico, passing just east of Los Angeles in the Cajon Pass area near San Bernardino. The fault reaches 10 miles (16km) deep into the earth, ranging in width from a few hundred feet to a mile.

Life Goes On

Los Angeles is so disaster-prone – between quakes, the city faces intermittent droughts, regular landslides, annual raging wildfires and daily traffic jams – that people have grown used to it. So Southern California's millions of fatalistic citizens carry on as if the "Big One" will never come – at least not in their lifetime.

The 1994 earthquake caused a section of Highway 14 to collapse onto Interstate 5

FIRST ANGELENOS
The Chumash and the Gabrielinos

Although many of the city's historic roots lie in Mexico, the early Angelenos were by no means here first. Native Americans inhabited California for thousands of years before the Spanish soldiers, settlers and missionaries showed up.

Chumash culture and traditions have been revived in recent years

In Southern California, along the Santa Barbara Channel from San Luis Obispo to Malibu and out in the Channel Islands, the ocean-going Chumash people thrived since well before BC became AD. The Tongva people, later known as the Gabrielinos, occupied villages on Santa Catalina Island (► 21) and in the regions around what is now LA.

Then Came the Colonizers

After a few brief encounters in the 16th and 17th centuries (Juan Cabrillo showed up off the Malibu coast in 1542) the Southern California natives were left alone until the late 18th century, when bands of settlers were sent in from Mexico to shore up Spain's claim to Southern California. Entire cultures were nearly wiped out by the usual imperialist suspects: European diseases, abuse of women, forced religious conversion, enslavement, wholesale theft of land and destruction of a way of life. By the 20th century, only a few Chumash remained. However, the last Chumash survivors reestablished bands of themselves as a recognized cultural group, with a revitalization of traditional languages and crafts and the creation of the Chumash Casino Resort Hotel, near Santa Barbara.

Happy Days

Research ranging from site excavations through oral histories to written accounts by Spanish explorers has created a fairly accurate account of life in pre-colonial Southern California. Not surprisingly, this life was relatively sweet. To some extent Southern Californians today appreciate the same regional verities that the Chumash reveled in 300 or 400 years ago: nature is bountiful and benevolent, but for the odd fire, drought or earthquake.

Cave paintings, a legacy of the Chumash, California's native inhabitants, in Kern County

Chumash rattles made from a variety of materials, including gourds and turtle shells

Coastal Crafts

Inhabiting coastal villages and the islands, the Chumash relied on ocean-going plank canoes with double-bladed paddles for travel. They developed high-quality stonework, including flint blades and large flat-rimmed mortars. The Chumash traded with the Gabrielinos of Catalina to the south for steatite (soapstone), using it to create animal figures, effigies, pipes, fancy beads and cooking pots. They also wove elegant baskets.

Cult and Christianity

The Gabrielinos were said to have initiated the Chinigchinich cult, a mission-era phenomenon that spread over Southern California. The cult's moral and ethical philosophies closely paralleled Christianity, leading many to suspect that it actually emerged after the first missions had been established. The Christians, however, did not take psychoactive herbs such as the toloache plant, or jimsonweed, used by the Gabrielinos to attain visionary states.

Chumash Calendar

The Chumash calendar parallels the Gregorian calendar of the Old World, except that their New Year begins on the winter solstice, around December 22. The Chumash year is divided into 12 months of 30 days each. As with Western astrology, Chumash individuals were assumed to be graced (or cursed) with personality traits inherent in the month of their birth.

What's in a Name

A number of Chumash villages survive in the names of modern California towns and places, including Point Mugu (Muwu), Simi Valley (Shimiyi), Lompoc (Lompo), Ojai (Ahwa'y), Pismo Beach (Pismu) and, most famously, Malibu (Humaliwo)

ON LOCATION

LA teems with film and video action, ranging from game shows, talk shows and sitcoms to location shoots for the latest new movie or commercial. Visitors to Los Angeles can get a piece of the action.

Action!

Plug into LA's movie culture by exploring the open-air set that is the city. Visit the Griffith Park Observatory (➤ 118), which served as the site of the climatic fight scene in *Rebel Without a Cause* (1955), and Grauman's Chinese Theatre (➤ 115), where scenes from the classic *Singin' in the Rain* (1952) and blockbuster *Blazing Saddles* (1974) were filmed. Take a spin down 1017 N Crescent Drive in Beverly Hills where John Travolta tracked down Danny DeVito (using a Star Map) in *Get Shorty* (1995). Make yourself scream at some of the heart-stopping rides at Knott's Berry Farm, which were used in the teen comedy *Knocked Up* (2007).

George Clooney and Brad Pitt starred in the 2001 remake of *Ocean's Eleven*

Musso & Frank Grill on Holywood Boulevard has featured in many films

Newman and Redford on the carousel on Santa Monica Pier in the 1973 film *The Sting*

Dinner and a Movie

Head to Musso & Frank Grill (► 131) on Hollywood Boulevard and sit at the table where George Clooney and Brad Pitt sat in *Ocean's Eleven* (2001). The restaurant was also used as a location in *Charlie's Angels: Full Throttle* (2003). Or tuck into sushi and sake at Yamashiro (► 131), which doubled as a Kyoto teahouse in *Memoirs of a Geisha* (2005).

At the Beach

Santa Monica Pier (► 57–59) was just one of the stars in the classic film *The Sting* (1973). In *White Men Can't Jump* (1992) Woody Harrelson holes up in the Shangri-La Hotel in Santa Monica's Ocean Avenue and plays basketball at the courts at Venice Beach (► 54–55). Fans of the surfside voluptuaries of *Baywatch* will fondly recall scenes from the television series as they tour the beaches of Santa Monica and Malibu. The initial scenes the terrifying *1408* (2007) were shot in South Bay (► 63) and featured Hermosa Beach Pier (► 63, 186) before the story moves to New York.

STUDIO SHOWS

A great way to get "on location" – aside from visiting the sets at Universal Studios (► 120–121) is to become a member of the audience taping for a sitcom, talk or game show. Demand is high, so make reservations as far in advance as possible. **Audiences Unlimited** (tel: 818/753-3470; www.audiencesunlimited.com) distributes free tickets online for *America's Funniest Videos* and some sitcoms starting 30 days prior to the show date. Well organized and sanctioned by the networks and production companies, Audiences Unlimited may be the best way into an actual show. Aside from the network **ABC** (www.abc.com), which uses Audiences Unlimited, some of the other networks may also have their own ticket offers. Consult **CBS** (www.cbs.com) for details of how to get tickets for the *Late Show with David Letterman, The Price is Right* or *American Idol* and **NBC** (www.nbc.com) for *Saturday Night Live* or *America's Got Talent.*

California's CHANNEL ISLANDS

The Channel Islands are easily accessible from Santa Barbara and Ventura: The Chumash used to paddle out here from the mainland in handmade canoes. Modern visitors come to hike, dive, kayak and relax in unspoiled nature.

These small, uninhabited islands are California's answer to the Galapagos Islands (where an assortment of unique animals shaped Darwin's Theory of Evolution), with 145 plant and animal species found nowhere else on Earth. Often these are simply smaller or larger versions of mainland animals – like the island fox, which is the size of a domestic cat, or pygmy mammoths just 4 feet (1.2m) tall.

The Channel Islands National Park

The national park covers 200 square miles (520sq km) of ocean and five islands. From north to south, they are San Miguel, Santa Rosa, Santa Cruz and Anacapa (forming the main cluster) and Santa Barbara Island farther south. Three other islands – San Nicolas and San Clemente, owned by the US Navy, and Santa Catalina (► 21) – are also part of the Channel Islands but do not fall within the national park.

Whales, dolphins, porpoises, sea lion and seal species, and sea otters thrive in the park's protected waters. Gray whales (December to April) and endangered blue whales (spring through summer) pass through as they make their annual migrations; whale-watching trips operate out of Ventura or Santa Barbara harbors.

San Miguel is a breeding ground for an incredible 70,000 California sea lions and 50,000 elephant seals every summer. These can be seen on channel crossings.

Santa Rosa is the second largest island off California's coast, rising to mountainous terrain in its center. A staggering 500 plant species grow here, including Torrey pine – one of the rarest pines in the world. There are also some 2,000 archaeological sites relating to Chumash settlements (► 12–14).

Santa Cruz, the largest island in the chain at 60,645 acres (24,543ha), is also the greenest, with two mountain ranges and a beautiful central valley.

Just 11 miles (17km) from Oxnard's Channel Islands Harbor, Anacapa's proximity to the mainland has made it a day-tripper's destination. Finally, Santa Barbara, the smallest island at 639 acres (258ha), boasts a rocky shoreline and raw landscape where wild flowers and birds thrive.

Advance planning is highly recommended as there is no public transportation, food or facilities on any of the five islands. The National Park Service for the Channel Islands (1901 Spinnaker Drive, Ventura, tel: 805/658-5730; Visitor Center; daily 8:30am–5pm; www.nps.gov/chis) provides information and offers free guided hikes.

Below: Santa Cruz Island scrub jay. Below right: The island fox

Santa Catalina Island

Avalon, on Santa Catalina Island

Twenty-two miles (35km) from the mainland, Santa Catalina Island is another world, as remote from the remoteness of the other Channel Islands as it is from the bustling towns of Long Beach (➤ 173–175) and Newport Beach (➤ 176), to which it is linked by boat services.

Avalon is a little jewel of a resort town, nestled into a balmy bay. Its waterfront restaurants and bars and colorful hillside homes attract many visitors. Displays of 1930s California tilework blanket the town, especially around the waterfront plaza, the walkways that climb the hilly town and at the Moorish Casino on Avalon Bay, an art deco masterpiece.

Two Harbors, in the middle of the island, is also popular, attracting campers and divers. Get off the boat in Isthmus Cove on the side facing the mainland, and stroll the half-mile trail to Catalina Harbor on the ocean side. It's an easy walk, but watch out for roaming buffalo (descendants of the 14 buffalo brought here for the 1924 movie *The Vanishing American*.

The Catalina Island Conservancy (tel: 310/510-2595; www.catalinaconservancy.org) provides permits for hiking (free) and bicycling (expensive). Available the day of your hike, they can be obtained at several locations – check the website for details.

A network of trails invites trekking and bicycling for anything from an hour to several days. In addition to the island's unusual ecosystems, you can take in the breathtaking 360-degree views of the ocean.

ISLAND TOURS

The following operators provide tours of the Channel Islands National Park:

Island Packers (1691 Spinnaker Drive, Ventura; tel: 805/642-1393; www.islandpackers.com) offers whale-watching tours.

Truth Aquatics (301 W Cabrillo Boulevard, Santa Barbara; tel: 805/962-1127; www.truthaquatics.com) specializes in several-day hiking trips and scuba diving in the clear kelp waters.

Channel Islands Aviation (305 Durley Avenue, Camarillo; tel: 805/987-1301; www.flycia.com) arranges flyovers and drop-offs.

Kayaking tours are increasingly popular. Several companies provide tours, including **Aquasports** (111 Verona Avenue Goleta; tel: 800/773-2309 or 805/968-7231; www.islandkayaking.com).

Surf City

Although LA's waves may not be considered first class by international standards, Southern California remains one of the primary centers for surf culture and LA, or a few of its coastal suburbs, continues to claim the crown of Surf City.

In big cities all over the US, far and near from the coast, trendy shops sell surfing gear to style-conscious wannabe surfers. Yet for all its international appeal, surfing is eternally linked with life in Southern California. For this we can thank the Beach Boys and a couple of movies about a girl named Gidget, a Beach Party and an Endless Summer. These pop-cultural products spawned in the late 1950s and 1960s produced a groove that has vibrated around the world ever since.

Point Break

Malibu Point (➤ 60–62) still offers those long, slow, perfect right-point break waves all summer long; Huntington Beach (➤ 176) not only hosts California's biggest surfing event, the Pro-Am, every summer, it also offers a consistent beach break year-round and is the home of the International Surfing Museum and Surfers Walk of Fame.

Sport for All

Aside from these two hot spots, you'll find surfers at almost every beach up and down the Southern California coast. Old guys on longboards, 10-year-olds on dinky shortboards, teenage girls carving up the waves: Surfing has been been an integral part of the LA scene for more than 50 years and the foundation for one of pop culture's most enduring myths. Since 1960, being a surfer, a babe or a dude has been "way cool."

Wave-riding LA style

LA by design

Something startling is happening to LA, particularly in the once down-at-heel downtown, with some stunning new buildings designed by such stellar architects as Frank Gehry and José Rafael Moneo transforming the urban landscape.

Eclectic Architects

The history of the city's construction begins with Hispanic influence – the adobe walls of sunny Spain and Mexico – but the shift from Hispanic to Anglo rule in the mid-19th century altered the design culture, with East Coast-style wood and masonry structures increasingly evident after 1850.

Since then, waves of immigration, benevolent weather and the ubiquitous influence of the car culture and the movies have cast a collective spell over the urban environment. Dozens of great designers and architects have raised their individualistic roofs all over town, from Aztec Modernism to the futuristic 1950s and '60s Googie design seen in many of the city's motels, bowling alleys and coffee shops. Mission Revival, Mediterranean Revival, Craftsman, neo-classic, *beaux-arts*, art deco, Streamline Moderne, Egyptian Revival, pre-Columbian Revival, Los Angeles Modernism and other stylistic trends have all left their mark. LA's architects and designers, like filmmakers, have always felt free to pursue their visions, however iconoclastic or non-contextual they might be.

Above: Cathedral of Our Lady of the Angels. Right: Richard Meier's Getty Center

Non-contextual is key: LA has never possessed a cohesive urban "design" – apart from downtown's relatively new skyline. The overriding visual image of the city is that of a shapeless sprawl of suburbs and subdivisions, a sea of low-rise buildings interrupted by an occasional skyscraper cluster or bank of hills scarred with strip malls and billboards. It all looks as if it were built without any clear plan.

Inspired Structures

The control tower at Los Angeles International Airport (LAX) was created by local architect Kate Diamond, whose 1995 design evokes a stylized palm tree. It makes a fine counterpoint to the nearby Theme Building, the spidery structure that has long been the symbol of LAX.

For buildings by the beach, head to 2709 Main Street in Santa Monica to Chinois on Main (➤ 70). Barbara Lazaroff's interior design here is a playful exercise in excess. At Bergamot Station (➤ 65), Fred Fisher transformed a light industrial complex into a lively arts complex.

Pacific Palisades

Charles and Ray Eames and several inspired Modernists and contemporary iconoclasts have created striking homes such as Lee Kappe houses at 715 and 680 Brooktree, 14629 Hilltree and 596 Dryad. The House at 444 Sycamore Road by Pierre Koenig and Eames House, at 203 Chautaqua Boulevard, are considered the greatest of the Case Study Houses from the late 1940s. These houses are all in or on the edge of Santa Monica Canyon.

In The Hills

Land of monied mansions, Beverly Hills has its share of fine buildings, beginning with its own Civic Center at Santa Monica Boulevard and Rexford, a 1930s creation with a 1980s remodel/expansion by Charles Moore. Not far away at 465 N Beverly Drive is the Paley Center for Media, designed by Richard Meier. The late Frank Israel executed a fine office

Landmark Union 76 gas station in Beverly Hills

building for Virgin Records at 338 N Foothill Road. Don't miss the classic 1950s Union 76 gas station, near the Civic Center. Anderton Court at 328 Rodeo is by Frank Lloyd Wright, one of a dozen high-design statements along "retail row." Nearby, the restaurant Kate Mantilini, by Morphosis, is one of LA's great contemporary statements at 9101 Wilshire.

Hollywood Greats

The standouts among hundreds of interesting buildings in Hollywood include four great old movie palaces: Grauman's Chinese Theatre (6925 Hollywood Boulevard), El Capitan Theatre (6838 Hollywood), the Pantages (6233 Hollywood) and the Egyptian Theatre (6712 Hollywood). The Hollywood Bowl (2301 N Highland) remains one of the country's most sublime outdoor music venues. Houses designed by Frank Lloyd Wright here include Ennis-Brown (2655 Glendower), Hollyhock House (4800 Hollywood Boulevard), Wright's first and some say his best, and the Storer House (8161 Hollywood Boulevard).

Downtown Design

Downtown's award-winning contemporary architecture combines stunning esthetics with cutting-edge technology. Morphosis' ingenious design for the CalTrans District 7 Headquarters (2004) enables the building to close out the midday sun, but at night allows it to open up and blend into the streetscape. In José Rafael Moneo's bold, post-Modernist Cathedral of Our Lady of the Angels (2002), soaring angled surfaces give way to sections of alabaster, which are used in place of traditional stained glass to prevent overheating. Frank Gehry's Walt Disney Concert Hall (2003) is a sculptural marvel of stainless steel sails. Lurking within is an auditorium designed by master acoustician Yasuhisa Toyota. So clear were the acoustics, that rehearsing in the new concert hall, the LA Philharmonic discovered printing errors in their music sheets that had gone unnoticed for years.

Alongside these high-art temples are blockbuster crowd pleasers like the Staples Center sports arena and the LA Convention Center.

ON TOUR

LA's architectural riches spread far and wide, so take it slow and use a map. To more fully explore the design scene, get Michael Webb's *Architecture and Design LA*, or *Los Angeles: An Architectural Guide* by David Gebhard and Robert Winter; alternatively, a number of tours are available.

- **Architours** (www.architours.com) offers focused tours for individuals or on specific topics.
- **The Los Angeles Conservancy** (www.laconservancy.org) has a dozen different tours of historic downtown.
- **Pasadena Heritage** (www.pasadenaheritage.org) offers tours of historic Pasadena architecture.

BEST of LA

Head to exclusive Rodeo Drive and prepare to be dazzled, put your finger on the pulse of city life at Venice Beach Boardwalk, or chill with stars in one the city's memorable restaurants. Experience the best of LA.

Best Day at the Beach

- Swim or snorkel in the clear waters off **El Matador Beach** (➤ 68), 10 miles (16km) north of Malibu on the Pacific Coast Highway. Bring food, drink and snorkeling gear as there are no beach facilities.
- Hit Malibu's **Surfrider Beach** (➤ 62) during a south swell and watch – or join – the surfers catching one of California's great waves.
- **Venice Beach Boardwalk** (➤ 54–56) on a sunny weekend offers lovers of urban craziness a full-tilt experience of this beachfront hangout.
- Take an early morning bicycle ride around **South Bay** (➤ 184–186) You'll love every waterfront mile.

Superlative Sports Event

- Any basketball game that features the Los Angeles Lakers, live at the **Staples Center** (➤ 164), including multimillion-dollar basketball stars on the court and megamillion-dollar movie stars courtside.

Most Memorable Meals

- **Best breakfast** Head to Patrick's Roadhouse (➤ 185), just off the South Bay beachfront, to enjoy home-cooked food with the sound of the ocean rolling across the wide beaches of the Palisades: This is coastal bliss.
- **Best brunch** Live the high life at the beautiful Hotel Bel-Air (➤ 95–96), with brunch by the Swan Pool.
- **LA lunch** Recapture Hollywood's golden era at The Polo Lounge (➤ 99), where you can watch the Hollywood gamesters in action.
- **Sublime steak** For a sophisticated take on the traditional steakhouse, try CUT (➤ 97) at the Beverly Wilshire hotel.
- **Afternoon tea** Luxuriate in the delights of a traditional high tea in Rose Garden Tea Room at the Huntington (➤ 155 and 162).
- **Superb French cuisine** Critics – and diners – agree that Sona (➤ 131) is one of LA's finest restaurants.

City Viewpoints

- Get a perspective of this sprawling city from the **Getty Center** (➤ 80–84), **Griffith Park Observatory** (➤ 118) or anywhere along **Mulholland Drive** in the Hollywood Hills (➤ 9).

Stellar Accommodation

- For old-school elegance, you can't beat the **Beverly Wilshire** (➤ 41). If you can't afford to stay, console yourself with a meal at BLD (➤ 91) or CUT (➤ 97), the hotel's two charming restaurants.
- For rock-star cool, take a villa by the pool at the **Sunset Marquis** (➤ 42) in West Hollywood.
- Sublime spas and general pampering are *de rigueur* at the **Langham, Huntingdon Hotel and Spa** (➤ 43), a grand old dame of a building in leafy Pasadena.
- For cheap chic, get a room at **The Standard Downtown** (➤ 43), where young wannabes hang out.

Grand Gardens

- LA may be a metropolis, but its gardens impress. The sublime **Chinese garden** at the Huntington Botanical Gardens (➤ 155) should not be missed. Combine art with the great outdoors at the **Franklin Murphy Sculpture Garden** (➤ 87) at UCLA or in the garden at the **Getty** (➤ 83).

Stylish Shopping

- The wealthy and flashy flock to **Rodeo Drive** (➤ 88–91); the young and trendy prefer **Melrose Avenue** (➤ 133–134); and pedestrians descend on Santa Monica's **Third Street Promenade** (➤ 72) and the **Old Pasdena** historic enclave (➤ 159, 163).

Cultural Life

- A concert at the Frank Gehry-designed **Walt Disney Concert Hall** (➤ 157–158), which is renowned for its superb acoustics, is a treat for the ears.
- Marvel at the encyclopedic collections from around the world at the **LA County Museum of Art** (➤ 108–111).
- Enjoy modern entertainment at the state-of-the-art **LA LIVE** (➤ 156).

Top: Surfrider Beach, Malibu. Center: Desert Garden, The Huntington. Bottom: Hip shoes for sale, Melrose Avenue

The greening of LA

Visitors to LA can rent an electric car, stay in a green hotel, eat locally grown produce at sustainable restaurants and even go to an eco nightclub. A million trees being planted over the next few years will result in a visibly greener city.

Good to Go

The United States may be not be at the forefront of the fight against global warming, but the citizens of LA are significantly greener than their fellow Americans, using around 30 percent less energy. In the wealthier parts of the city, fuel-efficient electric/petrol hybrids are prolific. Incentives such as free parking at all meters in the city for hybrid vehicles add to their popularity. Such cars are probably the best hope for the city with the highest per capita car ownership in the world; LA may boast one of the US's largest fleets of natural-gas buses, but hardly anybody uses them.

The Green Carpet

Never one to ignore the latest trend, Hollywood has jumped on the environmental bandwagon with great enthusiasm. Actress Julia Roberts, a spokesperson on environmental issues, made much of installing solar panels in her home, and stars like Jennifer Aniston and George Clooney are turning away from gas-guzzling stretch limos and instead are rolling up to prestigious events such as the Oscars in less-ostentatious, more environmentally friendly, hybrid "town cars."

Above: Living garden exhibit at Santa Monica Museum of Art. Right: Laguna Beach

A wind farm at San Gorgonio Pass, Palm Springs

Eating for the Environment

Forget about being a lactose-intolerant herbivore, if you want to join the latest food fad to hit the city you need to become a "locavore" and only consume food produced within a 100-mile (160km) radius. While you might not want to go that far, don't miss sampling delicious Californian produce from farmers markets and gourmet restaurants throughout the city. At The Lobster (► 70), diners can save two birds with one stone, tucking into Californian seafood and seasonal produce while sitting under a solar-paneled roof.

Eco Chic

Saving the planet no longer means wearing a hair shirt and no one knows this better than the glamorous Angelinos. In LA, green is very much the new black. Guests of the exquisite Venice Beach Eco Cottages (www.venicebeachecocottages.com) can relax in nontoxic, sustainable luxury, soaking away their troubles in an energy efficient hot tub made of plastic milk jugs, and congratulate themselves on the tiny carbon footprint resulting from their stay.

Drink to the Future

On sustainable wine tours (www.sustainablevine.com), you can travel in a biodiesel van, visiting vineyards that use organic and biodynamic techniques to grow their grapes. And, at the end of the day, you can make a paperless reservation for Ecco Ultra Lounge (www.eccohollywood.com), the country's first energy-efficient nightclub. Here, hedonists with a head for the environment can enjoy organic cocktails, dance in front of an eco amp and relieve themselves at the club's waterless urinals.

Finding Your Feet

First Two Hours

Arriving by Air: Los Angeles

- Most visitors to LA arrive at the vast, perpetually busy Los Angeles International Airport or LAX (tel: 310/646-5252; www.lawa.org), just 15 miles (24km) from Downtown LA near the beach south of Marina del Rey. LAX is huge but easy to manage, with shuttle buses connecting the airport's eight terminals.
- If you need help, inquire at one of 11 **Traveler's Aid** booths on the lower (Arrivals) level, which offer information on shuttles, cabs, buses, limousines and rental cars.
- Reasonably priced **taxis** are available from the lower (Arrivals) level. LA's obsession with driving means cabs are not as common as in other major cities, so you may have to wait. For trips between the LAX and downtown there is a fixed fee of US$46.50. Remember too that LA's size makes taxis costly for across-town journeys.
- **Shuttles** are a less expensive alternative to cabs, although the number of drop-offs means that they take much longer. Try Xpress Shuttle (tel: 310/323-7222 or 1-800/427-7483; www.xpressshuttle.com) or LAX FlyAway, which runs to Westwood, Union Station and Van Nuys (tel: 866/435-9529; www.lawa.org/flyaway).

Arriving by Air: Outside Los Angeles

- If you are flying in from **nearby states or cities,** you may arrive at one of the region's many smaller airports, which include **Bob Hope Airport** (tel: 818/840-8840; www.burbankairport.com); **John Wayne Airport** (tel: 949/252-5200; www.ocair.com); **Long Beach Municipal Airport** (tel: 562/570-2600); or **Ontario International Airport** (tel: 909/937-2700; www.lawa.org).

Arriving by Train

- **Amtrak** trains arrive from most major US cities at **Union Station** (tel: 213/683-6979) in Downtown Los Angeles. For information call Amtrak (tel: 800/872-7245; www.amtrak.com).

Arriving by Car

- If you're driving in, you'll probably come in on **Interstate 5, US 101, or US 1** from the north or south, or **Interstate 10 or 15** from the east.
- Most rental vehicles are fitted with an easy-to-use in-car navigation system, although a map is still useful for orientation.

Renting a Car

- The city sprawls, and without a rental car you're at the mercy of limited public transportation and taxis if you really want to see the sights.
- It's not normally necessary to reserve a car **in advance** except at the height of summer and around New Year, when the Tournament of the Roses Parade brings in big crowds.
- There are thousands of rental cars available through dozens of agencies (➤ 37); all you need to do is **call a couple of agencies** to track down the type of car you want, then take the agency's own free bus to the company office (the car rental agencies are all located within five minutes' drive of the airport) to pick up your car. Competition is fierce, so look for deals before you travel. All the major companies have websites where you

can shop in advance to track down specific models, prices and discounts. Look for links to Special Offers for the best deals.

- **Rates vary widely** depending on size and style of car and the time of year, as well as the number of days you're renting. You'll get a better deal on weekly rates. Prices follow demand, so they're higher in summer.
- By law, children aged under six, or weighing less than 60 lbs/27kg, must be in a child safety seat or booster. These are available on request for an additional fee. If you require a seat it is advisable to make arrangements in advance.

Orientation

- Aside from Pasadena to the north of Downtown and several excursions out of town, all the destinations in this guide can be found **north of the airport**, and west of Downtown.
- **From east to west** the areas lie as follows: Downtown (and Pasadena), Mid-Wilshire/Hollywood, Westside and Beverly Hills, the Beach.
- There are **distinct districts and neighborhoods** within each of the areas, and hundreds of other suburbs, separate cities and towns, districts and neighborhoods spreading in every direction from Downtown. They are all part of the Greater Los Angeles area.

Tourist Offices

Most LA districts have their own tourist offices. The following cover the primary areas:

- **Downtown**: Los Angeles Los Angeles Visitor Information Center, 685 S Figueroa Street between Wilshire and Seventh, tel: 213/689-8822; www.discoverlosangeles.com, Mon–Fri 9–5.
- **Beverly Hills**: Beverly Hills Visitors Bureau, 239 S Beverly Drive, Beverly Hills, tel: 800/345-2210 or 310/248-1015; www.beverlyhillsbehere.com, Mon–Fri 9–5.
- **Hollywood**: The Hollywood and Highland Center, 6801 Hollywood Boulevard, tel: 323/467-6412; www.discoverlosangeles.com, Mon–Sat 10–10, Sun 10–7.
- **Pasadena**: Pasadena Convention and Visitors Bureau, 171 S Los Robles Avenue, tel: 800/307-7977 or 626/795-9311; www.pasadenacal.com, Mon–Fri 8–5, Sat 10–4.
- **West Hollywood**: West Hollywood Convention and Visitors Bureau, 8687 Melrose Avenue, Suite M-38, tel: 800/368-6020 or 310/289-2525; www.visitwesthollywood.com, Mon–Fri 8–6.
- **Santa Monica**: Santa Monica Convention and Visitors Bureau, 1920 Main Street, tel: 310/393-7593; www.santamonica.com. The Santa Monica Visitors Bureau, tel: 310/467-6412 or 800/544-5319, has a kiosk in Palisades Park at 1400 Ocean Avenue (between Santa Monica Boulevard and Broadway), May–Oct daily 10–5; Nov–Apr 10–4.
- **Marina del Rey**: Marina del Rey Chamber of Commerce/Visitor and Convention Bureau, 4701 Admiralty Way, tel: 310/305-9545, www.visitmarina.com, Mon–Fri 9–5.

Admission Charges

The cost of admission for museums and places of interest mentioned in the text is indicated by the following price categories.

Inexpensive under $6 **Moderate** $6–$10 **Expensive** over $10

Getting Around

By far the easiest way to get around the city is by car. Don't be daunted by stories of the city's traffic. As long as you avoid driving between 7am and 9am and 4pm and 7pm and check local radio or television for the latest traffic news you should be fine. The website www.trafficreport.com/los-angeles also provides real-time traffic information. LA's drivers are some of the most polite in the world and the roads are in excellent condition.

Driving

There are surface street routes connecting all of LA. These "alternate" routes may be less crowded than the freeways at busy times. For example, to get to and from the Getty Center or the Skirball Center from Wilshire or Sunset Boulevard you can take Sepulveda, which runs parallel to the traffic-plagued San Diego Freeway (405). Most drivers rent an in-car navigation system with their car, and this is highly recommended. The following are basic freeway or street routes from LAX to the primary in-city areas.

- To reach **Marina del Rey, Venice, Santa Monica and Malibu**, follow the signs to Sepulveda Boulevard north; get off Sepulveda onto Lincoln Boulevard (here serving as Highway 1) and go north. Marina del Rey, Venice and Santa Monica are around 10–30 minutes away. Malibu lies another 20–30 minutes plus up the Pacific Coast Highway, Highway 1. (To reach the South Bay go south on Sepulveda.)
- To reach **Westside and Beverly Hills**, exit at the airport and follow the signs to the Century Freeway (105) or take Century Boulevard east to the San Diego Freeway (405). Head north on 405 until you cross 10 (the Santa Monica Freeway), then exit on Santa Monica, Wilshire or Sunset Boulevard, depending on your destination. This could take anywhere from 30 minutes to an hour.
- **Downtown Los Angeles** is roughly 20 minutes to an hour away from LAX. Take the Century Freeway (105) east to the Harbor Freeway (110) north; or take 105 to the San Diego Freeway (405) north to the Santa Monica Freeway (10) east to the Harbor (110) north. Take 110 north toward Pasadena to reach the Downtown LA exits.
- To reach **Pasadena** follow directions to Downtown and continue north on 110 (the name changes to the Pasadena Freeway once you're north of LA) to the end. From Downtown LA to Pasadena can take anywhere from 15 to 30 minutes plus.
- To reach **Hollywood or Mid-Wilshire**, take 105 east to 405 north to 10 east to 110 north (toward Pasadena), then take the Hollywood Freeway (101) toward Hollywood. It takes around 30–60 minutes.

Rules of the Road

- Pedestrians always have right of way.
- California state law forbids driving with 0.08 percent or more of alcohol in the blood.It is illegal to have any open bottles or cans of alcoholic drinks in any vehicle (as well as on the street).

Car Rental

- Most rental companies honor **foreign driver's licenses**, but you might want to make sure when making your reservation. It is also helpful to have your **passport** or **international driver's license** available.
- Most companies will only rent to drivers **over the age of 25.** Los Angeles Rent-A-Car (tel: 310/670-9945 or 1-800/441-7368; www.la-rentacar.com)

hires vehicles to those aged between 21 and 25 for a small premium.

- Check to see if your **insurance company** at home covers you for car rentals. Otherwise you may have to pay for per-day surcharges that all rental companies try to impose for liability insurance.
- The best places for specialty car rentals are: **Budget**, The Beverly Hills Collection, tel: 800/227-7117 or 310/274-9174; www.budget.com and **Beverly Hills Rent a Car**, tel: 800/479-5996 or 310/670-2020; www.bhrentacar.com

Car Rental Companies

Alamo tel: 800/327-9633; www.alamo.com
Avis tel: 800/331-1212; www.avis.com
Budget tel: 800/527-0700; www.budget.com
Dollar tel: 800/800-4000; www.dollar.com
Enterprise tel: 800/325-8007; www.enterprise.com
Hertz tel: 800/654-3131; www.hertz.com
National tel: 800/227-7368; www.nationalcar.com
Payless tel: 800/729-5377; www.paylesscarrental.com
Rent-A-Wreck tel: 800/535-1391; www.rent-a-wreck.com
Thrifty tel: 800/367-2277; www.thrifty.com

Public Transportation

Metro

- **Metro information**, tel: 800/266-6883 or 213/922-6000; www.mta.net
- LA's **subway** and **light-rail system** (the Metro) is useful if one of the stops happens to be convenient for you, but its four lines can be useless when trying to get from one part of town to another.
- Trains run every 5–10 minutes during rush hours, every 15–20 minutes otherwise, and the **cost is minimal**.
- **The Red Line** runs from Union Station near Downtown through Hollywood to North Hollywood and beyond into the San Fernando Valley. This line is useful for getting to Hollywood and Universal Studios (➤ 120–123) from Downtown.
- The above-ground **Blue Line** links Downtown with Long Beach and serves as the most heavily used commuter line. You can take this line to see the Watts Towers (➤ 157; get off at the 103rd Street stop) or to reach the *Queen Mary* and other sights in Long Beach (➤ 173–175).
- The **Green Line** connects Norwalk, southeast of LA, with Redondo Beach, southwest of LA.
- The **Orange Line** runs from valley communities to North Hollywood.

Buses

- The system covers the **entire metropolitan area** but can be a time-consuming way to travel due to distances and number of stops – not to mention traffic.
- Fares for bus rides are very economical. Downtown Area Short Hop (DASH) buses charge 25 cents; one travels around Hollywood, while five others go through Downtown every ten minutes or so. DASH routes also take in parts of Mid-Wilshire, Venice, South Central LA and Pacific Palisades. For more information, visit their website, www.ladottransit.com.
- If you're making more than one journey, a pass can save you money. Day, weekly or monthly Metro Passes can be used for unlimited rides on Metro Bus or Metro Rail. Alternatively, buy 10 Metro tokens for one-way bus or rail trips. Convenience stores and Metro Customer Centers sell both tokens and passes.

Cabs

- Traffic regulations make it illegal to hail a cab in LA, except at the airport, train station and major hotels. Phone ahead and have one dispatched by radio.
- Nine taxi companies are authorised to operate in the city (for more details visit www.taxicabsla.org). Vehicles belonging to these companies are easily identified by their **"Taxicab Seal."**
- Taxis can be called from: **Independent Taxi** (tel: 800/521-8294 or 323/666-0050) and **Bell Cab** (tel: 888/235-5222).

Walking, Cycling and Hiking

- Some **good areas for strolling** include Downtown LA, Old Pasadena, Hollywood Boulevard, Sunset Strip, Rodeo Drive and the Golden Triangle in Beverly Hills, and Main Street, the Third Street Promenade and Palisades Park in Santa Monica and the piers and boardwalks on the beach in both Santa Monica and Venice.
- The best cycle route by far is the beachfront path that covers a significant stretch of the **Santa Monica Bay** shore (➤ 184–186).
- The **Santa Monica Mountains and Griffith Park's Hollywood Hills** each have an extensive network of hiking and mountain-biking trails. For information call the **Sierra Club** (tel: 213/387-4287), the **Santa Monica Mountains National Recreation Area** (tel: 805/370-2301) or **California State Parks** (tel: 818/880-0350).

Tours

- The granddaddy of all tours in the city is the **Movie Stars' Homes Tour** run by Starline Tours (tel: 323/463-3333 or 1-800/959-3131; www.starlinetours.com). Starline's **Downtown LA Tour** (daily 9–5.30) is a hop-on hop-off service (over 24 or 48 hours) through downtown on a red, open-top double-decker bus. Its **Hollywood Tour** operates the same way.
- Other established mainstream tour companies include **Gray Line Tours** (tel: 714/978-8855; www.grayline.com) and **Hollywood Fantasy Tours** (tel: 323/469-8184; www.hollywoodfantasytours.com).
- **Los Angeles Conservancy Tours** (tel: 213/623-2489; www.laconservancy.org) take visitors on foot to landmark buildings and historic parts of the city.
- **Los Angeles by Night**: tel: 310/831-1761; www.specialeventsservices.com. Special Events Services takes you to the Grauman's Chinese Theater, Universal City Walk and down the Sunset Strip; expensive.
- **NBC Studio Tour**: 3000 W Alameda, Burbank, tel: 818/840-3537, Mon–Fri 9–3; moderate.
- **Warner Bros VIP Studio Tour**: 4000 Warner Boulevard, Burbank, tel: 818/972-TOUR, Mon–Fri 8:20–4, extended hours during spring and summer; expensive.
- **Universal Studios**: The Studio Tour is one of the many rides at this theme park/studio (➤ 120–121).

  Also visit www.hollywoodtours.us for city, studio and private tours.

CityPass

LA is part of the CityPass network, a multiattraction pass that gets discounted admission at four LA attractions (Hollywood Entertainment Museum, Starline Tours, Red Line Tours and the Hollywood Museum). Available for 30 days from the first use, and priced at $49.95 ($39 for kids under 12), passes can be bought at any of the attractions or online at www.citypass.com. The ticket can be used at either the Hollywood Museum or Red Line Tours, not both. For information tel: 888/330-5008.

Accommodations

When choosing a hotel in LA, first decide where you want to stay, as each of the city's main neighborhoods has its own character and offers a very distinct experience.

The city encompasses the Downtown business district, surf-and-sun beaches, the chic Westside and Beverly Hills, traditional old Pasadena and the undeniable lure of Hollywood.

A celebrity haunt on the Westside or Beverly Hills will be accompanied by sky-high rates, while a less flashy motel or hotel in Downtown or even at the beach may be positively seedy. LA caters to all budgets. If you're here for a convention or business, one of Downtown's full-service high-rises may serve well, but for ocean breezes with your latte try Santa Monica. All of the major hotel and motel chains are here. Additional options include bed-and-breakfasts and apartments.

Visitors should take into consideration the city's vast size – and its inadequate (and, in places, nonexistent) public transportation system. A Metro subway system now links Downtown to Hollywood, and buses operate in many parts of the city; nonetheless, almost everyone will want a car to make the most of a visit. Most types of accommodations provide parking facilities, but some tack on surcharges, and others offer only valet parking. Accessible rooms are readily available for travelers with disabilities, and smokers can sometimes request a smoking room.

When to Go

Weather is rarely a factor in LA's moderate climate. Summer months and holidays usually glean the most visitors, especially to the beaches and theme parks. Flexible travelers will often be able to pick up some great deals during off-peak times. At any time, it's best to make advance reservations – especially if you have your heart set on staying in one of the more glamorous spots.

Information

- AAA, Automobile Club of Southern California, 2601 S Figueroa Street, 90007, tel: 213/741-3686 or 800/222-1333; www.aaa-calif.com).
- Los Angeles Visitor Information Center, 685 South Figueroa Street, tel: 213/689-8822; www.discoverlosangeles.com

Diamond Ratings

- AAA tourism editors evaluate and rate lodging establishments based on the overall quality and services. AAA's diamond rating criteria reflect the design and service standards set by the lodging industry, combined with the expectations of our members.
- Our one (💎) or two (💎💎) diamond rating represents a clean and well-maintained property offering comfortable rooms, with the two-diamond property showing enhancements in decor and furnishings. A three (💎💎💎) diamond property shows marked upgrades in physical attributes, services and comfort and may offer additional amenties. A four (💎💎💎💎) diamond rating signifies a property offering a high level of service and hospitality and a wide variety of amenities and upscale facilities. A five (💎💎💎💎💎) diamond rating represents a world-class facility, offering the highest level of luxurious accommodations and personalized guest services.

Hotel/Accomodations Prices
The price ranges below are for the least expensive double room per night, excluding 14 percent hotel tax.
$ under $200 **$$** $200–$300 **$$$** over $300

At the Beach

Beach House Hermosa $$$

A boutique hotel, the Beach House Hermosa enjoys a wonderful location right on the coastal path of the relaxed Hermosa beach. The rooms are supremely comfortable, with balconies, real fire places and kitchens, and prices reflect this. The complimentary breakfast is a simple, no-nonsense affair. If you can afford it, the Beach House Hermosa is a great choice for both romantic and family holidays.

202 E1 1300 The Strand, Hermosa Beach 310/374 3001; www.beach-house.com

Best Western Gateway Hotel Santa Monica $$

As those familiar with the Best Western chain will know, the reason to stay here is no-frills accommodation at a very affordable price. This hotel is a mile (0.5km) from Santa Monica beach, but for those without a car, a shuttle bus (until 8pm) and local bus service run from outside the hotel. The free underground parking is a real bonus and the staff is generally very friendly.

198 A1 920 Santa Monica Boulevard, Santa Monica 310/829 9100; www.gatewayhotel.com

Channel Road Inn Bed-and-Breakfast $$

Tucked into Santa Monica Canyon, just one block from the beach, this architectural prize consists of the original 1915 shingle-clad Colonial Revival house plus a third-floor addition. The house is filled with period antiques, and all 15 rooms are individually decorated and have private baths; some rooms boast fireplaces, views and decks, although there are no real ocean views. Breakfast is served on the patio or in the cozy breakfast room. A hot tub is on hand, bikes are provided, and some fine restaurants are within walking distance. The staff is as charming as the accommodations.

202 D2 219 W Channel Road 310/459-1920; www.channelroadinn.com

Fairmont Miramar Hotel Santa Monica $$$

Known locally as the "Miramar," this fine property evolved from Santa Monica founder Sen John P Jones's private mansion. Past guests have included such notables as JFK (when he was a senator) and Jackie, Greta Garbo and Clark Gable. Today's Miramar draws international visitors and families primarily. Accommodations are in the original character-soaked brick building, charming bungalows or contemporary Ocean Tower. The lushly landscaped property is just across from the Palisades bluff and beach access, and a short walk from Santa Monica Promenade.

202 D2 101 Wilshire Boulevard 310/576-7777 or 800/441-1414; www.fairmont.com

Hotel Casa Del Mar $$$

Sitting directly on the sand, this local landmark sprang to life in 1929 as the glamorous Club Casa Del Mar. After a $60 million renovation, the eight-floor Italian Renaissance building reopened in time for the millennium. Many of the rooms and suites face the water, while others are just a tiptoe away. All units are beautifully appointed, with fresh flowers, excellent sound

ystems and fabulous white marble bathrooms. The seafood and sushi restaurant is worth a visit in itself. Relaxing massages can be had in a cabana facing the bay or in the privacy of your own room.
202 D2 1910 Ocean Front Way
310/581-5533 or 800/898-6999;
www.hotelcasadelmar.com

The Inn at Venice Beach $
This modern motel sits just a couple of blocks from the beach and the delightfully eccentric Venice Boardwalk. Though not luxurious, the flavor is that of a European inn, making it a sterling choice for moderately priced accommodations near the ocean. Airy rooms feature high-beam ceilings, and complimentary continental breakfast is served.
202 E2 327 Washington Boulevard
310/821-2557 or 800/828-0688;
www.innatvenicebeach.com

Westside and Beverly Hills

Avalon Hotel $$$
The Avalon manages to combine retro '50s chic with contemporary cool. Most of the one-time motel's rooms have been renovated to a funky modern standard: Check when making a reservation, as some have yet to be overhauled. The hotel is just moments from the heart of Beverly Hills, the staff is charming and the Blue on Blue restaurant and bar attracts the beautiful people.
198 B1 9400 W Olympic Boulevard
310/277-5221 or 800/670-6183;
www.avalon-hotel.com

Beverly Hills Hotel $$$
Known as the "Pink Lady," this has been the quintessential Los Angeles glamour spot since 1912. Just about anyone who is, was or wants to be anyone in Tinseltown has either stayed, dined or cocktailed in this classic property. Impeccably renovated, the hotel still sports its signature banana-leaf wallpaper in the corridors, and acres of lush tropical landscaping. Most of the celebs bed down in one of the high-priced bungalows, but all rooms are beautifully appointed, with pampering staff at your beck and call. Dealmakers and stargazers still congregate in the famous Polo Lounge (► 99).
199 D3 9641 Sunset Boulevard, 90210
310/276-2251;
www.thebeverlyhillshotel.com

Beverly Hilton $$
The Beverly Hilton, a venerable Beverly Hills hotel that had become embarrassingly lackluster, found a savior in celebrity-owner Merv Griffin. A complete renovation re-glitzed this popular behemoth, with 570 guest rooms, elegant ballroom and Trader Vic's Polynesian restaurant (one of LA's long-time favorite haunts) for tiki ambience and knockout rum concoctions.
198 C3 9876 Wilshire Boulevard
310/274-7777 or 800/922-5432;
www.beverlyhilton.com

Beverly Wilshire $$$
Right in the heart of the Beverly Hills triangle, this Four Seasons hotel sits on Rodeo Drive like a glamorous grand old dame. For nearly 75 years, the well-heeled have swept into its splendid lobby, an area graced with Greek columns and armfuls of fresh flowers. Ask for one of the rooms in the old building, which are infinitely better than those in the newer, more modern annex. The spa is slick, although the pool area is rather cramped. The BLD restaurant (► 91) is perfect for any time of day, while the CUT steakhouse (► 97) is a must – if you can get a table. A free silver Rolls Royce taxi service operates within 3 miles (5km) of the hotel.
199 D3 9500 Wilshire Boulevard
310/275-5200 or 1-800/545-4000;
www.fourseasons.com

Élan Hotel $–$$
In a great location between Beverly Hills and West Hollywood, the Élan Hotel offers very reasonably

priced rooms and genuinely friendly staff. It is just minutes away from the Beverly Shopping Center and a short walk from the numerous eateries of Restaurant Row. The rooms are spotlessly clean with good amenities, although there is no swimming pool. A basic buffet breakfast is included in the price, and the wine and cheese reception every evening between 5 and 7pm is a lovely touch.
199 E3 8435 Beverly Boulevard 866/203-2212 or 323/658-666; www.elanhotel.com/

Luxe Hotel Rodeo Drive $$$

The Luxe Hotel offers contemporary elegance in a prime spot on Rodeo Drive. Although the rooms are on the small side, there are some that have spacious balconies. Others overlook the luxury shops of the most famous stretch of Beverly Hills (try to avoid the so-called "courtyard view" rooms). The hotel has an attractive restaurant and provides guests with free internet connection, as well as the use of a business center with two computers.
199 D3 360 N Rodeo Drive, Beverly Hills 310/273 0300; www.luxehotelrodeodrive.com

Hollywood, Midtown and Universal Studios

Best Western Sunset Plaza Hotel $

It doesn't draw the hippest crowd in town, but the Best Western Sunset Plaza, with its heart-of-the-Sunset-Strip location and reasonable rates, is hard to beat. All of the hotel's 100 rooms have modern appointments, while some have Jacuzzis. Complimentary continental breakfast, a swimming pool and tours that depart from the hotel lobby make this a particularly attractive choice.
199 E4 8400 Sunset Boulevard 323/654-0750 or 800/421-3652; www.bestwestern.com

Chamberlain West Hollywood $$$

An apartment complex transformed into a boutique hotel, the Chamberlain is in a pleasant residential part of West Hollywood. The hotel has 114 spacious rooms, a fitness center and a rooftop pool with stunning views of the city. Close to the Sunset Strip and Santa Monica Boulevard.
199 D3 1000 Westmount Drive, West Hollywood 310/657-7400 or 800/201-9652; www.chamberlainwesthollywood.com

Dunes Inn Sunset $

Dunes Inn is a no-nonsense, no-frills motel-style operation. It may not offer star quality, but what it lacks in luxury, it more than makes up for in price; accommodations here are some of the most competitively priced you will find in Hollywood. Rooms are on the small side and functional, but with plenty of singles on offer. There is a bar and restaurant, as well as free Wi-Fi and ample parking. It is easy to check availability and prices, and even make reservations, online. There is a sister property at 4300 Wilshire Boulevard in the city.
200 B3 5625 Sunset Boulevard, Hollywood 323/467-5171; www.dunesla.com

Hollywood Roosevelt Hotel $$

Site of the first Academy Awards presentation since opening in 1927, the legendary Hollywood Roosevelt is synonymous with stardom. Across from Grauman's Chinese Theatre, the hotel reeks with Tinseltown's glory years when the likes of Ernest Hemingway, F Scott Fitzgerald, Errol Flynn and WC Fields were permanent fixtures. The guest rooms vary in size, but all have comfortable decor, and some even come with resident ghosts. Teddy's Lounge provides strong cocktails and a taste of old Hollywood glamour.
199 F4 7000 Hollywood Boulevard 323/466-7000 or 800/950-7667; www.hollywoodroosevelt.com

Sunset Marquis $$$

The Sunset manages to be both cool and incredibly comfortable. It is rock-star fabulous (there's even a recording studio downstairs), with helpful, welcoming staff. Suites, highly desirable villas and two swimming pools are set in peaceful, tropical gardens. The full-menu room service (with perhaps the best burgers on the planet) is available around the clock, although there is also a small and rather formal restaurant. Don't miss a cocktail or two in intimate, low-lit Bar 1200 where musicians and music business types gather.

199 E4 1200 Alta Loma Road, West Hollywood 310/657-1333 or 800/858-9758; www.sunsetmarquishotel.com

Downtown and Pasadena

The Langham, Huntington Hotel & Spa, Pasadena $$$

The historic hotel building surrounded by extensive gardens has been a landmark in leafy Pasadena since 1907. Formerly a Ritz Carlton hotel, the Langham still retains the grand interiors and traditional service of its forerunner. There is a full service spa where guests can rent bicycles for trips to nearby Old Pasadena, and during the summer you can indulge in martinis and manicures by the pool. Enjoy a meal in the award-winning restaurant, The Dining Room, as well as breakfast and lunch on the poolside terrace.

201 E3 1401 South Oak Knoll Avenue, Pasadena 626/568-3900; http://pasadena.langhamhotels.com

Millennium Biltmore Los Angeles $$

The Biltmore, opened in 1923, is one of LA's most cherished hotels. Designated a Historical Cultural Landmark, the restored Italian Renaissance-style structure was used for early Academy Awards presentations, headquarters for JFK's 1960 presidential campaign, and other high-profile events. Public areas are exquisite and ornate, but many of the units are smallish. Thoughtful service, a health club and an upscale bistro-and-sports bar add to the allure.

197 D4 506 S Grand Avenue 213/624-1011 or 800/245-8673; www.millennium-hotels.com

The Standard Downtown $–$$

A youngish, sophisticated crowd flocks to this hotel that does something rare: it succeeds in being both chic and inexpensive. Deliberately defying expectations, the hotel promotes itself as "anything but standard." Choose from six types of rooms; those with a bath, instead of just a shower, cost more. Hotel guru André Balazs is responsible for the interior, with funky beanbags and shag-pile carpets – even on the walls. Events, including DJs and performance art shows, take place regularly, adding to the cool, contemporary vibe. There are plenty of comforts too, from minibars to a 24-hour restaurant, as well as a swimming pool.

197 D4 550 S Flower Street 323/650-9090; www.standardhotels.com

Westin Bonaventure Hotel and Suites $$$

The 35-floor-tall, futuristic-looking Bonaventure is usually filled with conventioneers and business travelers – many trying to find their way around. The dramatic lobby and "cylinder-like" glass towers can be confusing to maneuver (and easy to get lost in), so helpful staff are usually on hand to set you straight. The hotel is always bustling, and many people drop in just for a ride on the exterior glass elevator, a drink in the 34th-floor revolving bar, or a meal in the sky-high restaurant with panoramic views of the city.

197 D4 404 S Figueroa Street 213/624-1000 or 800/937-8461; www.starwoodhotels.com

Food and Drink

Angelenos are devoted "foodies" – in fact this is where the label originated. Celebrity chefs Wolfgang Puck, Michel Richard, Joachim Splichal and many others rose to superstar status at their LA restaurants. While plenty of places are relegated to the "see and be seen" crowd, they are still outnumbered by a staggering assortment of casual cafés and inexpensive eateries, many specializing in local, seasonal produce.

- Thanks to LA's diverse population, a wide range of restaurants, serving cuisines from around the world, can be found in just about every neighborhood.
- The mild climate and low rainfall mean that **alfresco dining** is available in every season, and many establishments have outdoor heaters on their patios.
- **Vegetarians** need not worry about finding suitable fare; both casual eateries and fine restaurants offer meatfree dishes, and vegetarian cafés and health food stores are prevalent in most areas of the city.
- You can choose from **trendy clubs, clubby lounges, hip bars, neighborhood pubs and local dives**. California wine, imported beer, martinis and margaritas are perennial favorites. However, in this land known as the "cocktail nation," you'll be able to order just about any concoction.
- Make **reservations** in advance for the most popular spots, especially those that cater to celebrities.

Eating and Drinking on a Budget

- Many of the finest restaurants allow walk-ins to **sit at the bar** and order off a far **less expensive**, yet still high-quality **bar menu**.

Guide to Neighborhoods

Most neighborhoods have a conglomeration of eateries, ranging from inexpensive and quick to savor-every-crumb. Here's a snapshot.

- **At The Beach** The Santa Monica Promenade is full of restaurants, bars and sidewalk cafés. The Venice Boardwalk is great for cheap eating. Many plush seaside hotels combine fine dining with ocean views. Along the Pacific Coast Highway, you'll find some pricey seafood restaurants, though the occasional supermarket (on the east side of the highway) offers picnic supplies for a pittance.
- **Westside and Beverly Hills** Dress up and dig deep in your wallet for the famous restaurants near Rodeo Drive and those associated with glamorous hotels. Dine with the less-affluent student population in Westwood Village and on the UCLA campus.
- **Hollywood** The Hollywood-Highland complex is filled with dining outlets, and Hollywood Boulevard offers more. Sunset Strip's luxury hotels and the notable restaurants on and around Melrose Avenue are the places to go for trendy food and star clienteles.
- **Downtown and Pasadena** Nearly all of the large hotels and boutique operations feature multiple dining facilities – from refined, white-glove service to brasseries and poolside terraces. Old Pasadena is dotted with popular bistros and sidewalk cafés.

- **Lunch** at the smarter spots is often as delightful as dinner (particularly when there's an ocean or city view) and can reduce the cost significantly.
- **Early-bird dinners** can be especially good value and are offered by many restaurants, including some of the high-end establishments.
- **Fast food and take-out** in LA doesn't necessarily mean a trip into one of the international chains. You'll find many one-of-a-kind ethnic food stands.
- Put together a **picnic** to eat at the park or beach. Groceries are relatively inexpensive, and fruits and vegetables are fresh year-round.

Practical Tips

- **Dress codes** are rarely enforced in this casual town; however, some of the more elegant restaurants require that men wear jackets and ties, otherwise "smart casual" reigns.
- **Lunch** is usually served from around noon to 2pm, **dinner** from 5pm until 10 or 11pm. Various **coffee shops, delis and take-outs** work 24 hours a day, as do a large number of **supermarkets**.
- The legal **drinking age** is 21 and ID is often required. Most bars stop serving alcohol at 2am, but some after-hours clubs continue until dawn.
- **Sales tax** will be added to the check. Expect to leave a 15 to 20 percent tip, depending on service. Restaurants often automatically add a tip for groups of six or more.

Recommended Places to Eat and Drink

Each of the major chapters features a list of recommended places to eat and drink. This is by no means exhaustive, but rather a select group of some of the more interesting, memorable and famous locales.

Diamond Ratings

As with the hotel ratings (➤ 39), AAA tourism editors evaluate restaurants on the overall quality of food, service, decor and ambience – with extra emphasis given to food and service. Ratings range from one diamond (💎), indicating a simple, family-oriented establishment to five diamonds (💎💎💎💎💎), indicating an establishment offering such culinary skills as an ultimate dining experience.

Bests...

...all-day dining: BLD (➤ 91)
...beachside hangout: Beachcomber Café (➤ 71)
...celebrity spotting: Spago Beverly Hills (➤ 98)
...dim sum: Empress Pavilion (➤ 160–161)
...nostalgia bar: The Polo Lounge (➤ 93, 99)
...Old Timer: Musso & Frank Grill (➤ 131)
...snack: Pink's Famous Chili Dogs (➤ 132)
...sophisticated Sunday brunch: Hotel-Bel Air (➤ 95)
...seaside seafood: The Lobster (➤ 70)
...steak: CUT (➤ 97)
...sushi: Matsuhisa (➤ 98)

Restaurant Prices

The $ amounts indicate the average price for a three-course meal, excluding tax, drinks and service, for one person.

$ under $30 **$$** $30–$60 **$$$** over $60

Shopping

Enormous malls, elite shopping "streets," ethnic districts and street vendors all provide a bounty of goods running the gamut of the price scale.

Malls and Department Stores

- The five-floor Hollywood and Highland complex (➤ 127–128) adjacent to Grauman's Chinese Theatre combines shopping with entertainment and nightlife.
- **Other popular malls** are located throughout the city and include Beverly Center, Westfield Century City and Westside Pavilion (Westside and Beverly Hills); Santa Monica Place; and ARCO Plaza, Broadway Plaza, and Seventh Market Place (Downtown).
- **The Grove at Farmers Market** is an open-air shopping center near the Mid-Wilshire area. There is a 14-screen movie theater here and places to eat.
- Almost all the malls are anchored by at least one department store. **Macy's** and **Robinsons-May** are the biggest entries in the mid-price category. **Nordstrom, Neiman Marcus, Barney's Beverly Hills** and **Saks Fifth Avenue** are the high-end stores.

Specialty Districts

- Both sides of **Rodeo Drive** in Beverly Hills are lined with exclusive (and expensive) jewelers, boutiques, designer showrooms and salons.
- **Melrose Avenue** has shifted gears from the old "super hip" days, with vintage wear and trinkets dominating the strip between La Brea and Citrus avenues and high-end home decor showcased along the western edge near the Pacific Design Center.
- Though still a tourist haven, Santa Monica's **Third Street Promenade** has usurped Melrose. This three-block, pedestrians-only thoroughfare (anchored by Santa Monica Place mall) is lined with mid-price and chain stores, cafés and takeouts, and always seems to throng with visitors.
- You'll find even more shops and art galleries along **Montana Avenue** and **Main Street** (both in Santa Monica), or join the **UCLA** crowd in **Westwood Village**, where Westwood Boulevard and adjacent streets still offer a "village-type" shopping experience.
- In **Pasadena**, Colorado Boulevard and South Lake Avenue are centers of shopping action.
- **Universal CityWalk** at Universal Studios Hollywood (➤ 122–123) features an eclectic mix of retail outlets among the nightclubs and eateries.

Ethnic Shopping

- **Olvera Street**, a pedestrians-only historic park across from Union Station, is steeped in Mexican clothing, trinkets, pottery and other goods.
- **Chinatown and Little Tokyo**, both nearby, are the perfect areas to pick up exotic treasures from the Far East.
- Near Museum Row, **Fairfax Avenue** – headquarters for the Jewish community – is the place to purchase Judaica, curios and deli, deli, deli.

Other Shopping Options

- Don't overlook **museum shops**, rich in books, prints and other items.
- For discounted merchandise head to Downtown's **Garment District**, making the Cooper Building (860 S Los Angeles Street) your first stop.
- On the first Sunday of each month **Pasadena's Rose Bowl** becomes a vast **flea market** (open 8–3) where you can barter for just about anything.

Practicalities

- Most shops are **open** daily from 10–9. Some shops, particularly in Beverly Hills, close earlier. Those in the tourist areas often **keep later hours**.
- Some of the more exclusive Rodeo Drive establishments are **open by appointment only**.
- An **8.25 percent sales tax** will be added to any purchase price.

Bests...

...accessories: Fred Segal (➤ 72, 134)
...book store: Book Soup (➤ 134)
...department store: Barney's Beverly Hills (➤ 101)
...designer shopping: Rodeo Drive (➤ 100–101)
...jewelry: Tiffany & Co (➤ 100)
...museum shop: Getty Center (➤ 80–84), LACMA (➤ 108–112)
...shopping mall: Beverly Center (➤ 134)
...pedestrian-only shopping: Third Street Promenade, Santa Monica (➤ 71), Old Pasadena (➤ 163)
...vintage clothing: Aardvark's Odd Ark (➤ 133)

Entertainment

As the undisputed entertainment capital of the world, Los Angeles stands at the forefront of the movie, television and music industries.

Movies and Television

- Many of the **Golden Era movie theaters** still reside on Hollywood Boulevard, with others in Westwood Village and the Downtown area.
- **Independent movie houses**, although a rare breed, can be found in the Los Feliz, Westside and Santa Monica areas.
- **Multiplexes** are found at most malls and shopping centers. Check out **UCLA** (tel: 310/206-3456; www.cinema.ucla.edu), **USC** (tel: 213/740-2311; www.usc.edu) and the **American Film Institute** (tel: 323/856-7600; www.afi.com) for independent releases and film festivals.
- For a **behind-the-scenes** look at the movie-making process visit **Universal Studios Hollywood** (tel: 800/864-8377; www.universalstudioshollywood.com) and **Warner Bros** in Burbank (tel: 818/ 972-8687; www.warnerbros.com). For more information on city tours ➤ 38.
- **Television** runs nonstop, offering choices from movie classics and foreign films to sports and sitcoms. **Cable** is available at most hotels, and premium pay-for-view stations are often thrown in as a bonus. To be part of the television audience, **tickets** to most shows (free and on a first-come basis) should be requested in advance (➤ 17).

Theater, Dance and Music

- Made up of four venues, including the prestigious Walt Disney Concert Hall (tel: 323/850-2000; www.laphil.com), Downtown's **Performing Arts Center** (tel: 213/972-7211) hosts major musicals, comedies, dramas and new works, and is the seasonal home to the Los Angeles Opera, Los Angeles Philharmonic Orchestra and the Los Angeles Master Chorale.

- The **Pantages Theater** (➤ 135) in Hollywood also hosts spectacles.
- Other notable venues include the **Kodak Theatre** (➤ 128) at the Hollywood and Highland complex, the landmark **Pasadena Playhouse** (➤ 164) and the **Geffen Playhouse** near UCLA (➤ 102).
- Major **concerts** are held at the **Staples Center** (➤ 164) and **Shrine Auditorium** (➤ 164) and in the **Gibson Amphitheater** (➤ 123). Come May or June, locals pack picnics for the extraordinarily popular **Hollywood Bowl** (➤ 128) concerts with a roster of jazz and classical music series, top-name individual performances and the Philharmonic's summer season.
- The **Greek Theatre** (➤ 136) in Griffith Park also presents well-known performers in an **outdoor** setting.
- **Clubs, lounges and bars** around town (particularly in West Hollywood and along Sunset Strip) are filled with blues, jazz, rock and dance music every night of the week.

Outdoor Activities

- **Water** enthusiasts can surf, swim, windsurf and kayak from Venice to Malibu. (Some **beaches** are designated for swimmers or surfers only, and lifeguards are not always on hand, so be wary of riptides.)
- **Cyclists and joggers** will find specially designated paths throughout the entire city (Palisades Park, Brentwood's San Vicente Avenue and the Venice Boardwalk are local favorites) and in **Griffith Park** (➤ 118).
- **Golf and tennis** can be played at public courses and parks. Many top-class hotels have tennis facilities and can arrange country club access.
- **Hikers** will find excellent trails at **Will Rogers State Historic Park** (➤ 66–67) in Pacific Palisades or farther afield in the **Angeles National Forest** (north of Pasadena, in the San Gabriel Mountains, tel: 626/574-1613; www.r5.fs.fed.us/angeles).
- In winter, **skiing** and other **snow sports** can be enjoyed in the San Gabriel or San Bernardino mountains.

Spectator Sports

- Downtown's **Staples Center** (➤ 164) is home to the **Los Angeles Lakers** and **Los Angeles Clippers** basketball teams as well as the women's **Los Angeles Sparks**. The NHL's **Los Angeles Kings** play hockey at Staples.
- The National League's **Los Angeles Dodgers** play professional baseball at **Dodger Stadium** (near Downtown; www.dodgers.com) and the American League's **Los Angeles Angels of Anaheim** hold forth at **Edison International Field** (near Disneyland, tel: 714/634-2000, http://losangeles.angels.mlb.com).
- LA still lacks a professional **football** team, but you can watch the **UCLA Bruins** at the Rose Bowl in Pasadena (tel: 310/825-2101, http://uclabruins.cstv.com/) and the **USC Trojans** at the Coliseum (tel: 213/740-GOSC, http://usctrojans.cstv.com). The Galen Center is the new USC basketball arena. For information: www.usc.edu/neighborhoods/galencenter.
- Play the **ponies** at Hollywood Park (in Inglewood, near LAX; tel: 310/419-1500; www.hollywoodpark.com) or famous Santa Anita Park (in Arcadia, tel: 626/574-7223; www.santaanita.com), both with seasonal schedules of thoroughbred racing.

Practical Information

The "Calendar" section in Sunday's *Los Angeles Times* provides complete listings for all events (www.latimes.com). The Los Angeles Convention and (tel: 213/689-8822; www.discoverlosangeles.com) has detailed information on current events, or ➤ 193–194.

At the Beach

Getting Your Bearings

The beaches of Los Angeles stretch from the northwest end of Malibu down to the south end of Santa Monica Bay and beyond, but connoisseurs generally agree that those strands north of LAX, from Marina del Rey to Malibu, provide visitors with the most compelling selection of seaside activities. The ritzy Marina gives way to Bohemian energy at the Venice

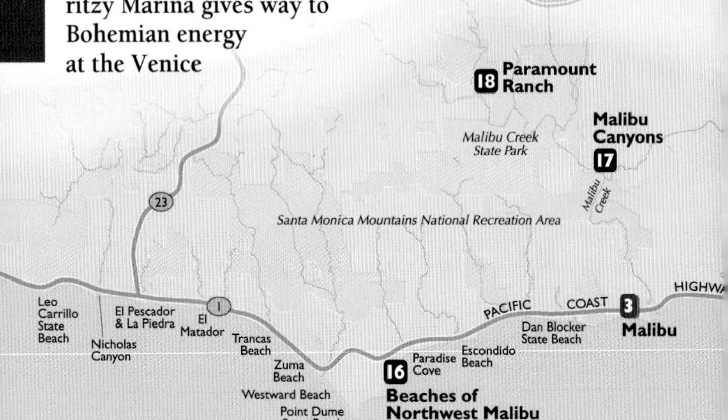

Boardwalk, while Santa Monica and its Pier, Promenade and Palisades Park offer laid-back beach-town vibes. Farther north, visitors ogle Malibu's movie-star colony and miles of pricey waterfront real estate. The once-dilapidated pier is in action again and there are some magnificent public beaches ranging from crowded surf spots to deserted coves. The Santa Monica Mountains loom over Malibu, a vast rural sanctuary on the edge of the city. Whales and dolphins frolic offshore.

This western edge of LA consists of small, primarily wealthy towns: Malibu, Pacific Palisades, Santa Monica, Venice and Marina del Rey northwest of the airport (the focus here), and a tight cluster of other towns to the south. Some are independent cities, others are tentacles of the vast LA octopus; together they form an extensive urban waterfront, one unlike any other place on earth. Here you'll find surfers with dreadlocks and aspiring movie stars, jugglers with chain saws and guitarists singing the blues. On LA's wild and wacky beaches, the circus is in town every day.

Page 49: Lazy days at Venice Beach

At Your Leisure

★ Don't Miss

In a Day

If you're not quite sure where to begin your travels, this itinerary recommends a practical and enjoyable day at LA's beaches, taking in some of the best places to see using the Getting Your Bearings map on the previous page. For more information see the main entries.

8:00am

Enjoy breakfast in Venice or Santa Monica (Patrick's Roadhouse, ➤ 185, is a great spot), then drive northwest on the Pacific Coast Highway. You'll pass 14 **Will Rogers State Beach** (➤ 67; take a quick jag up Sunset Boulevard for a look at the 13 **Self-Realization Fellowship Lake Shrine,** ➤ 67, below). Continue on to Malibu. Lined with super-expensive waterfront housing on your left and the Santa Monica Mountains on your right, the Pacific Coast Highway (PCH) offers a scenic cruise into this starstruck beach town. Weekdays, the rush-hour traffic headed the other way serves to remind of the price people pay to live in paradise.

9:30am

Stop at Malibu Surfrider Beach just north of the Malibu Pier for a walk along the California surf scene. Stroll around the point to glimpse the 3 **Malibu Lagoon** (➤ 61) and the 3 **Malibu Colony** (➤ 62). Take a little time to walk up the Colony beach (stay below the high tide line and you won't be trespassing) and you just might see a few movie or TV stars catching some early rays.

11:00am

Enjoy a tour of the **Adamson House and Museum** (➤ 61). The tile decoration is stunning, and the museum offers an intriguing look at life on the old Spanish ranchos of Malibu.

12:00noon

Stop for lunch locally at Beachcombers Café, right on Malibu Pier for a Kobe burger or healthy salad in an atmospheric spot. Then head to one of the gorgeous **beaches** farther northwest (➤ 68): La Piedra, El Matador, El Pescador and Nicholas Canyon beaches are especially appealing. Drive up one of the canyons, spend a couple of hours on the beach or explore the mountains.

3:00pm

Head back to Venice (below) or Santa Monica. Stroll **Palisades Park** (➤ 182), **2 Santa Monica Pier** (➤ 57–58), and/or **1 Venice Boardwalk** (➤ 54–56). Enjoy a cycle ride or an inline skate tour along the beach. If art's your thing, head up to **9 Bergamot Station** (➤ 65) and check out Santa Monica's lively gallery scene.

5:30pm

Savor a sunset cocktail with a view on the Santa Monica Pier (the Mexican place at pier's end has good margaritas), on the boardwalk or in one of the restaurants on Ocean Avenue.

6:30pm

Dine at one of the fine restaurants on **11 Montana Avenue** (➤ 66), **7 Main Street** (➤ 64 and 70–71) or elsewhere in Santa Monica or Venice. After dinner, stroll **Santa Monica's Third Street Promenade** (➤ 72) – it's a lively scene.

Venice Beach and Boardwalk

The Venice Beach Boardwalk has been a bohemian beachfront hangout since it opened in 1905. Over the decades it has seen good times and bad, but has always attracted a spirited, pleasure-seeking crowd. Today, that crowd unselfconsciously puts on a show, creating one of the most entertaining public spectacles in all of Southern California.

The history of Venice stretches back to 1904, when a "visionary" real-estate entrepreneur named Abbot Kinney took control of 160 acres (65ha) of marshy beachfront land south of Santa Monica, and decided to create a town modeled after the great Renaissance city-state of Venice, Italy. Kinney drained the marshes and created an 18-mile (29km) network of working canals. He imported a few authentic gondoliers, built a pier, added theaters, planned restaurants and cafés, and erected a fancy hotel designed after St Mark's Basilica in Venice. He threw a Grand Opening party on July 4, 1905, and sold many an overpriced canal-front lot; but then most of his investors built bungalows instead of mansions, and his vision of palazzos lining the canals never came to pass.

Visitors enjoy Venice's laid-back vibe

Bicycling is a good way to see Venice and there are rental outlets all along the Boardwalk

Venice's Decline

Subsequently, when Venice visitors demanded cheaper thrills, Kinney obliged, enhancing his fiefdom with amusement park rides, a casino, arcades and other attractions. In the 1920s, pollution from oil derricks to the south began to wreak havoc in the canals and soon, although the Boardwalk continued to thrive, many of the canals were filled in and the city began a long, slow slide into decay.

New Life

In the late 1950s and 1960s, artists began moving into the area, and it took on some bohemian cachet. The money always follows the artists, and so it went in Venice. With ritzy Marina del Rey to the south and pretty Santa Monica to the north, Venice has been transformed. Today, real estate along the Boardwalk is outrageously expensive, and the neighborhoods clustered around the last of the canals (now dredged and cleaned) have emerged as expensive residential enclaves.

Anything Goes

Venice can be pricey, yes, but exclusive, no. On a hot summer day, just about anything goes here, from Hare Krishnas chanting to Rastafarians juggling, to street vendors plying their wares, most of it legal. A trip through this informal performance-art spectacle is a must for any visitor curious about LA's cultural *zeitgeist*. If you want to see Venice on skates or a bicycle, you'll find them for rent all up and down the Boardwalk. On foot or on wheels, you'll encounter a constant stream of interesting characters. Wheelers and walkers are separated, so you won't have to worry about being flattened by cyclists, bladers or skateboarders. There are plenty of restrooms along the way, where you can change if you want to swim, or have a go at surfing on one of the soft-top (safer) surfboards or boogie boards for rent at various stands along the Boardwalk.

A WALK THROUGH THE VENICE CANALS

Abbot Kinney's grand Venetian vision, ironically enough, has been partly realized in the millennium, with new, expensive residences fronting Venice canals. There are only a few canals left, in a small enclave just south of South Venice Boulevard; and many of the decades-old homes here are relatively modest. However, there's no denying that this bucolic neighborhood has undergone a renaissance, powered by skyrocketing real-estate values and the inventive flair of some imaginative architects. Focus on the homes along Dell Avenue. Roam up and down the Courts, enjoy views from the bridges and admire the ducks and boats in the canals. It is a lovely, pleasantly tranquil scene, a wonderful assemblage of old houses mingled with the occasional ultra-contemporary architectural marvel. You can stroll the district in an hour, then head back to the beach.

A body-building contest at Muscle Beach

By Design

Check out the last colonnaded remnants of Kinney's vision of Venice on and off the Boardwalk on **Windward Avenue.** On the beach south of Windward, musclemen flex their pecs, pumping heavy iron in the **Muscle Beach** outdoor weight-lifting center. Among the houses lining the Boardwalk between Windward Avenue and Washington Boulevard to the south are several designed by architectural superstars such as Frank Gehry and Antoine Predock.

Slip over to Main Street for a stroll, head east on Venice Boulevard and right on Dell Avenue for a tour of the Venice Canals (► 55) or walk south from Washington onto the quieter sands of the Marina Peninsula.

TAKING A BREAK

Figtree's Café, on the Boardwalk (429 Ocean Front Walk; tel: 310/392-4937; www.figtrees.com; daily 9–9, inexpensive–moderate) offers everything from great French toast and homemade muffins for breakfast to pasta and burritos for lunch.

---

202 E2

Santa Monica Visitors Bureau and Santa Monica Convention & Visitors Bureau (► 35)

VENICE BEACH AND BOARDWALK: INSIDE INFO

Top tips Don't hang out on or near the Venice Boardwalk **at night**. After dark the area can be unsafe.

- LA's beaches are often **overcast** until midday, especially in spring and early summer ("June gloom"). If you want guaranteed sunshine, stay inland in the morning and hit the beach in the afternoon (and wear **sunscreen**; even with a cooling breeze off the ocean that California sun can fry your skin).
- Don't be surprised if the **water feels cool**, even cold; it rarely reaches 70 degrees Fahrenheit (21 degrees Celsius) before late summer.
- If you're **driving** come early, especially in summer, and especially on weekends. The parking lots fill up very fast at the beaches at these times.

2 Santa Monica Beach and Pier

Less than half an hour's drive from central LA is the relaxed resort of Santa Monica. With its 2.5-mile (5.5km) stretch of sandy Pacific beach, and its pedestrian-only shopping, long promenade and old-fashioned pier – complete with amusements, aquarium, and even a solar-powered Ferris wheel – it's the perfect spot to shop, walk and play.

Santa Monica Pier, rebuilt and restored, still retains its old-world charm

Santa Monica Pier

A hundred years after its 1874 debut, the Santa Monica Pier was in danger of being swallowed up by history – and the ocean. In the winter of 1982 a series of powerful storms knocked half of the Pier into the ocean; what remained was seriously damaged and in danger of collapse. Fortunately, it was restored, rebuilt and tidied up. The wonderful **old sign** arching over the entrance to the Pier at the foot of Colorado Boulevard beckons the fun-seeking multitudes, as it has done for the past 50 years or more.

For a taste of old-time beachfront resort atmosphere, the Pier is the place to go. The recent changes have not undermined its carnival-like ambience, generated by fast-food stands, arcades, curio shops, drinking and dining spots, amusement park rides and one fine carousel. The beautifully restored **Looff Carousel**, built in 1922, features 44 handcarved wooden horses. With calliope music setting the mood, you can take a rollicking 50-cent ride into history.

Pacific Ocean Park, a fantastic, shambling giant of an amusement park pier just down the beach, competed with the Santa Monica Pier for decades, until it was demolished in the 1970s. In a nod to remembered glories, the Santa Monica Pier's amusement park section is named **Pacific Park.** It offers a scaled-down sampling of the rides, including the roller coaster and a Ferris wheel that take riders on a thrilling and scenic ride over the water's edge.

At the end of the Pier, stoic anglers still drop their lines in search of perch, rockfish or whatever else lurks around the pilings below. Note that the waters here are not very clean, especially after rainfall: nearby storm drains flush whatever comes off the streets into the ocean.

Get close to the creatures of the sea at the **Santa Monica Pier Aquarium**, where different tanks are filled with underwater creatures including octopus, sea stars and crabs. On Shark Sundays at 3:30pm, visitors can see sharks being fed and hear an informative presentation.

On Thursday nights in summer, swing bands and other musical stylists draw crowds of revelers and dancers for twilight concerts.

STEPPING OUT
If you're up for a walk in non-beach territory, go up or down the **Adelaide Steps** on Fourth Street – the view from either top or bottom is awesome (► 183).

North of the Pier

North of the Pier, the parallel cycle and walking paths skirt the sands of Santa Monica Beach on one side, with a mix of old-time mansions, modest bungalows, beach clubs and architect-designed pads of the *nouveau riche* on the other.

The rides of Pacific Park on Santa Monica Pier illuminated at night

The Looff Carousel, immortalized in the 1973 film *The Sting*

This so-called **Gold Coast** once boasted a 120-room house owned by William Randolph Hearst, that flamboyant newspaperman, and one of the larger houses still standing once belonged to Peter Lawford, a Kennedy in-law (the house reportedly served as a trysting place for John F Kennedy and Marilyn Monroe).

South of the Pier

South of the Pier, the beach offers a children's playground, with stone sculptures for climbing. Nearby, volleyball courts feature world-class action, and gymnastic apparatus conjures another bit of historic lore: the original **Muscle Beach** was here. In the 1930s and 1940s, the first "hardbodies" of the modern world strutted their stuff on the Santa Monica sand.

Several swanky new hotels have opened south of the Pier, but the old-time charm lingers. Cyclists, bladers, walkers, skateboarders and joggers jostle for space on the boardwalk and cycle path, while surfers hit the waves, sun-worshipers bake in the sands, and seagulls vie for leftover fast food.

TAKING A BREAK

One of the few restaurants in Santa Monica with a sea view, **The Lobster** (1602 Ocean Ave, tel: 310/458-9294; www.thelobster.com, $$) lets you feast on fine seafood and strong cocktails while surveying the beach scene. There's casual, bar-stool dining at the back if you just fancy a beer and a bowl of crispy squid.

---

202 D2

Pacific Park

202 D2 310/260-8744; www.pacpark.com Summer Sun–Thu 11–11, Fri–Sat 11am–12:30am; winter/spring Mon–Thu noon–6, Fri noon–midnight, Sat 11am–midnight, Sun 11–9 Free; rides inexpensive–moderate

Santa Monica Pier Aquarium

202 D2 1600 Oceanfront Walk 310/393-6149; www.healthebay.com Tue–Fri 2–6pm, Sat–Sun 12:30–5 Inexpensive

SANTA MONICA BEACH AND PIER: INSIDE INFO

Top tip Park in one of the public parking structures on Second or Fourth streets (flanking the Promenade on Third Street), and **walk** to the Pier, rather than fighting the crowds of cars going into the beach lots.

3 Malibu

Native Americans, Spanish colonists, American ranchers, movie stars and surfers have all planted their flags on or near Malibu Point, laying claim to what has become some of the world's most expensive turf. Malibu Point, the little curve of beach tucked in between the pier (built in 1945) and the lagoon, remains one of California's premier summer surf breaks – famous as one of a handful of beaches whose denizens created the surf culture in the 1950s and 1960s.

For centuries, the Chumash (➤ 12–14) had a settlement at Malibu Point, which they called *Humaliwo*, "the place where the surf sounds loudly." Then, Spanish explorer Juan Cabrillo anchored offshore in October 1542, while an overland expedition from Mexico came in 1775, seeking to shore up Spanish claims. One member of the expedition was José Bartóleme Tapia. Expedition diaries established that the group camped in Malibu Creek on February 22, 1776.

Years later, Tapia was granted "rights of concession" (a sort of property lease) to Rancho Malibu Topanga Sequit. Tapia Park, a few miles up the road in Malibu Canyon, honors his memory. The ranch changed hands several times over the decades and ended up in the hands of the Rindge family.

The iconic Malibu Pier and Surfrider Beach, Malibu

A tiled fountain at the Adamson House

Malibu Origins

Frederick Hastings Rindge, a wealthy poet, philosopher and philanthropist, and his wife, May, purchased the 13,350-acre (5,400ha) Malibu Ranch in 1892. They built a big house in Malibu Canyon and created a successful cattle- and grain-raising operation. Then a run of bad luck hit: The original house burned down in 1903, a victim of a Malibu brush fire. (Such fires have been torching expensive Malibu houses ever since.) Two years later Rindge died. His wife struggled to keep the ranch intact, but after a 17-year legal battle the Pacific Coast Highway sliced through her land. Undaunted, at the age of 65 she began construction of a family "castle" on a ridge behind Malibu Point. Mrs Rindge died in 1941 before the castle was completed, and it was sold to the Franciscans in 1942. It has served as the Serra Retreat since; the monks even rebuilt after another raging fire burned much of it to the ground in 1970.

Adamson House and Malibu Lagoon

Lost in that fire were thousands of irreplaceable Malibu tiles that had been created in the Malibu Pottery, founded by the Rindges in 1927 on Carbon Beach to produce Mediterranean-style tiles. The pottery turned out magnificent work, much of which decorates the **Adamson House** on Malibu Point. This Moorish-Spanish Colonial Revival house, built in 1929 by the Rindge's only daughter, Rhoda Rindge Adamson, features an impressive array of Malibu tiles both inside and out, on walls, floors and ceilings, along with hand-carved teak doors, lead-framed bottle-glass windows and other refinements.

Since 1981, the house and grounds have been open to the public. A gift shop on the grounds sells reproductions of Malibu tiles, and a small museum in the house explores Malibu history. Colorful gardens and sweeping lawns roll down to the edge of the **Malibu Lagoon** (now a bird refuge and state park) on one side, and the surfing beach on the other. The house's guided tour comes highly recommended; the Persian "carpets" made of tile are worth the price of admission, as is the view of the Malibu surf from the living room and veranda.

Malibu Colony

Malibu Lagoon is now a state park and bird refuge

The Malibu Colony started in the late 1920s, when the Rindges sold the beach to Art Jones, who promoted it by leasing lots to movie stars. Residents in the 1930s included such old-time stars as Clara Bow, Ronald Colman, Gloria Swanson, Gary Cooper and Barbara Stanwyck. Today the colony is a gated private enclave, every house is worth millions and movie stars and other very rich people still live there. Stroll up from Surfrider Beach – stay below the high-tide line on the beach and you can't be accused of trespassing.

Surf Colony

Ronald Colman played a role in promoting Malibu's other contribution to American culture: surfing. He was great friends with the Hawaiian surfer/promoter Duke Kahanamoku. The Duke taught surfing to Colman and other members of the Santa Monica Swim Club, and soon they had "colonized" the break at Malibu.

Malibu Pier

New life was breathed into the old beach haunt when Malibu Pier was reopened in 2008. Built in 1905 and closed in 1995 due to severe storm damage, the iconic pier was reopened at a cost of $10 million. Visitors can now not only take a stroll down the historic construction, but also drink or dine at its café, and take a memorable whale-watching or coastal tour.

TAKING A BREAK

Feel the breeze in your hair at the **Beachcomber Café** (tel: 310/456-9800; www.thebeachcombercafe.com, $$), on Malibu Pier.

---

202 C2

Adamson House and Malibu Lagoon Museum
23200 Pacific Coast Highway, PO Box 291, Malibu 310/456-8432; www.adamsonhouse.org Museum and House: Wed–Sat 11–3 (also tour 2). State Park: daily 9–7 Inexpensive; parking free on the Coast Highway or moderate in the parking lot just south of the entrance

MALIBU: INSIDE INFO

Top tip The Pacific Coast Highway gets crowded even on weekdays in summer. To avoid traffic try to get on the road to the beach before 11am and plan on returning late.

At Your Leisure

4 The South Bay

Heading south from Marina del Rey, the southern half of the Santa Monica Bay beachfront consists of a series of small towns, including (from north to south) Playa del Rey, El Segundo, Manhattan Beach, Hermosa Beach, Redondo Beach, Torrance and the Palos Verdes Peninsula, which forms the bay's southern edge. All have their charms, but the most pleasant are Hermosa Beach and Manhattan Beach, small cities steeped in seaside surf culture. Each has an attractive municipal pier (Manhattan's features a small aquarium), and low-key retail areas with restaurants, bars and stores right off the beach. Parking is often hard to find, so one good way to get here is via the cycle path from Venice and Santa Monica to the north (➤ 184–186). Farther south, King's Harbor at Redondo combines the tacky, fast-food/curio-shop pleasures of an old-time wharf with a yacht harbor; beautiful Palos Verdes replicates the overpriced waterfront real estate of Malibu, *sans* movie stars. South Bay waters are cleaner than Santa Monica's, so this is a good area to swim or surf.

202 E1

5 Marina del Rey

Home to several thousand boats and several hundred flight attendants and pilots (LAX is 10 minutes away), Marina del Rey has one claim to fame: the world's largest man-made yacht harbor. Fisherman's Village (13855 Fiji Way) is a pseudo-Cape Cod-style shopping and dining complex. It's also the embarkation point for a variety of boat tours, ranging from high-speed catamaran trips to leisurely cocktail cruises. If you are after physical activity, head to the marina, where there is windsurf, pedal-boat and surfboard rental, as well as fishing trips.

Sitting at the halfway point of a 22-mile (35km) coastal cycle path, with Santa Monica to the south and Venice beach to the north, it's

Fisherman's Village, Marina del Rey

the perfect spot to rent a bicycle or skates. Circle the marina via Washington, Lincoln and Culver boulevards and make your way to the northwest corner of Playa del Rey, the quiet, out-of-the-way beach town on the marina's south side.
202 E2 310/305-9545; www.visitmarina.com

6 California Heritage Museum

Any museum that features an exhibition called "COWABUNGA – The Santa Monica Bay Surfing Experience 1907–1967" can't be all bad. Other California-inspired topics explored at the CHM include Malibu tiles, Depression glass, Arts and Crafts furniture, Mexican folk art and Hawaiiana. The museum's mission is to inspire collectors with displays of American decorative and fine arts, California-style. The building itself is worth a look: The museum is housed in an 1894 Queen Anne-style house (now a historic landmark) designed by renowned architect Sumner P Hunt for Roy Jones, son of a Santa Monica founding father.
202 D2 2612 Main Street at Ocean Park Boulevard, Santa Monica 310/392-8537; www.californiaheritagemuseum.org Wed–Sun 11–4 Inexpensive; free parking

The 1894 building housing the California Heritage Museum is an historic landmark

Giant binoculars mark the entry to the former Chiat/Day/Mojo Headquarters on Main Street, Santa Monica

7 Main Street, Santa Monica

An eclectic shopping and dining artery that parallels the beach, Main Street is noteworthy for a couple of Frank Gehry buildings: the Edgemar complex (2435 Main), and the former Chiat/Day/Mojo Headquarters building (340 Main) between Brooks and Clubhouse to the south. Start and end a stroll with these two and you will have done Main Street. Chiat/Day/Mojo presents the street with an eccentric, formidable facade: Giant black binoculars by artists Claes Oldenburg and Coosje von Bruggen mark the entry, flanked by a forest of copper pillars on one side and bowed white "ocean liner" decks on the other. At Edgemar, Gehry makes art of the mini-mall. An ice-cream store and a gourmet restaurant, among others, hold down the neo-constructivist fort, once an egg-packing facility. Between the two Gehrys, enjoy assorted oddball stores, the California Heritage Museum, a high concentration of boutiques and restaurants and the compelling *Ballerina Clown* statue on the Renaissance Building at Main and Rose.
202 D2 www.mainstreetsm.com

8 Santa Monica Museum of Flying

A pleasure for airplane buffs and families with children, the Santa Monica Museum of Flying occupies an old hangar on the north side of the Santa Monica Municipal Airport. The converted hangar was once part of Douglas Aircraft. The museum houses over 30 vintage aircraft, including a 1924 Douglas World Cruiser Biplane (the first airplane to circle the earth), World War II fighters and modern jets – all flight ready. The original Douglas Aircraft Boardroom upstairs includes an impressive 22-seat round table with an illuminated globe at its center. When you've had enough of the aviation-related exhibits, videos, books and gifts, head upstairs to the sleek DC-3 restaurant overlooking the runway.

198 B1 2772 Donald Douglas Loop North, off 28th Street, Santa Monica 310/392-8822; www.museumofflying.com Closed temporarily: check website for latest info Suggested donation moderate

9 Bergamot Station/ Santa Monica Museum of Art

When architect Fred Fisher converted an old train shed into the gallery complex known as Bergamot Station, Santa Monica's art world was transformed, as Bergamot quickly took over as the most dynamic outpost of arty LA. With 40 galleries and art-related ventures occupying a series of light industry structures in a nondescript section of eastern (away from the beach) Santa Monica, Bergamot has something artistic for everyone. The artists range from unknown to world famous. Top galleries include Robert Berman, Patricia Faure, Rosamund Felsen, Track 16 and a dozen others.

The Santa Monica Museum of Art, occupying one of the buildings of the Bergamot complex, showcases local artists and hosts lively special events, including Friday night Salons featuring artists discussing their work. Email reservations and sometimes pre-payment are required for these.

198 B1

Bergamot Station

2525 Michigan Avenue 310/828-4001; www.bergamot-station.com Tue–Fri 10–6, Sat 11–5 Inexpensive

Santa Monica Museum of Art

Bergamot Station, 2525 Michigan Avenue 310/586-6488; www.smmoa.org Tue–Fri 11–6, Sat 11–8 Inexpensive

10 Uplifters Club and Rustic Canyon Recreation Center

Harry Haldeman helped found the club in 1913, when he and a group of pals bought 120 acres (48ha) of woods in Rustic Canyon (across Sunset and below the Will Rogers ranch). Decades later, his grandson H R Haldeman masterminded Nixon's Watergate fiasco.

Another famous name is Frank L Baum, who penned *The Wizard of Oz* and also named "The Lofty and Exalted Order of Uplifters," so-called because their mission was to "uplift art and promote good fellowship." They built a Spanish-style clubhouse and several cabins in their private forest, where members such as Walt Disney, Harold Lloyd and Darryl F Zanuck uplifted many a glass right through Prohibition.

Today the clubhouse anchors the 8-acre (3ha) Rustic Canyon Recreation Center, a lovely spot for a picnic or a walk. The neighborhood features examples from every period of 20th-century residential architecture. Don't get too intrusive: celebrities abound, and they value their privacy.

202 D2 600–700 Latimer Road, off Brooktree below Sunset in Rustic Canyon 310/454-5734 Free

11 Montana Avenue, Santa Monica

Montana was once a sleepy, mixed retail-residential avenue slicing through the rich north side of Santa Monica. Then, sometime in the 1980s, the leafy residential neighborhood around Montana woke up to its own bucolic charms; soon designer coffee shops, antiques stores, yoga studios, gourmet diners and chic boutiques moved in, displacing the old guard and creating a topflight shopping destination. From Seventh Street to 17th Street, high prices and high style prevail. If you like to spend money and spot celebrities, this is a good place to indulge; unique, individually owned stores still outnumber the chains. In the middle of it all an old-fashioned movie house, the Aero Theater (➤ 74), shows first-run movies on a single screen.

202 D2
www.montanaave.com

A tiled fountain at the Uplifters clubhouse in Rustic Canyon

12 Will Rogers State Historic Park

The 187-acre (75ha) Will Rogers State Historic Park nicely reflects the populist leanings of its former owner and namesake, America's beloved cowboy-philosopher; there's something here for everyone. Rogers and famous aviator Wiley Post were killed in a plane crash in 1935 and the ranch was willed to the state in 1944. The park and its historic buildings are currently undergoing extensive renovation work; the ranch house and much of the landscape has already been restored to its pre-war state. Hikers and naturalists explore trails linking the old ranch with the adjacent parklands in the Santa Monica Mountains. Enthusiasts of Western lore and California history find Mission furniture and an eclectic collection of cowboy memorabilia to admire in Rogers' unpretentious ranch house, now a museum. But the biggest draw continues a tradition begun by Rogers: open-to-the-public weekly professional and amateur polo matches on the park's polo field (weekends April through October).

202 D2 1501 Will Rogers State Park Road off Sunset Boulevard, Pacific Palisades 310/454-8212; www.parks.ca.gov Park: summer daily 8–7; other seasons 8–6. House/museum: daily 10:30–5 except major holidays Ranch house tours: Tue–Sun 11am, 1pm, 2pm Free; parking moderate

13 Self-Realization Fellowship Lake Shrine

Southern California has always had a reputation for cultivating New Agers, spiritualists and oddball gurus. One of the most popular was Paramahansa Yogananda (1893–1952), who still has his followers. Since 1950 his foundation has owned the Self-Realization Fellowship Lake Shrine, tucked behind high hedges off Sunset, less than a mile off the PCH in Pacific Palisades. Given the commercialism scarring the nearby intersection, the shrine offers a tranquil little hideaway with gorgeous gardens, a windmill-shaped chapel, a golden dome-topped lotus arch, gazebos and a houseboat (Yogananda's former home) drifting on a small lake. The Court of Religions honors five world faiths and in Mahatma Gandhi's World Peace Memorial, some of the spiritual leader's ashes have been enshrined. Walk the lake trail and sit in the gardens, then hit the gift shop. There's also a small museum to learn about Yogananda and his philosophy. On a hill overlooking the lake sits a large temple for the resident monks.

202 D2 ✉ 17190 Sunset Boulevard, Pacific Palisades ☎ 310/454-4114; www.lakeshrine.org 🕐 Tue–Sat 9–4:30, Sun 12:30–4 Free

The Self-Realization Fellowship Lake Shrine is a tranquil retreat from the bustle of the modern city

14 Will Rogers State Beach

If you're feeling energetic, leave your car in Rustic Canyon and hike down to Will Rogers State Beach. There you'll find public sands stretching from the northwest edge of Santa Monica almost all the way to Topanga Canyon. The waters are somewhat polluted at the foot of Rustic Canyon, but otherwise the swimming and lounging here are very good. Big parking lots, clean public restrooms and fast-food stands make a day at the beach fun and easy; come early in summer, because the lots fill up fast. Alternatively, rent a bicycle and cycle in: the South Bay Cycle Path (➤ 184–186) that runs south all the way to Palos Verdes terminates near the northwest end of Will Rogers State Beach, by the private Bel Air Bay Club. Be warned though: The path can get busy, particularly on summer weekends. The cliffs across the PCH, which slide onto the road during rainstorms or earthquakes, edge the high-priced suburb of Pacific Palisades.

202 D2 ✉ Along the Pacific Coast Highway, northwest of Santa Monica, southeast of Malibu

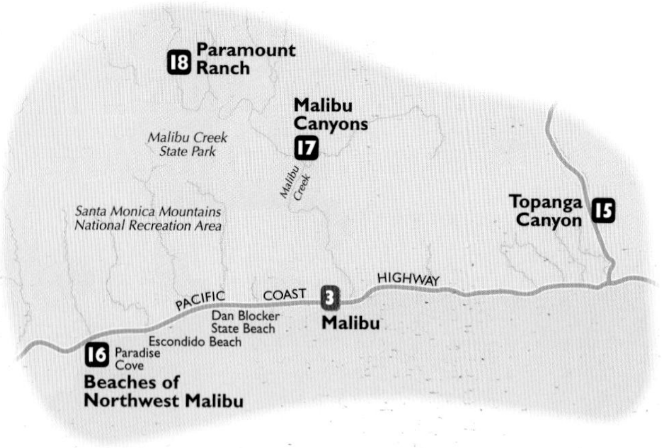

15 Topanga Canyon

Native Americans called it "the place where the mountains meet the sea," an apt description. Topanga Canyon Boulevard, connecting the San Fernando Valley to the coast, has unfortunately evolved into a commuter throughway, but Topanga State Park and its miles of trails offer rural adventure close to the city. At the foot of Topanga, the state beach's point break provides surfers with some of the best waves south of Malibu. Up the canyon, the primary entrance to the park is at the old Trippet ranch off Entrada Road. The Backbone Trail follows the Santa Monica Mountains' ridge line (spectacular views), then turns toward the ocean to end in Will Rogers State Historic Park. Long a bastion of artists, musicians and old hippies, the canyon wears the aging garb of the Age of Aquarius gracefully, with restaurants such as the Inn of the Seventh Ray (128 Old Topanga, Canyon Road) serving refined natural foods. The Topanga Community House (1440 Topanga Canyon Boulevard), once the scene of impromptu concerts by local residents like The Byrds and Neil Young, now offers primarily children's entertainment. In summertime, the nearby Theatricum Botanicum (1419 Topanga Canyon Boulevard, tel: 310/455-2322), founded by *The Waltons* actor Will Geer, delivers Shakespeare and other classic and modern plays as well as hosting workshops.

202 D2 North on Highway 127 (Topanga Canyon Boulevard) off the PCH west of Pacific Palisades, east of Malibu

16 Beaches of Northwest Malibu

Once you're past the private movie star residential enclave of Malibu Colony and the build-up around Pepperdine University, heading northwest on the coast highway, Malibu's residential and commercial density thins. Here, you'll find a number of public beaches offering varying degrees of privacy. While Zuma Beach, northwest of Point Dume, is crowded with day-trippers from the San Fernando Valley, the beaches beyond (beginning with Trancas Beach and including El Pescador, La Piedra, El Matador, Nicholas Canyon and Leo Carillo) offer wonderful opportunities for sunning, swimming, beachfront strolling, kayaking, fishing and scuba and skin diving. The waters are a little colder here than in Santa Monica Bay, but they are also cleaner. On or south of Point Dume you'll find numerous public beaches: Westward Beach, Point Dume State Beach, Paradise Cove, Escondido Beach, Dan Blocker State Beach and

others nearer Malibu. To find these gems, watch for the names on road signs or small "coastal access" signs. Bring your own food and drink. Note: Some of the beaches, especially Zuma, have large, dangerous surf and attendant riptides.
202 A2–C2

17 Malibu Canyons

Between Topanga Canyon and the Los Angeles county line where it meets the ocean, Malibu's coastline offers a multitude of beaches and seaside diversions. Less traveled but more appealing for those who want to get off the beaten path and drive are the many canyons that wander north and east from the coast through the mountains to the valleys on the other side. The drives take you up into the Malibu Mountains, where pull-offs frequently provide spectacular views of valleys, mountains, the coastline and the Pacific. It is easy to do a loop drive rather than backtrack, since most of the canyon roads link up high in the hills, via Mulholland Drive (► 9), which winds along above and through the mountains all the way from Hollywood to the northwestern reaches of Malibu, where it hits the beach near the Los Angeles/Ventura county line.

Some of the more intriguing roads for drives, views, trail access or interesting destinations include Tuna, Las Flores, Malibu, Latigo and Decker canyons. All roads begin at the Pacific Coast Highway.
202 C3

18 Paramount Ranch

The Malibu Mountains contain residential areas, great swatches of parkland and working movie and television studio backlots, the most significant one still in use being the Paramount Ranch. The ranch has been used for cowboy flicks since the 1920s.

Sights include a permanent set called "Western Town," complete with railroad station and tracks, cemetery, general store and saloon. The set has been used in plenty of films and TV series including *Have Gun, Will Travel*, *The Dukes of Hazzard*, and more recently, *Dr Quinn, Medicine Woman*. Beyond the movie sets, the Ranch offers picnic grounds and trail hiking.

The half-mile-long (0.8km) Coyote Canyon Trail is short enough for children to manage and beckons with wildflower meadows and oak forests for picnicking, plus bird's-eye views of Western Town.
202 C3 ✉ 2813 Cornell Road off Dume-Kanan Road, not far from Mulholland Drive north over the hills from Malibu (access is quicker from the Ventura Freeway on the other side) ☎ 818/597-9192 ⏱ Daily 8am– dusk; sets closed to the public during the week if filming is underway 💲 Free

A Western movie set at Paramount Ranch

Where to... Eat and Drink

Restaurant Prices
Expect to pay per person for a three-course meal, excluding tax, drinks and service
$ under $30 **$$** $30–$60 **$$$** over $60

RESTAURANTS

Chinois on Main $$$
Wolfgang Puck's long-established fusion restaurant still draws the crowds. Enjoy signature dishes such as warm sweet curried oysters and grilled squab with pan-fried noodles. Watch the wizards wield their magic from a counter seat.
202 D2 2709 Main Street, Santa Monica 310/392-9025; www.wolfgangpuck.com Wed–Fri 11:30–2, Mon–Thu 6–10, Fri–Sat 6–10:30, Sun 5:30–10

Geoffrey's $$
The location on a cliff above the Pacific Ocean is reason enough to come; the creative California cuisine is another. Celebrities will be your dining partners for such delights as ahi tartare, stuffed rack of lamb and two-pound Maine lobsters. Prime time here is during sunset hours or Sunday brunch.
202 C2 27400 Pacific Coast Highway, Malibu 310/457-1519; www.geoffreysmalibu.com Mon–Fri noon–10, Sat 10:30–10, Sun 11–10

Hal's Bar & Grill $$$
Venice locals flock to this neighborhood restaurant, which serves up a seasonal menu of American classics, cocktails at the long bar, and jazz on Sunday and Monday evenings. Weekend brunch is a local institution.
202 E2 1349 Abbot Kinney Boulevard, Venice 310/396-3105; www.halsbarandgrill.com Mon–Fri 11:30–3, 5:30–10:30, Sat–Sun 10–3, 5:30–11

The Hump $$$
Raw fish dishes served in a chic setting draw diners to the Santa Monica Airport for a first-rate meal accompanied by fabulous views. Soft-shell crab and stuffed eggplant (aubergine) are among the specials.
198 B1 3221 Donald Douglas, Loop 5 310/313-00977; www.thehump.biz Tue–Thu noon–2, Fri noon–2, 6–10:30, Sat 6–10:30, Sun 6–10

The Lobster $$
Perhaps one of the best views in Santa Monica can be had through the floor-to-ceiling windows at this restaurant at the beginning of Santa Monica pier. The seafood and fish here are as fresh as you would expect from the name and location, although the steak and pasta are just as good. Enjoy full flavors: ahi with wasabi, spicy crab enchiladas and teriyaki sea bass, or perhaps a simple lobster sandwich or steak and mango salad. There are fine wines and winning cocktails, which can be enjoyed from the bar area if you don't want to eat.
198 A1 1602 Ocean Avenue, Santa Monica 310/458-9294; www.thelobster.com

Ocean Avenue Seafood $$
This lively eatery with an ocean-view patio serves a broad range of quality seafood. You'll find delicious fish selections from all over the world, and the menu changes daily. Oyster lovers can select from a treasure chest of delights, while the choice of other dishes

might include Hawaiian ahi, Maine lobster, and mainstay crab cakes and clam chowder.
202 D2 1401 Ocean Avenue, Santa Monica 310/394-5669; www.oceanave.com Sun–Thu 11:30–10, Fri– Sat 11:30–11

Valentino Restaurant $$$
Get dressed in your best and order from a menu of carpaccio or seared ahi appetizers, heavenly pastas, veal and seafood entrees, or a seasonal risotto. With 2,000-plus choices, and a 140,000-bottle cellar, choosing the wine may be difficult.
202 D2 3115 Pico Boulevard, Santa Monica 310/829-4313; www.valentinorestaurant.com Mon–Thu 5–10, Fri 11:30–2:30, 5–10:30, Sat 5–10:30

CAFÉS

The Beachcomber Café $$–$$$
The Beachcomber on Malibu Pier is no ordinary café. Brave the outdoors wrapped in one of the blankets provided and tuck into clam chowder or a burger for lunch, or even just a coffee. For supper, there's seafood pot pie and steak on the menu, best enjoyed with a Coastal Breeze or Surfrider cocktail.
202 C2 Malibu Pier 310/456-9800; www.thebeachcombercafe.com Daily 7.30am–10pm for food (11pm for drinks)

Newsroom Café $
This is one of the best places in town for the smoothies, salads and vegetarian food. Celebrity sighting is almost guaranteed.
202 D2 530 Wilshire Boulevard, Santa Monica 310/319-9100 Mon–Fri 8am–10pm, Sat–Sun 9am–10pm

Novel Café $
This colorful coffeehouse is the perfect place for reading, recovering, surfing the net or writing the next *Catcher in the Rye*.
202 D2 212 Pier Avenue, Santa Monica 310/396-8566; www.novelcafe.com Mon–Fri 7am–1am, Sat 8am–1am, Sun 8am–midnight

BARS

Cameo Bar at the Viceroy
This hotel bar is billed as a contemporary take on an English lounge. Come for a drink by the pool or to admire the green, gray and chrome decor inside.
202 E2 1819 Ocean Avenue, Venice 310/260-7500; www.viceroysantamonica.com Mon–Wed 11–midnight, Thu–Sun 11am–1am

Duke's Malibu
Beachfront Duke's provides an authentic taste of Malibu surfer life, complete with *aloha* atmosphere and terrific views. Slowly sip on a cocktail and watch the waves crash.
202 C2 21150 Pacific Coast Highway, Malibu 310/317-0777; www.dukesmalibu.com Mon 5–9pm, Tue–Thu 11:30–9, Fri–Sat 11:30–10, Sun 10–9

Hotel Casa Del Mar
A cocktail on the elegant ocean-view veranda of this restored 1929 landmark on the beach will lull you back to LA's Golden Era. Explore the martini menu and enjoy the live music.
202 D2 1910 Ocean Front Walk, Santa Monica 310/581-5533; www.hotelcasadelmar.com Daily 7am–midnight

The Library Alehouse
Choose from over two dozen microbrews on tap and another dozen bottled beers. Finger food, light meals and snacks are also on offer.
202 D2 2911 Main Street, Santa Monica 310/314-4855; www.libraryalehouse.com Fri–Sat 11:30–2, Sun–Thu 11:30–midnight

Ye Old King's Head
Anglophiles can't get enough of this friendly pub where you can down a pint, throw some darts and order up bangers and mash.
202 D2 116 Santa Monica Boulevard, Santa Monica 310/451-1402; www.yeoldekingshead.com Sun–Thu 11–10, Fri–Sat 11–11

Where to... Shop

The beach area affords a wonderfully casual shopping experience complete with ocean breezes. Santa Monica Place and the adjacent Third Street Promenade combine mall action with a pedestrians-only stretch of eclectic stores and chains. Shops here have a reputation for being hip, and it is a popular haunt for visitors and locals alike. Main Street nearby has its own brand of uniqueness with specialty stores galore, while Montana Avenue (between Seventh and 17th streets) is a hidden enclave of upscale boutiques. Additional choices include Marina del Rey's harborfront Fisherman's Village, funky Venice Beach and decidedly non-funky Malibu.

SANTA MONICA

Frank Gehry's new-look **Santa Monica Place** mall (Broadway at Second Street; www.santamonicaplace.com) is scheduled for completion in 2010. With stores like Macy's and Nordstrom to tempt shoppers and a restaurant deck overlooking the ocean, it will connect with the pedestrian-only shopping streets.

Stores at **Third Street Promenade** (between Broadway and Arizona Avenue; daily 10–10) include popular chains such as Banana Republic, Benetton, Foot Locker and Abercrombie and Fitch.

Fred Segal (500 Broadway), one of LA's beloved merchants, offers clothing, hats and a dizzying array of interesting items.

Within the **Segal complex** are: **Zero Minus Plus**, with fine tableware and stationery; **Life Size at Fred Segal**, with kid-size versions of adults' designer duds; and **Fred Segal Essentials & Scentiments**, with bath and body products, aromatherapy candles and custom-blended fragrances. The complex is open Monday to Saturday 10–7 and Sunday 10–6.

Pass up the big-name booksellers for **Hennessy & Ingalls Art and Architecture** (214 Wilshire Boulevard; Mon–Sat 10–8), which stocks books, magazines and journals devoted to those topics.

Art, architectural and photography books, as well as out-of-print volumes and exhibition catalogs, are the focus of **Arcana Books on the Arts** (1229 Third Street Promenade; Mon–Sat 10–6, Sun noon–6).

Surfwear, flip-flops and board shorts are in stock at **Rip Curl** (1451 Third Street Promenade).

Zara, the ever-growing Spanish brand, has an outpost (1338 Third Street Promenade) here. The line is known for changing frequently, giving the clothes a fresh look.

Puzzles galore, along with action figures and other toys are available at **The Puzzle Zoo** (1413 Third Street Promenade).

Broadway Deli (1457 Third Street Promenade) has hundreds of Californian and international wines, as well as one of LA's largest selections of grappa. It also sells a variety of salads, cheeses and plenty of other ingredients for a fine picnic.

Bergamot Station (➤ 65) is the hub for many of LA's contemporary art scene and also home to the **Santa Monica Museum of Art**. You'll find exceptional collections of paintings, prints, photography, sculpture, glasswork, jewelry, art furniture and other media spread throughout approximately 30 galleries under one roof. Among the residents are the Rosamund Felsen

Gallery, Shoshona Wayne Gallery, Peter Fetterman Photographic Works of Art, Patricia Faure Gallery, Sculpture To Wear and the Gallery of Functional Art. Most galleries in the complex are open Tuesdays through Saturdays.

Antiques lovers will want to browse the **Santa Monica Antiques Show and Sale** (Santa Monica Civic Auditorium, 1855 Main Street; tel: 209/358-3134; Fri, Sat 11–7, Sun 11–5; moderate). Expect high-quality antiques and collectibles, including fine art, furniture and jewelry, with few real bargains to be found.

Patagonia (2936 Main Street) will prepare you for outdoor adventures with quality active wear, beach wear and its trendy signature surfboards.

Movie addicts should visit **Vidiots** (302 Pico Boulevard), a tiny place but with a vast and formidable collection of rare and foreign movies, scripts and movie-related books.

MONTANA AVENUE

Around 150 boutiques line this street, which attracts well-heeled locals as well as interested visitors. Choose from designer labels, fine wines and home furnishings. American artists create the whimsical, one-of-a-kind items sold at **Raw Style** (No 1511).

You'll find lingerie, bed and bath accessories and jewlry at **Only Hearts** (No 1407) and unique furnishings and home accessories at **The Blue House** (No 1402).

If you like knitting, **L'Atelier** (No 1202) will thrill you with its top-of-the-line imported yarns and chic patterns.

Parisian designer Emile Lafaurie fashions French and Italian fabrics into the menswear sold at **Sean** (No 1609).

Hemisphere (No 1627) is a great place to browse for home furnishings from the Far East. Gorgeous silks, fine Chinese cabinets and Burmese Buddhas have all been lovingly chosen by the owner (for larger items, shipping can be arranged).

VENICE

Venice may seem like an unlikely area for quality stores; nonetheless, visitors will find some happy surprises. Most of these small stores open daily, although times vary.

French country furnishings at **Bountiful** (1335 Abbot Kinney Boulevard) include chandeliers, mirrors, bed frames and sundry wicker items.

Neptina, at No 1329, features showstopper window displays, designer glass and ceramics, along with standout furniture.

Immortalize your LA cycling experience with a custom-designed bicycle, Spandex apparel and protective helmets at **Helen's Cycles** (2472 Lincoln Boulevard).

Cycle on down to **Small World Books** (1407 Ocean Front Walk), where you can browse fiction, literature and mysteries, then read your purchase on the beach.

OTHER AREAS

Farther afield, the **California Map and Travel Center** (3312 Pico Boulevard) is the perfect place for travel guides, maps and atlases, hiking and cycling directories as well as travel accessories.

Just down the street, **Caprice** (3213 Pico Boulevard) will tempt you with some of the city's finest French pastries, truffles and fruit tarts – all freshly made.

Santa Monica has no fewer than four weekly **farmer's markets** that together form one of the best sources for fresh produce and flowers on California's coast. Some also sell crafts and host live music. Wednesdays 8:30–1:30, Arizona Avenue and 2nd Street; Saturdays 8:30–1:30 Arizona Avenue and Third Street; Saturdays 8–1pm 2200 Virginia Avenue; Sundays 9:30–1 2460 Main Street.

Where to... Be Entertained

THEATER

Morgan-Wixson Theater
Operettas, contemporary plays, musical comedies, literary events and other performances.
202 D2 ✉ 2627 Pico Boulevard, Santa Monica ☎ 310/828-7519; www.morgan-wixson.org

Santa Monica Playhouse
Musicals, comedies and innovative works, including many family-oriented productions.
202 D2 ✉ 1211 4th Street, Santa Monica ☎ 310/394-9779; www.santamonicaplayhouse.com

Santa Monica Puppet and Magic
Puppeteers and magicians mesmerize all ages at this fascinating place.
202 D2 ✉ 1255 2nd Street, Santa Monica ☎ 310/656-0483; www.puppetmagic.com

MUSIC

14 Below
Mostly unknown rock and acoustic performers appear nightly.
202 D2 ✉ 1348 14th Street, Santa Monica ☎ 310/451-5040

Harvelle's
There's nothing pretentious or touristy about this little blues joint, with live sounds and good vibes.
202 D2 ✉ 1432 Fourth Street, Santa Monica ☎ 310/395-1676

Malibu Performing Arts Center
This contemporary cultural space for both the creation and enjoyment of the arts hosts a rich program of music, dance, film and theater.
202 C2 ✉ 23825 Stuart Ranch Road, Malibu ☎ 310/456-6722; www.malibuperformingartscenter.com/

McCabe's Guitar Shop
This 1960s icon continues presenting legendary and local folk artists in an intimate back-of-the-store performance space.
202 D2 ✉ 3101 W Pico Boulevard, Santa Monica ☎ 310/828-4497; www.mccabes.com

Pacific Park
Entertainment is often on hand during peak hours, with dance concerts and a music series during summer months (➤ 58).
202 D2 ✉ 380 Santa Monica Pier, Santa Monica ☎ 310/260-8744

Zanzibar
A Morrocan-themed dance bar with a variety of styles and sounds.
202 D2 ✉ 1301 Fifth Street, Santa Monica ☎ 310/451-2221

MAGIC

Magicopolis
Professional magicians mix comedy and magic during weekend shows.
202 D2 ✉ 1418 Fourth Street, Santa Monica ☎ 310/451-2241; www.magicopolis,com

MOVIE THEATERS

If you want to see a movie in Santa Monica, head to Third Street Promenade, where you will find the four-screen **AMC Loews Broadway** (No 1441), the six-screen **Mann Criterion 6 Theaters** (No 1313) and **AMC Santa Monica 7** (No 1310).

Aero Theater
An old-fashioned, single-screen neighborhood movie house showing first-run movies, the Areo Theater draws locals and often celebrities.
202 D2 ✉ 1328 Montana Avenue, Santa Monica ☎ 323/466-FILM

The Westside and Beverly Hills

Getting Your Bearings

LA's Westside, including Beverly Hills, is a place defined not so much by geography as by economy: just about everybody who lives in this area is doing quite well, thank you. The neighborhoods include Brentwood, Westwood, Bel Air, Century City, parts of West Los Angeles and the fabled city of *Beverly Hills 90210*. The inexact "borders" lie around 26th Street to the west, Olympic Boulevard to the south, Mulholland Drive to the north and La Cienega Boulevard to the east.

The Westside counts among its pleasures the Getty Center, an architectural tour de force and one of the world's most important cultural institutions. Not far from the Getty, visitors can explore the Skirball Cultural Center, another majestic piece of contemporary architecture, designed to celebrate the richness of the Jewish experience. The Holocaust is touched on here but explored more thoroughly and eloquently at the Museum of Tolerance, in another part of the Westside.

This well-to-do section of LA also offers pleasant walks and intriguing drives. With or without a map to the stars' homes, after window-shopping on Rodeo Drive or strolling the student haunts of Westwood Village and UCLA, you can tour the residential streets of Brentwood, Bel Air and Beverly Hills for a voyeuristic taste of The Good Life, Southern California-style. North of Sunset, take a spin up into loftier precincts for lovely panoramas of the city and peer through banks of immaculate greenery in front of elegant homes, ranging from rustic ramblers to massive mansions, which house the city's privileged classes.

Skirball Cultural Center 10
Mulholland Dri
SAN DIEGO FREEWAY
North Sepulveda Boulevard
Getty Center 1

Page 75: The legendary Beverly Hills Hotel on Sunset Boulevard

Below left: The azalea maze in the Getty Center's Central Garden

★ Don't Miss

At Your Leisure

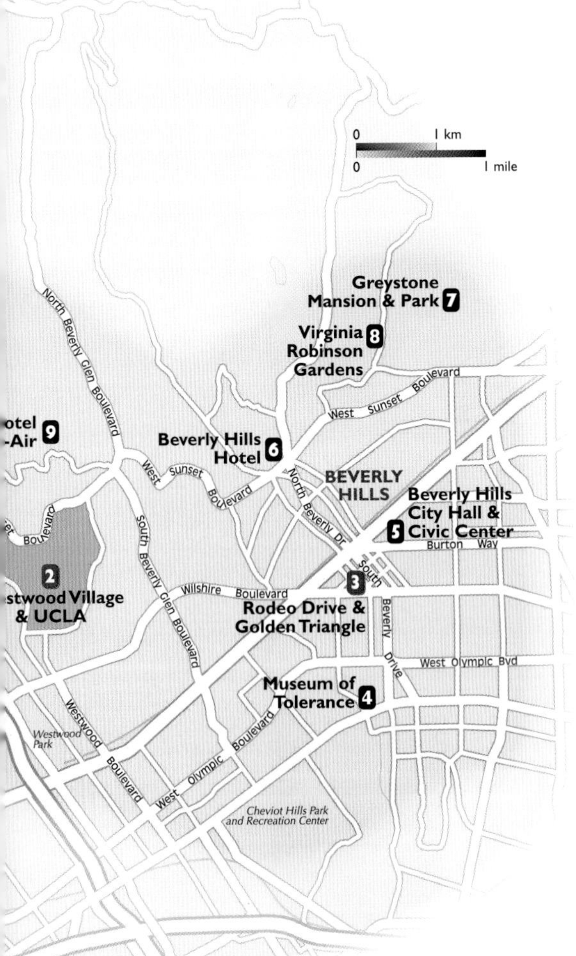

In a Day

If you're not quite sure where to begin your travels, this itinerary recommends a practical and enjoyable day in the West Side and Beverly Hills, taking in some of the best places to see using the Getting Your Bearings map on the previous page. For more information see the main entries.

8:00am

Breakfast in 3 **the Golden Triangle** (➤ 88–91), soaking up the atmosphere at BLD (➤ 91). Whether you go for a bruléed grapefruit or a hearty steak and eggs, you'll enjoy one of the best breakfasts in the city (served until a civilized 3pm) and a captivating view down Rodeo Drive.

9:00am

Kill some pre-Getty time exploring a few nearby notable addresses: the Schnabel House at 526 Carmelina, by Frank Gehry; the Sturges House, at 449 Skyway, by the one and only Frank Lloyd Wright; and the modest little house at 12305 Fifth Helena Drive, off Carmelina, where Marilyn Monroe died.

10:00am

Opening time at the 1 **Getty Center** (➤ 80–84, left). Spend at least two or three hours exploring the collections, buildings, gardens and views. There's enough here to keep you busy all day.

1:00pm

Lunch at The Restaurant (➤ 84) in the Getty Center. Reservations are highly recommended.

1:30pm

Drive to 2 **Westwood** (➤ 85–87), park you car and take a stroll through the village and at least a small part of 2 **UCLA campus** (➤ 86–87). Or drive up to the 10 **Skirball Cultural Center** (➤ 96), five minutes from the Getty, for an hour

well spent in this beautifully designed museum and cultural complex that celebrates Jewish history and life. Or for a different look at Jewish life, drive just south of Beverly Hills and spend an hour at the 4 **Museum of Tolerance** (➤ 92).

2:30pm

Head to 3 **Rodeo Drive** (➤ 88–91, above) and soak in the ambience of one of the world's most chic retail districts. Even if you can't afford to buy, it's worth it for the window-shopping alone.

5:00pm

Explore **Bel Air** and **Beverly Hills** (➤ 27) by car; if you want to take the celebrity tour, get out your movie star map and start looking for street names and numbers.

6:00pm

Indulge in a cocktail at the legendary 6 **Beverly Hills Hotel** (➤ 41 and 93) or drive up Stone Canyon and have that cocktail at the exclusive 9 **Hotel Bel-Air** (➤ 95–96), surely one of the most beautiful hotels in America, if not the world.

7:00pm

Stay on at the Hotel Bel-Air for dinner at one of LA's most romantic restaurants, the Dining Room, or switch from one fabulous hotel to another and have dinner at the Polo Lounge at the Beverly Hills Hotel. Either way, you'll need a reservation, you'll eat great food, and it is very possible that you'll see a few famous faces.

0 Getty Center

Opened in 1997, the Getty Center has quickly assumed a richly deserved position as the single most compelling attraction in Los Angeles. Don't miss it! This massive museum, education and art conservation complex proffers the pleasures of great classical art from the fabulously well-endowed Getty Collections (remember that this complex alone cost about $1 billion to construct), inspired contemporary architecture by Richard Meier and drop-dead views from a mountaintop setting just minutes off Sunset Boulevard near Bel Air.

All this and a garden created by Robert Irwin, one of Southern California's premier contemporary artists, add up to a great way to spend a day or a couple of hours. The Getty campus covers less than a quarter of the 110-acre (44.5ha) hilltop site, and the building complex itself is shaped in response to the contours of the two ridges that form the site. The highlight of the landscaping is Robert Irwin's enormous (134,000 sq ft/12,450sq m)) Central Garden, a piece that occupies a ravine between the museum proper and the nearby Research Institute.

Plazas and gardens surround the buildings

Skylights and glass walls establish a light, airy ambience

Winning Architecture

Architect Richard Meier's finest projects – and the Getty ranks high among them – offer a compelling integration of classical proportion and contemporary style. Composed primarily of off-white marble and white metal panels, the Getty's low-rise buildings attain a pleasingly rich, dense complexity. The heart of the center is the museum itself, consisting of 54 galleries contained in five two-floor pavilions around a central courtyard. Linked by bridges and open passageways, the gallery buildings are accessed from a cylindrical entry pavilion. These museum structures are clad in Italian travertine marble to distinguish them from the nearby non-museum buildings, which are finished in white aluminum and clear glass, and they house offices and education and conservation facilities.

Works of Art

The generous Getty endowment will in time elevate the museum's collections to a place among the world's finest. Meanwhile, you can trip through the galleries at whatever speed feels comfortable, lingering on the masterpieces and skimming the rest at your chosen pace. Take 10 minutes to view the **orientation film** in the entry hall; it'll help you focus on what you want to see.

The holdings include the work of 1,145 artists dating from before 1600 to the present day, grouped in collections representing pre-20th-century European paintings, drawings, illuminated manuscripts, sculpture, decorative arts and American and European photographs, all arranged chronologically.

The museum's expansive chronological range is its greatest strength: While the famous masterpieces are admittedly few, almost every period of Western history has been represented in some way. If you have only limited time, the museum offers printed guides for those in a hurry.

Among the must-see (and so usually crowded) "stars" of the collection are Van Gogh's ***Irises*** (1889) and Belgian James Ensor's raucously teeming, pre-Expressionist ***Christ's Entry into Brussels*** (1889). For those drawn to masterpiece-makers, the collection offers 16 Rembrandts, 19 Rubens, an intriguing selection of Degas' drawings and photographs, and works by Millet, Raphael and others. The impressive photography collection includes more than 100 pieces by Man Ray and works by David Hockney, Moholy-Nagy, Tina Modotti, Walker Evans and Lucas Samaras. Due to their light-sensitive nature, not all of the drawings and photographs are on view.

HOW TO GET THERE

Metro Rapid line 761 has a stop outside the Getty Center's main entrance on Sepulveda Boulevard. Taxis will also drop you here.

Van Gogh's *Irises* is perhaps the Getty's single most famous work of art

THE GETTY VILLA

J Paul Getty had a clear vision for the Getty Villa in Pacific Palisades: he wanted to re-create the perfect setting for his works of art. It was designed as a country house museum, in the style of the Roman Villa dei Papiri (Villa of the Papyrus) in modern-day Ercolano, Italy. Expanded and renovated, it is now an antiquities museum that focuses on ancient Greek, Roman and Etruscan art and culture. Each room has its own distinct theme: one may be dedicated to gods and goddesses and another to the Trojan War. Visitors experience the building as they would a private home. Advance, timed tickets are required: Reservations for these can be made online or by phone up to three months in advance. A limited number of same-day tickets available.

17985 Pacific Coast Highway, Pacific Palisades 310/440-7300; www.getty.edu. Thu–Mon 10–5 Free; parking moderate Metro Bus 534 stops at Coastline Drive and Pacific Coast Highway opposite the Getty Villa entrance. Entrance only from northbound (right-hand) lane of Pacific Coast Highway.

Period Rooms

A somewhat provocative design decision led to the installation of "period" rooms to house "period" works. As a result, you'll find yourself passing from the cool contemporary ambience of Meier's pale marble courtyards and passageways into galleries decorated with richly colored walls, heavy moldings and other rococo embellishments, evoking a kind of postmodern eclecticism perfectly attuned to the anything-goes design scene of Los Angeles.

The Central Garden

Artist Robert Irwin created the Getty's Central Garden, the heart of which consists of a tree-lined walkway descending through layers of artfully planted gardens.

The walkway crosses a stream winding downhill amid a diverse assortment of grasses and other plantings, with arbors draped with bougainvillea that establish intimate seating areas around a small plaza. Below the plaza, waterfalls splash in a pool ringed with beds planted for color and reflectivity.

The attractive Garden Terrace Cafe overlooks the Central Garden

The Central Garden neatly bridges the aesthetic space between Meier's classically modern buildings and the rough, chaparral-covered terrain of the site.

You can see a thrilling contrast here between the garden's intimate, colorful plantings and the panoramic views of Greater LA and the Pacific. Hope for a fog- and smog-free day when you visit.

TAKING A BREAK

The Restaurant (tel: 310/440-6810; Tue–Fri 11:30–2:30, Sat 11:30–2:30, 5–9, Sun 11–3) at the Getty offers elegant dining with views of the Santa Monica mountains. Reservations are highly recommended.

198 A3 · 1200 Getty Drive, near the intersection of the San Diego Freeway (405) and Sunset Boulevard · 310/440-7300 for all information, parking and restaurant reservations; www.Getty.edu · Tue–Fri 10–5:30, Sat 10–9, Sun 10–5:30; closed Mon and major holidays · Free. Parking: moderate

GETTY CENTER: INSIDE INFO

Top tips The Getty's art and architecture are certainly world class and the reason that the museum is famous. But many visitors find the **spectacular views**, **landscaped gardens** and **breathtaking location** just as memorable. Stay for lunch and make a day of it.

- Take advantage of the Getty's well-trained staff and tour guides by taking one of the several tours offered. One-hour **gallery tours** are offered Tuesday to Sunday at 11am. Meet by the stairs in the entrance hall. **Architecture tours** take place continuously every day (30 minutes). Meet to the left of the museum entrance doors. **Garden tours**, which last between 30 and 45 minutes, are organized six times daily Tuesday through Sunday. Sign up at the information desk in the entrance hall.
- **Bring sunglasses!** You don't often think of a museum as a place requiring them, but you'll probably spend a lot of time outside here, admiring the buildings, gardens and views. The endless expanses of white marble and white-painted metal make for a blinding experience if you don't have shades.

2 Westwood Village and UCLA

In spite of clusters of massive towers thrown up nearby over the past 40 years, Westwood Village maintains an enticingly low-key "village" ambience. Bordered on the south by Wilshire Boulevard and on the north by the UCLA campus, it offers a lively array of eateries, stores and student-oriented businesses, and a couple of stand-out theaters from the glory days of movie-house design.

Disentangle yourself from the brutal traffic along and around Wilshire by parking your car, and explore the low-rise Village streets and the UCLA campus on foot. Dating from the 1920s, the Spanish Revival-style Village was planned as a shopping district, and remains one, more or less: The main drag, Broxton Avenue, is lined with restaurants, movie theaters and retail stores.

Theater District

What lends Broxton visual distinction are three theaters: the neon-spired **Fox Westwood Village**, at 961 Broxton, with its 1931 Spanish Revival glories still intact, and the 1937 **Bruin** across the street at 948, along with the landmark Dome, at 1099 Westwood Boulevard. The **Dome** originally housed the offices of Janss Investment Corporation, responsible for transforming part of the original 3,300-acre (1,335ha) Rancho San Jose de Buenos Aires into Westwood Village.

Hammer Museum

After a disagreement with the LA County Museum of Art, billionaire oilman Armand Hammer moved the bulk of his art collection to his own museum, called the Hammer

The neon spire of the 1931 Fox Westwood Village movie theater

Westwood Memorial Park, where notables such as oil tycoon Armand Hammer are buried

Museum, on Wilshire. The reception area and several galleries devoted to changing exhibitions are contained in the tower, with other exhibition galleries housed in a windowless, horizontally striped extension of the tower that nudges north into Westwood Village.

Since UCLA took over the operation of the museum in 1994, the curated shows have become more contemporary in focus. Some critics have argued that Hammer's collection consists primarily of lesser works by greater artists, but there are a number of real masterpieces here, like Van Gogh's *Hospital at St Remy* and John Singer Sargent's *Dr Pozzi at Home*.

South of Wilshire, behind the Avco Cinema, the miniscule **Westwood Memorial Park** shelters the grave of Armand Hammer, along with an impressive array of the famous dead, including Peter Lorre, Natalie Wood, drummer Buddy Rich and the immortal Marilyn Monroe.

UCLA

The University of California at Los Angeles arrived in its present-day Westwood location in 1925. Architect George Kelham masterplanned the original campus, inspired by northern Italian Romanesque architecture. The original grassy central quadrangle remains the heart of the campus, surrounded by the university's central cluster of early buildings. The best of these originals include **Royce Hall**, constructed in 1929 from a design by architect David Allison, and inspired by a Milanese basilica; **Powell Library**, also from 1929, by George Kelham after the Church of San Zenove in Verona; **Kerckhoff Hall**, a 1931 neo-Gothic beauty housing the Student Union; and the **Fowler Museum of Cultural History**, adjacent to Royce Hall and home to a vast collection of artifacts, including masks from every part of the globe, a 10,000-piece textile collection and extensive artworks from Mexico, Africa and Polynesia. The nearby **Athletic Hall of Fame** houses a different sort of artifact: the countless awards won by UCLA teams over the years. Of special note is the tribute to John Wooden, the UCLA basketball coach recognized as the greatest in the history of the sport.

The verdant splendors of UCLA call for walking. Get a map and self-guided tour brochure from one of the information kiosks and take a walk around.

Mathias Botanical Garden provides a verdant retreat on the east side of UCLA campus

Close to Westwood Village, the **Mathias Botanical Garden** (open daily, free) conjures a country glade on the east side of campus, with lilies, fern grottoes and redwood trees. Abutting the Wight Art Gallery in the northeast campus, the 5-acre (2ha) **Franklin Murphy Sculpture Garden** offers the best selection of sculpture in LA, with more than 70 pieces by Rodin, Joan Miró, Jean Arp and Deborah Butterfield, among others. A free tour can be reserved (tel: 310/443-7041).

TAKING A BREAK

Though you may hate to give up your Westwood parking spot, get in your car and head down to **The Apple Pan** (10801 Pico Boulevard, just east of Westwood Boulevard; tel: 310/475-3585; Tue–Thu and Sun 11am–midnight, Fri–Sat 11am–1am, closed Mon; $, no credit cards) for a classic LA burger. Save room for a piece of homemade apple pie.

---

198 B3 Westside Village

UCLA
Guided UCLA campus walking tours can be booked (reservations required)
310/206-3719 or 825-8764 Free Mon–Sat. Parking inexpensive

UCLA's refurbished Ackerman Union building

UCLA Hammer Museum
10899 Wilshire Boulevard
310/443-7000; www.hammer.ucla.edu Tue–Sat 11–7, Thu 11–9, Sun 11–5. The Grunwald collections can be seen by appointment only (tel: 310/443-7078) Inexpensive; free Thu

Fowler Museum of Cultural History
310/825-4361; www.fowler.ucla.edu Wed–Sun noon–5 (also Thu 5–8pm) Free

WESTWOOD VILLAGE AND UCLA: INSIDE INFO

Top tip An especially noteworthy part of Armand Hammer's collection in Westwood is in the **Grunwald Center for the Graphic Arts**, home to some 35,000 drawings, prints and photos.

Hidden gems **UCLA Film and Television Archive** (Melnitz Hall, on UCLA; by appointment at Powell Library, or tel: 310/206-5388, Mon–Fri 9–5 for access, free). This vast archive contains classic, foreign and art films, TV shows from the medium's early days to the present day, and journalism footage from local and state news, including newsreels dating back to the turn of the 20th century.

- Another great alfresco destination is the **UCLA Hannah Carter Japanese Garden** off the UCLA campus (tel: 310/794-0320; www.japanesegarden.ucla.edu; Tue, Wed, Fri 10–3; free; by appointment only, self-guiding tours from entrance). The garden is an inspired exercise in Zen tranquility.

3 Rodeo Drive and the Golden Triangle

Even if you don't like to shop, you have to do Rodeo Drive, if only to gawk at the Bentleys and Benzes lining up for parking spaces or the tastefully executed monuments to excess that line the streets.

First, get located. The Golden Triangle is a wedge-shaped commercial district bordered by Wilshire Boulevard to the south, Santa Monica Boulevard to the west and Rexford Drive to the east. Along with the crème de la retail crème, the 20 blocks of the Triangle contain a few architecturally significant historic and modern buildings, a couple of ultra-chic restaurants, a classy hotel or two and the offices and salons of the high-priced service industries that cater to the rich and famous: psychiatrists, cosmetic surgeons, agents and celebrity hairstylists.

The exclusive stores that line Rodeo Drive attract a well-heeled clientele

To the Mall

The primary activity here is shopping if you can afford it, and window-shopping if you can't. The excitement starts at **Two Rodeo**, a kind of hyper-upscale mini-mall at the foot of Rodeo between Wilshire Boulevard and Dayton Way. Along with top-of-the-line stores – Tiffany & Co, Jimmy Choo and other famous names – Two Rodeo is distinguished by the Spanish Steps linking Wilshire with Via Rodeo, a cobblestone, pedestrians-only passage that dates from Beverly Hills' founding in 1914.

Each of Two Rodeo's two- and three-floor buildings have been designed to stand out individually, evoking not only different styles but different historic moments. The other "mall" on Rodeo lies up the street at No 421, home of the **Rodeo Collection**. Lording it over the Rodeo sidewalks between

Rodeo Drive's Spanish Steps

the two "malls" are several dozen of the most expensive and well-known temples of consumerism on the planet, including Van Cleef & Arpels (300), Cartier (370), Polo/Ralph Lauren (444) and Giorgio Beverly Hills (327).

Side Streets

While the stores along high-rent Rodeo all sport recognizable names, many of the side streets offer less pricey, more adventurous action. Stroll along Little Santa Monica Boulevard for specialty shops, and also check out the hipper-looking row of retailers on Brighton Way. Then drop in for tea at the Beverly Wilshire (➤ 41) and plot another walk through the Golden Triangle.

You can backtrack up Rodeo to 322 Anderton Court, for example, to see what Frank Lloyd Wright did in the realm of retail architecture. With a ramp winding up around a metal mast, it smacks of a warm-up for the Guggenheim in New York, and at the same time conjures a kind of nautical Streamline Moderne look.

Centers of History

Farther afield, the **Beverly Hills City Hall** and adjacent **Civic Center** (➤ 92–93) hold the fort on Rexford, close to a post office housed in an Italian Renaissance-style building at 9300 Santa Monica Boulevard. Even gas stations get the treatment here: Check out the Unocal station at 427 N Crescent, a flashback to the golden age of gas in the 1950s and 1960s. At one corner of the Triangle, the intersection of Wilshire and Santa Monica, the **Electric Fountain** offers a circular frieze depicting scenes from early California history, beneath a statue symbolizing a Native American rain prayer. Look for the sleek marble and glass building at 9830 Wilshire. This ode to the power of the Hollywood agent was designed by I M Pei for the Creative Artists Agency in 1989.

A nice counterpoint to Pei's contemporary cool can be found at 507 N Rodeo: the **O'Neill House** (closed to the public), a neo-art nouveau 1986 home by architect Don Ramos. Another fairy-tale house can be found at 516 N Walden Drive at Carmelina. Called the **Witch's House**, the privately owned Spadena House served as the headquarters building for a Culver City movie studio in the 1920s. Its name was inspired by the steeply pitched roof, jagged fences, gnarled windows and broomstick entrance.

Architect Don Ramos took art nouveau as his inspiration for the 1986 O'Neill House

Paley Center for Media

Back in the heart of the Triangle, the Paley Center for Media draws visitors into an assemblage of the soothingly bright, angular white spaces that signify the work of architect Richard Meier. Along with special exhibitions devoted to topics like "The Sounds of Silents" (silent films restored with full orchestration), "Hello, Goodbye" (three months of pilots, premieres and final programs from series television archives)

A trolley tour bus takes visitors down Rodeo Drive

Italian designers Dolce & Gabbana are among the high-end fashion houses with outlets on Rodeo Drive

and "The Role of the Media in Creating the News," the collections feature more than 140,000 programs: films, TV and radio shows, including documentaries, commercials and newscasts.

TAKING A BREAK

It's hard to fault the **BLD** at the Beverly Wilshire hotel (7450 Beverly Boulevard; tel: 323/930-9744; www.bldrestaurant.com, Mon–Sat 8am–11pm; Sun 8am–10pm). Take your spot on the terrace outside on the cornerstone of Rodeo Drive, or on the comfortable chairs inside, and order a healthy "eggless egg sandwich" like a local or a more robust steak salad.

---

199 D3
www.rodeodrive-bh.com

Two Rodeo
Mon–Sat 10–6, Sun 11–5 310/247-7040; www.tworodeodrive.com

Rodeo Collection
Mon–Sat 10–6 www.rodeocollection.net

The Paley Center for Media
465 N Beverly Drive, Beverly Hills 90210 310/786-1091; www.paleycenter.org Wed–Sun noon–5 Free; contributions welcome

RODEO DRIVE AND THE GOLDEN TRIANGLE: INSIDE INFO

Top tip Admirers of architect Richard Meier's work can see another example at the **Gagosian Gallery**, 456 N Camden Drive, a spartan, garage-like volume that shows the work of modern-day art stars, among them Cindy Sherman, David Salle and Eric Ruscha.

At Your Leisure

A neo-baroque dome crowns the Spanish-style Beverly Hills City Hall

4 Museum of Tolerance

The tragic subject of the Holocaust has been handled with sensitivity and resourcefulness at this powerful museum, associated with the Simon Wiesenthal Center. One of its strong suits is the state-of-the-art technology employed in making the exhibits highly interactive. Along with the powerful exploration of the plight of the Jewish people in Nazi Germany, the museum examines the ways different political, religious and social systems contribute to racism, prejudice and other forms of intolerance. The enormous four-level complex includes a permanent exhibition level; a multimedia learning center containing documents, photographs, artifacts, testimonies and maps; an archival exhibit with Holocaust materials; gallery space; and theaters, shops, cafeterias and courtyards. The museum is currently being expanded, with new space devoted to an educational and cultural resource center and exhibition galleries.

The Tolerancenter offers several clever interactive exhibits focusing on different aspects of prejudice, including The Point of View Diner, a 1950s-style diner with video jukeboxes exploring various controversial subjects. The Holocaust Exhibit is also interactive and can be painfully moving: Each visitor is issued a photo passport of a Nazi-era child, and as you tour the exhibit, the passports are updated. After you've seen and heard the story of the Nazis and the resulting Holocaust, you finally learn the fate of the child whose passport photograph you've been carrying.

199 D2 ✉ 9786 West Pico Boulevard (between Overland Avenue and Beverly Drive) ☎ 310/553-8403; www.museumoftolerance.com Apr–Oct Mon–Fri 10–5, Sun 11–5; Nov–Mar 10–3, Sun 11–5. Closed Jewish holidays Moderate Photo ID is required for admission

5 Beverly Hills City Hall and Civic Center

Beverly Hills' ornate City Hall dates from 1932, which goes to show that this particular neighborhood was not exactly suffering even in the

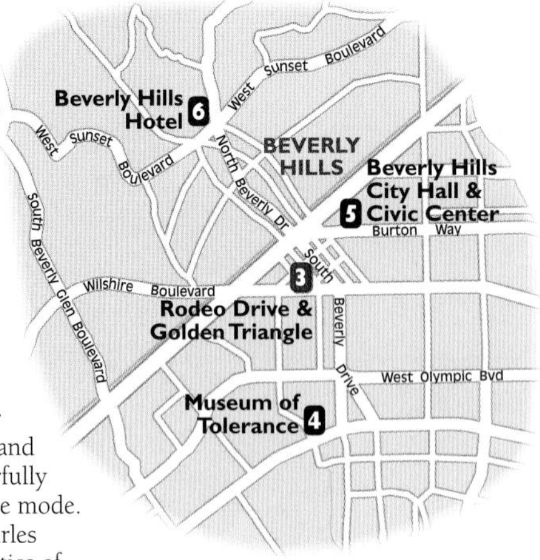

middle of the Great Depression. Architect William Gage's mid-rise confection has a classic civic form: low base signifying government, high tower signifying business. The look is pure Southern California eclectic; the overall style is Spanish Revival with art-deco touches, while the tower evokes Moderne design and the dome on top is colorfully detailed in a neo-baroque mode. Next door, architect Charles Moore used the retro tactics of postmodernism to excellent effect here, in the expansion of City Hall known as the Beverly Hills Civic Center. Built in the 1980s, the Civic Center exhibits an appealing Spanish flavor, richly seasoned with art-deco influences. The whole composition, including a large public library, fire and police departments and a parking garage, has been artfully arranged around elegantly landscaped courtyards.

199 D3 444 & 455 N Rexford Drive, Beverly Hills 310/285-1000 First floor daily 9–5; library Mon–Thu 10–9, Fri–Sat 10–6, Sun noon–6

6 Beverly Hills Hotel

The legendary "Pink Palace" opened in 1912 when developer Burton Green constructed the Mission Revival-style hotel to attract wealthy visitors to the new town of Beverly Hills, population 500. With its ideal location on Sunset Boulevard at the foot of the northern hills and canyons, the 12-acre (5ha) property soon claimed its place as the social nexus of the movie industry and symbol of the glamorous life lived by the stars. The classic pink and green hotel was purchased by the Sultan of Brunei in 1987; he invested a bit more than $100 million in a complete makeover in 1995, bringing the old queen up to contemporary standards without sacrificing an iota of her low-keyed, high-toned style. The Polo Lounge remains at the center of deal- and scene-making in Hollywood, while the hotel's 21 bungalows, nestled among immaculately tended gardens, are still the hideaways of choice for visiting celebrities. Just about every famous name in Hollywood history made history here, for better or worse, from Marilyn Monroe to John Belushi. Partake of the excellent fare at the Polo Lounge, and witness

The Beverly Hills Hotel still reigns over Hollywood society

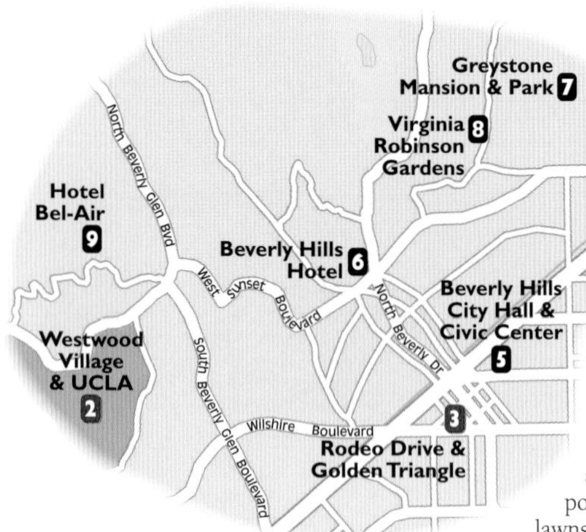

Hollywood at work while you eat; have a milk shake or sandwich downstairs at the cozy little Fountain Coffee Shop. You might find yourself (literally) rubbing elbows with someone you've seen in the movies.

199 D3 9641 Sunset Boulevard (at Rodeo Drive), Beverly Hills 310/276-2251 or 800/283-8885; www.thebeverlyhillshotel.com

7 Greystone Mansion and Park

The massive, rambling Greystone Mansion looks as if it might have been airlifted from the English countryside and planted on a Beverly Hillside: the 46,000-square-foot (4,270sq m), 55-room house is in a classic English Tudor style. In the late 1920s oilman Edward S Doheny built the house on a 415-acre (168ha) tract north of Sunset, thus claiming title to the largest family estate in Beverly Hills. Most of the land was sold off in the 1950s, but the 18 acres (7ha) of landscaped gardens that remain with the house have been transformed into a lovely public park.

The house is not open to visitors, but you can get close enough to admire the intricacies of the chimneys and the fine limestone facades, and you can peek in the windows. The formal and informal gardens circling the house are worth exploring; along with koi ponds, a swimming pool and expansive lawns, there are splendid views of the house and grounds in the foreground and the city in the distance.

199 E4 905 Loma Vista Drive (off Doheny Drive), Beverly Hills 310/550-4796; www.greystonemansion.org Park: summer daily 10–6; winter 10–5 Free

The Greystone Mansion, a bastion of Tudor grace in Beverly Hills

The lush and elegant Virginia Robinson Gardens

8 Virginia Robinson Gardens

Nestled at the end of a cul-de-sac in a quiet residential neighborhood near the Beverly Hills Hotel, the Virginia Robinson Gardens, which can be visited by appointment only, rank high on the list of under-visited parks in the LA area, to your great good luck if you take the time to make your reservations in advance – preferably two weeks ahead of your intended visit.

Designed in 1911 in classic *beaux-arts* style by architect Nathaniel Dryden (landscape design by Charles Gibbs Adams), the house and 6-acre (2.5ha) estate was built for the heiress to the Robinson department store empire. Mrs Robinson willed the property to Los Angeles County; the Department of Parks and Recreation manages the site, offering tours by appointment only.

While the house is not open to the public, the 1924 Renaissance Pool Pavilion serves as the starting point for the 75-minute docent-guided garden tours. The gardens are glorious, with five distinct zones: the Italian Terrace Garden, the Formal Mall Garden, the Rose Garden, the Kitchen Garden and the magnificent Tropical Palm Garden. Dominated by hundreds of Australian king palms, the palm garden is the largest collection of its kind in the country.

199 D4 · 1008 Elden Way, Beverly Hills · 310/276-5367; www.robinsongardens.org · By appointment for tours only, Tue–Fri 10am and 1pm · Moderate

9 Hotel Bel-Air

Tucked into a lush, wooded canyon in the hilly upper reaches of Bel Air, the secluded, mission-style Hotel Bel Air surely ranks as the most charming hotel in Los Angeles. Even if you can't afford an overnight stay, a visit for a cocktail or tea on the Terrace, or better yet, Sunday brunch by the Swan Pool or dinner in the hotel Dining Room, comes highly recommended. With its Sunset Boulevard address, the Beverly Hills Hotel has always had more attention, but many well-heeled visitors and celebrities find the quieter, more intimate Bel Air a better choice. Set

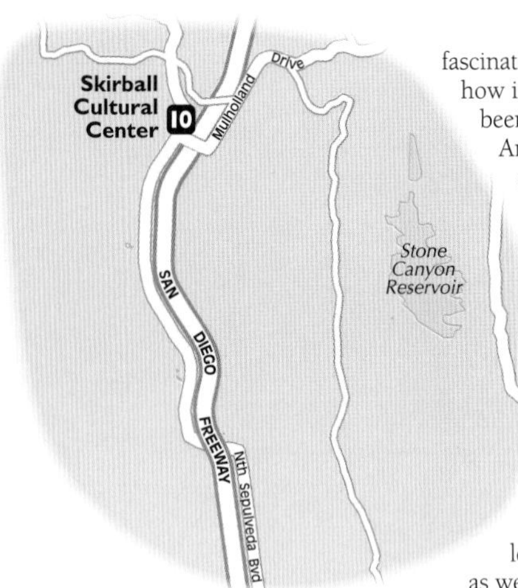

in verdant grounds with thousands of flowers, laced with streams, ponds and fountains making water music at every turn, the hotel is delightfully relaxed and glamorously elegant. The new, luxurious spa completes the sense of sanctuary.

198 B3 701 Stone Canyon Road (north off Sunset) 310/472-1211 or 800/648-4097; www.hotelbelair.com

10 Skirball Cultural Center

Canadian architect Moshe Safdie crafted this spacious, light-saturated cultural complex devoted to Jewish life in America. Located on a 15-acre (6ha) site at the crest of Sepulveda Pass in the Santa Monica Mountains (a couple of miles from the Getty), the Skirball covers a lot of ground, both physically and culturally. At the heart of the Center lies the museum dedicated to exploring "Visions and Values: Jewish Life from Antiquity to America." Here, 12 galleries organized in chronological order take visitors on a journey from the origins of Judaism through life in the Old World, immigration and assimilation into modern society. The Holocaust, a topic that tends to dominate museums devoted to Jewish culture, is handled delicately in the larger context of Jewish history. The exploration of Jewish assimilation into contemporary American life is fascinating, reminding visitors of how immensely significant has been that culture's influence on America's democratic values and self-image.

The Center has something for everyone: The mock archaeological digs and the hands-on activities in the Discovery Center will fascinate kids. The Tapler Courtyard serves as a wonderful setting for outdoor concerts, while the auditorium offers a regular series of lectures, films and concerts as well as readings. There is also a multicultural museum store, a lively indoor/outdoor café, provocative temporary exhibitions, a resource center with high-speed Internet access to over 150 related websites and a well-stocked research library.

198 A5 2701 North Sepulveda Boulevard 310/440-4500; www.skirball.org Tue–Fri noon–5 (also Thu 5–9), Sat–Sun 10–5 Moderate; under 2s free. Free Thu

Visitors play with the automated animals at the Noah's Ark at the Skirball exhibit

Where to... Eat and Drink

Restaurant Prices
Expect to pay per person for a three-course meal, excluding tax, drinks and service
$ under $30 **$$** $30–$60 **$$$** over $60

RESTAURANTS

The Belvedere $$$
Set inside the ritzy Peninsula Beverly Hills Hotel, the Belvedere offers fine, formal dining throughout the day, but it's the dinner menu that's really stellar. The daily changing menu, comprising small bites, small and large plates and Chef Sean Hardy's suggestions, are a melange of modern American creations – all exquisitely presented and perfectly executed. Opens at 11 on Sundays for brunch.
198 C2 9882 Little Santa Monica Boulevard, Beverly Hills 310/975-2736; www.peninsula.com Daily 6:30–11, 11:30–2:30, 6–10:30 (opens Sun 11am for brunch)

La Cachette Restaurant $$
A delightful dining experience awaits all those who seek out this charming hideaway. Owner-chef Jean-Francois Meteigner welcomes guests to his oasis of calm, then treats them to nouvelle French creations such as sautéed squab, farm-raised venison and pan-roasted salmon. *Tarte Tatin* is a big hit on the dessert list.
198 C2 10506 Santa Monica Boulevard, Century City 310/470-4992 Mon–Thu noon–2, 6–9:30, Fri–Sat 6–10:30

CUT $$$
Celebrity chef Wolfgang Puck has successfully taken the traditional American steak house and made it one of the slickest in the city. In a corner of the Beverly Wilshire hotel (➤ 41), CUT has made quite a name for itself. The contemporary design and melt-in-the-mouth choice cuts and Kobe steaks consistently draw in an appreciative crowd – many of them locals – making it often hard to get a table.
199 D3 9500 Wilshire Boulevard, Beverly Hills 310/275-5200; www.wolfgangpuck.com Mon–Thu 5:30–10, Fri–Sat 5:30–10:30

The Grill on the Alley $$
Classic American grill fare is served to Hollywood heavyweights. An industry power lunch might include chicken pot pie, steak or fresh seafood. The concept and decor were modeled after traditional New York-style grills.
199 D3 9560 Dayton Way, Santa Monica Boulevard, Beverly Hills 310/276-0615; www.thegrill.com Mon–Thu 11:30–11, Fri–Sat 11:30–midnight, Sun 5–9

Il Moro $$
Preparing northern Italian fare in a cheerful space on the first floor of a high-rise building, Il Moro chefs work their magic in an open kitchen. Dine inside or on the greenery-filled patio.
198 B1 11400 W Olympic Boulevard 310/575-3530; www.ilmoro.com Mon–Thu 11:30–3, 5–10, Fri 11:30–3, 5–10:30, Sat 5–10:30, Sun 4:40–9:30

Il Pastaio $$
This popular trattoria is run by Sicilian-born chef Giacomino Drago. Al dente pasta, authentic osso bocco and melt-in-the-mouth desserts do not disappoint.

Lunchtimes are particularly popular; be sure to reserve.
199 D3 400 N Canon Drive, Beverly Hills 310/205-5444; www.giacominodrago.com Mon–Wed 11:30–11, Thu–Sat 11.30am–midnight, Sun 11.30–10

Jaan $$$

Housed in the Raffles L'Ermitage Beverly Hills, Jaan fuses French and Asian flavors to create a sophisticated menu. The minimalist room has a domed ceiling and chairs draped in handwoven silk that change with the season. Offerings may include kobe beef steak tartar, chorizo-crusted halibut and spiced marinated duck.
199 D3 9291 Burton Way, Beverly Hills 310/278-3344; www.jrsdeli.com Mon–Sun 7–2:30, 6–10

Junior's Restaurant $

If you're craving authentic Jewish deli, Junior's offers some of the finest "tastes-like-someone's-mother-made-it" recipes. The *matzoh* ball soup and *blintzes* are the high points, along with generous sandwiches, smoked fish platters and the usual lengthy menu of goodies morning, noon or night. They not only deliver within a 50-mile (80km) radius but will ship anywhere in the world.
198 C1 2379 Westwood Boulevard, West LA 310/475-5771 Mon–Thu 6:30am–11pm, Fri 6:30am–midnight, Sat 7am–midnight, Sun 7am–11pm

Lawry's The Prime Rib $$

Lawry's draws locals and tourists with its magnificent and succulent prime rib, accompanied by whipped-cream horseradish and Yorkshire pudding. You can also choose savory steaks or fresh seafood and such comforting side dishes as creamed spinach and mashed potatoes.
199 E2 100 N La Cienega Boulevard, Beverly Hills 310/652-2827; www.lawrysonline.com Mon–Fri 5–10, Sat 4:30–11, Sun 4–9:30

Matsuhisa $$$

It may be incredibly expensive but at Matsuhisa you'll experience Japanese food at its very best. The *sushi* practically defies description and includes artistically prepared renderings of the freshest squid, salmon and sea scallops, all with an international twist. Chef Nobu Matsuhisa's 25-page menu of cooked seafood is mind-boggling, and you might want to opt for one of the daily specials.
199 E3 129 N La Cienega Boulevard, Beverly Hills 310/659-9639; www.nobumatsuhisa.com Mon–Fri 11:45–2:15, 5:45–10:15, Sat–Sun 5:45–10:15

Spago Beverly Hills $$$

Reservations are not easy to come by, but if you are lucky enough to get in you'll be lifted into gastronomic heaven. Stained-glass windows, contemporary art and a central patio graced with a fountain are the backdrop for the exquisite cuisine and the fine wines. Delicious preparations of lobster, veal, filet mignon and others are on the menu, along with Wolfgang Puck's famous signature pizzas. Expect perfect service and an expert sommelier to select your wine.
199 D3 176 N Canon Drive, Beverly Hills 310/385-0880 Mon–Thu, Sun 11–2:15, 5:30–10:30, Fri–Sat 11–2:15, 5:30–midnight

The Stinking Rose $$

This fun restaurant takes garlic as its theme. Californian and Italian dishes are all laced with garlic, right down to the ice cream and martinis. Seafood is a specialty, including Dungeness crab and mussels, with decent ribs also on the menu. There are some intimate corners in the cozy, kitsch interior, although the restaurant is a popular venue for large parties, so a romantic atmosphere is by no means guaranteed.
199 E3 55 N La Cienega Boulevard, Beverly Hills 310/652-673; www.thestinkingrose.com Daily 11–11

CAFÉS

Barney Greengrass $

Atop Barney's Beverly Hills department store, this is a pricey pit stop for clientele who need a break. Smoked fish, chopped liver, and bagels and cream cheese are among the deli fare. The view is free.

199 D3 · 9570 Wilshire Boulevard, Beverly Hills · 310/777-5877 · Mon–Wed 8:30–6, Thu–Fri 8:30–7, Sat 9–7, Sun 9–6

Brighton Coffee Shop $

This is a real 1950s coffee shop, improbably plunked in the middle of Beverly Hills. Savor the taste of nostalgic Americana with a meatloaf or tuna sandwich and a slice of pie and other past-era favorites.

199 D3 · 9600 Brighton Way, Beverly Hills · 310/276-7732 · Mon–Sat 7–5, Sun 10–3

The Farm of Beverly Hills $

Take a break from high-end shopping at this casual café specializing in salads, pizzas, pasta and burgers. The brownie sundae is a signature dessert.

199 D3 · 439 North Beverly Drive, Beverly Hills · 310/273-5578; www.thefarmofbeverlyhills.com · Mon–Fri 7:30am–10pm, Sat–Sun 8am–10pm

New York Bagel $

Brentwood residents stop in for fresh bagels and all the trimmings, as well as egg dishes and a variety of other deli delights.

198 A2 · 11640 San Vicente Boulevard, Brentwood · 310/820-1050 · Daily 7–7

BARS

Bar Nineteen 12

In the lobby of the glamorous Beverly Hills Hotel (➤ 41), the chic Bar Nineteen 12 is curently one of LA's coolest hotel bars. Pose on the terrace overlooking the pool with one of the fine signature cocktails.

199 D3 · 9641 Sunset Boulevard, Beverly Hills · 310/276-2251; www.barnineteen12.com · Daily 5pm–2am

Bel-Air Bar & Grill

After a day at the Getty Center or Skirball Cultural Center, drop in for a drink at this secluded bar with a lovely garden patio.

198 A3 · 662 N Sepulveda Boulevard, Bel Air · 310/440-5544; www.belairbarandgrill.com · Daily 11:30–3, 5:30–late

Blue on Blue

Enjoy poolside cocktails in an intimate setting. Specialty cocktails include the "pomegranate mojito" and the "blue avalon." Nibbles and snacks available from the bar menu.

199 D2 · Avalon Hotel, 9400 West Olympic Boulevard, Beverly Hills · 310/277-5221 · Daily 2pm–midnight

Liquid Kitty

Locals gather for martinis in this popular, dark and crowded nightspot.

198 B1 · 11780 W Pico Boulevard, West LA · 310/473-3707; www.liquidkitty.com · Mon–Fri 5pm–2am, Sat–Sun 8pm–2am

Peninsula Hotel Bar

This ultra-chic hotel bar, known as Club Bar, is a favorite respite for celebrities, their agents and other industry types. Look the part and you'll be welcomed.

198 C2 · 9882 Little Santa Monica Boulevard, Beverly Hills · 310/551-2888; www.peninsula.com · Mon–Sat 1pm–1am, Sun 3pm–midnight

The Polo Lounge

You can recapture a smidgen of Hollywood's golden era, as you recline with costly wine or cocktails at this legendary watering hole.

198 C3 · 9641 Sunset Boulevard, Beverly Hills · 310/276-2251; www.beverlyhillshotel.com · Daily 7am–1:30am

Q's Billiard Club

A youngish UCLA crowd frequents this upscale pool hall with tons of billiards tables and other games.

198 B2 · 11835 Wilshire Boulevard, West LA · 310/477-7550 · Daily 11:30am–2am

Where to... Shop

Most people head straight for Beverly Hills and Rodeo Drive, the world's most famous shopping thoroughfare, with other highbrow retailers on the adjacent streets. Student-oriented Westwood Village and smart Brentwood (along San Vicente Boulevard) offer additional shopping experiences, or you can tackle the select Westfield Century City (Santa Monica Boulevard, at Avenue of the Stars, in Century City) and unpretentious Westside Pavilion (Pico and Westwood boulevards, West LA). Antiques and art hounds may not find bargains but will certainly find top-of-the-line merchandise carefully shipped in from around the world. The Getty Center has one of the best museum stores, with a magnificent array of books, cards, fine art, toys and other items. Even if you're on a tight budget, you can shop with the rich and famous at the Beverly Hills farmers market.

RODEO DRIVE/BEVERLY HILLS

Rodeo Drive – the center of the shopping universe, filled with ritzy designer boutiques, jewelers and salons – is where you'll encounter chauffeur-driven limos and Rolls Royces, depositing celebrities outside their favorite couturier or stylist's door. Take a deep breath and begin your trek where Rodeo Drive meets Wilshire Boulevard. Make **Two Rodeo Drive** (www.tworodeo.com) your first stop. Considered one of the most expensive retail complexes ever constructed, it houses branches of Tiffany & Co, Jimmy Choo, Versace and Gucci Fine Jewelry. Here Gianfranco Ferre offers the Milanese designer's fashions for men and women including his gorgeously detailed women's blouses, and Vilebrequin brings quality men's swimwear from St Tropez to Beverly Hills.

Prominent tenants at **One Rodeo Drive,** across the street, include Bulgari and Louis Vuitton – both great favorites with the city's in-crowd.**Ermenegildo Zegna** (301 N Rodeo Drive), a quality Italian fabric-maker since 1910, incorporates its luxurious goods into beautifully tailored clothing for both men and women.

Amphora Art & Antiques (308 N Rodeo Drive) will send you home with fabulous paintings, bronzes and heavy antique silver. The finest antique and estate jewels are showcased at **David Orgell** (320 N Rodeo Drive), while **Frances Klein** (310 N Rodeo Drive) specializes in astounding art-deco and art-nouveau jewels – many designed by Tiffany, Bulgari and other famed names. You're practically guaranteed an approving nod from LA's fashion police, garbed or accessorized by the hip Milanese boutique **Prada** (343 N Rodeo Drive).

Fendi (355 N Rodeo Drive), a Roman family-owned business since the 1920s, stocks signature handbags, luggage, watches, women's clothing and furs. Italian designers **Dolce & Gabbana** (312) bring show-stopping, bold fashions to their Beverly Hills boutique. **Harry Winston** (371 N Rodeo Drive), provider of celebrity jewels on Oscar night, could make anyone feel like a star in his necklaces, earrings and rings. At sleek-boutique **Chanel** (400 N Rodeo Drive) women will find traditional

Chanel suits, accessories, fragrances and makeup. Designer **Giorgio Armani** (436 N Rodeo Drive) provides elegant surroundings for acclaimed clothing and accessories.

Both **Gucci** (347 N Rodeo Drive) and **Hermès** (434 N Rodeo Drive) are world-famed for purses, leather goods and their signature silk scarves.

Expensive and beautiful intimate apparel is the draw at **La Perla** (433 N Rodeo Drive), but for sheer exquisite extravagance you can't beat **De Beers** (401 Rodeo Drive), where diamonds and other fine jewelry are a girl's best friend. **Frette** (459 N Rodeo Drive) will spoil you forever with their worth-every-cent luxurious Italian sheets – the same you'd sleep on in the world's most elegant hotels.

Branches of the finest elite department stores (generally open Monday to Saturday 10–6, Sunday noon–6, although times may vary) line the stretch of Wilshire Boulevard near Rodeo Drive. Referred to as "Department Store Row," shoppers can whisk among a delicious assortment of under-one-roof retail outlets. **Barney's** of Beverly Hills (9570 Wilshire Boulevard) – West Coast cousin of Barney's New York – is the most impressive, with bleached-oak floors, winding staircases and an enormous skylight for that natural look. But don't look too natural, because this is a store for the young and thin, with five levels of hip designer labels and a collection of Vera Wang bridal gowns.

Texas-based **Neiman Marcus** (9700 Wilshire Boulevard) carries a more typical and exclusive range of goods including high-end fashions for men, women and children, cosmetics, lingerie, shoes and more. Revive yourself with a martini in the fourth-floor men's department or a relaxing lunch and a glass of California wine at Mariposa, in the store's lower level.

Famous **Saks Fifth Avenue** (9600 Wilshire Boulevard) carries both American and European designer fashions, fine jewelry, millinery and cosmetics. Discover the perfect fragrance at **Beverly Hills Perfumery** (9555 Wilshire Boulevard), with colognes and perfumes from all over the globe, or timeless (and expensive) tailored men's and women's wear at **Faconnable** (9680 Wilshire Boulevard).

If you have deep pockets and itchy fingers, and you haven't yet found the perfect souvenir to take home, try the auction houses. Both **Christie's** (360 N Camden Drive) and **Sotheby's** (9665 Wilshire Boulevard) conduct auctions throughout the year where you can bid for such items as an original Picasso, vintage automobile or a bottle of fine wine.

If you love eating cheese, head to The **Cheese Store of Beverly Hills** (419 N Beverly Drive) where you can choose from hundreds of of different types of cheese, yielded from cows, goats and sheep, from all over the world. For a choice of more than 250 teas and a plethora of tea accoutrements **Le Palais des Thés** (401 N Cañon Drive) is the place to go. This is the only US outpost for the French shop. Stock up on fresh-roasted coffee beans and Swiss water-process decaf at **Graffeo Coffee Roasting Company** (315 N Beverly Drive).

Delicious handmade chocolates and melt-in-your-mouth truffles are just some of the tempting sweet-tooth goodies to be found at **Edelweiss Chocolates** (444 N Cañon Drive), in business since the 1940s.

Dutton's Beverly Hills Books (447 N Cañon Drive), with a great selection of titles and frequent author signings, is a great place for bookworms. **Al's News** (216 S Beverly Drive), with periodicals geared toward screenwriters and playwrights, is the newsstand to hit if you've got the bug to write your own classic.

Where to... Be Entertained

THEATER

Geffen Playhouse
Celebrated actors perform contemporary off-Broadway-type plays, one-person shows and other works.
198 B2 10886 Le Conte Avenue 310/208-5454; www.geffenplayhouse.com

Odyssey Theater Ensemble
Odyssey continually draws raves for its well-executed avant-garde and contemporary plays.
198 C2 2055 S Sepulveda Boulevard 310/477-2055; www.odysseytheatre.com

Wilshire Theatre
Called the Fox Wilshire when it opened in 1930, this often serves as a venue for the Broadway/LA series and hosted Billy Crystal's one-man show.
199 E3 8440 Wilshire Boulevard 323/468-1770

UCLAlive
Concerts, theater, dance, opera and other performances. Venues include the sumptuous 1919 Royce Hall and other hallowed halls.
198 B3 Various venues 310/825-2101; www.uclalive.org

MUSIC AND DANCE

Chamber Music in Historic Sites
From November through May, Mount St Mary's College hosts a series of top-class chamber music ensembles in diverse settings.
213/477-2929; www.saintmarys.edu

Jazz Bakery
A converted bakery is now a small, nonprofit venue showcasing a variety of stellar jazz acts. Bring in drinks, or buy beer and wine in the lobby.
199 D1 3233 Helms Avenue 310/271-9039; www.jazzbakery.com

Skirball Cultural Center
This museum and cultural enclave has a program of concerts, film series and lectures. The focus is on Jewish culture, although other ethnic groups are also featured (➤ 96).
198 A5 2701 N Sepulveda Boulevard 310/440-4500; www.skirball.org

MOVIE THEATERS

AMC Century City 15
These revamped theaters boast 15 auditoriums with Stadium seating, surround sound, and a food court.
198 C2 10250 Santa Monica Boulevard 310/277-3898; www.amctheatres.com

Laemmle's Royal Theatre
Independent and foreign films are usually on the bill here.
198 B2 11523 Santa Monica Boulevard 310/477-5581; www.laemmie.com

Mann Bruin
You can't miss the wrap-around marquee at this 1930s Westwood icon, now showing first-run flicks.
198 B2 948 Broxton Avenue 310/208-8998; www.manntheatres.com

Mann Village
This popular 1920s movie theater primarily shows first-run titles. The modernized interior still affords viewers balcony seating.
198 B2 961 Broxton Avenue 310/208-5576; www.manntheatres.com

Nuart Theatre
This excellent revival house offers independent movies, classics, cult numbers and documentaries.
198 C2 11272 Santa Monica Boulevard 310/281-8223

Hollywood, Midtown and Universal Studios

Getting Your Bearings

Northwest of Downtown and east of the wealthy suburbs lies Hollywood. Tinseltown's iconic status as the heart of the movie industry has survived the near disappearance of actual filmmaking. The Hollywood Sign, Grauman's Chinese Theatre, the Walk of Fame and Universal Studios all feed the film-world fantasy. But Hollywood is not all tinsel: world-class art, LA's Museum Row and the largest city park in the United States all have their home here.

The glory days may be gone, but Hollywood still bears traces of its glamorous heritage. There are many attractions worth exploring, including Universal Studios in North Hollywood. Nearby, the chaparral-clad hills of Griffith Park offer endless acres of natural refuge and at least one legendary movie location.

Moving south from Hollywood down La Brea, Fairfax or La Cienega, you meet Midtown, also known as Mid-Wilshire. Here, a strip of once-grand retail real estate bordering the elegant community of Hancock Park was dubbed the "Miracle Mile."

This stretch of Wilshire offers few miracles today, but just steps west you'll findthe city's densest concentration of museums.

Anchored by the brilliant LA County Museum of Art (LACMA), Museum Row has something for just about everybody, from a facility devoted to that LA icon, the automobile, to the amazing La Brea Tar Pits, primal pools of prehistoric ooze absolutely stuffed with the well-preserved bones of creatures from Hollywood's Ice Age.

★ Don't Miss

At Your Leisure

- **7** Farmers Market ➤ 124
- **8** Petersen Automotive Museum ➤ 124
- **9** Craft and Folk Art Museum ➤ 125
- **10** Hollywood Forever ➤ 125
- **11** Hollyhock House ➤ 126
- **12** Sunset Strip ➤ 127
- **13** Schindler House ➤ 127
- **14** Hollywood and Highland ➤ 127
- **15** Freeman House ➤ 128
- **16** Hollywood Bowl ➤ 128
- **17** Autry Museum of Western Heritage ➤ 129
- **18** Los Angeles Zoo ➤ 129

Page 103: The Walk of Fame

Opposite: LA County Museum of Art

In Two Days

If you're not quite sure where to begin your travels, this itinerary recommends a practical and enjoyable two days in Hollywood, Midtown and Universal Studios, taking in some of the best places to see using the Getting Your Bearings map on the previous page. For more information see the main entries.

Day One

Morning

Breakfast on cheese omelet or a melt-in-the-mouth buttermilk pancake at Du-pars (6333 W 3rd Street; tel: 323/933 8446; open 24 hours; $). There are also plenty of open-air cafes at the 7 **Farmer's Market** (below, ➤ 124), which opens at 9am. Take a spin east on Third Street and then down La Brea to Wilshire Boulevard to admire the art deco beauties that grace the Miracle Mile. Of note are the E Clem Wilson Building at 5217, featured as the *Daily Planet* building in the 1952 television series *The Adventures of Superman*), the Darkroom, an old photographic shop whose facade is a huge camera, at 5370, and the still functioning El Rey Theatre at 5515 (➤ 136). Visit 2 **La Brea Tar Pits** (➤ 113–114), making sure to have a look at the "fish bowl" laboratory to see scientists making discoveries before your eyes.

Lunch

Make your way to the 2 **LA County Museum of Art** (➤ 108–112), which only opens at noon, or 11am at weekends. Have a quick lunch at LACMA's outdoor café, or grab a hot dog at the landmark Pink's Famous Chili Dogs (➤ 132), then spend a few hours exploring the museum's superb collections.

Afternoon

Time for some star gazing: take a look at the prints in the cement left by celebrities outside 3 **Grauman's Chinese Theatre** and the stars of the world-famous **Walk of Fame** (➤ 115–117). Then take to the great outdoors at 4 **Griffith Park and Observatory** (above right, ➤ 118), perhaps

walking one of the scenic trails. A visit to the newly renovated observatory is a must. From here you can see the famous 5 **Hollywood Sign** on Mount Lee (➤ 119), actually within the park, although it is illegal to get close to it.

Evening
Have a drink and a meal fit for a Hollywood star, either at Ca'Brea (➤ 130) or Sona (➤ 131)

Day Two

Morning
Make your way to 6 **Universal Studios Hollywood** (Globe fountain below, ➤ 120–122), the movie theme park for all ages. If you are keen to experience a number of rides, you may want to buy a Front of Line Pass (➤ 123) as long lines are common. Those interested in the movie-making process should consider the VIP Experience (➤ 123), which takes a full six hours. Spend the morning seeing the special-effects stages and visiting the studio lots.

Lunch
Grab a quick lunch at any of the fast-food outlets offering pizzas, burgers and salads.

Afternoon
Take your pick from any number of thrilling rides and perhaps catch one of the many shows.

Evening
Enjoy a casual dinner at 6 **CityWalk** (➤ 122–123) in the fun, Texan-themed Saddle Ranch Chop House. Then take in a movie at one of its many cinema screens to complete your Hollywood experience.

LA County Museum of Art

The collections at the LA County Museum of Art offer virtually global coverage of the history of art. It may be less glitzy than the Museum of Contemporary Art (MOCA) and the Getty Center, but LACMA's collections are generally superior and more extensive than those of the newer institutions.

The first phase of LACMA's Transformation project, an expansion and renovation program that aims to unify the existing museum buildings, was completed in 2008. This added the new Broad Contemporary Art Museum (BCAM), creating an additional 60,000 square feet (5,574sq m) of exhibition space. The new BP Grand Entrance is fronted by the stunning *Urban Light*, a sculpture cunningly made from reclaimed streetlights. Plazas allows easy access to a series of other buildings, the Ahmanson, the Art of Americas, the Hammer, a Pavilion for Japanese Art and the Bing Center.

A view across to the Pavilion for Japanese Art, on the periphery of the museum complex

Entrance staircase from Wilshire Boulevard leading to the museum

The Transformation is moving into its next stage, which means that gallery displays may change often. So be prepared that works may not be on display. Check ahead with the museum first to avoid disappointment.

Ahmanson Building

The Ahmanson, to the west of the BP Grand Entrance, is a treasure house. At plaza level (Level 2) is the Modern Art collection, some 250 paintings and sculptures mainly from Europe. The artists read like a roll call of modern art and it is hard to pick favorites. Works not to be missed include Picasso's *Portrait of Sebastian Juner Vidal* (1903) and the later *Weeping Woman with a Handkerchief* (1937), Magritte's iconic 1929 painting *Treachery of Images (This is Not a Pipe)* and Matisse's huge *Tea* (1919). Braque, Leger, Miró and Schwitters are also well represented.

German Expressionism gets a gallery to itself. The Robert Gore Rifkind Gallery specializes in works on paper, with an extensive collection of works by Beckmann, Dix, Grosz, Kirchner, Marc, Nolde and others. Additionally, the Ahmanson has works of Klee, Kandinsky and Feininger from the Bauhaus period, as part of a US$100 million bequest from Janice and Henri Lazarof in 2007.

African art is displayed on the Plaza level. The collection includes an array of stunning masks and ritual objects, many dating from the 20th century. Look to see if the splendid 17th-century Benin bronze plaque of a warrior is on view when you visit.

Upstairs again (at Level 3) there is a vast range of European art from the ancient Romans and Greeks to the 19th century. Among the hundreds of masterpieces on display are Rembrandt's paintings *The Raising of Lazarus* (*c*1630) and *Portrait of Marten Looten* (1632), Hans Holbein's *Portrait of Young Woman with a White Coif* (1541), Georges de la Tour's striking *The Magdalen with the Smoking Flame* (*c*1630) and Rodin's *Nude Study of Balzac*. Also on this floor are fine objects from the Hearst bequest, including the beautiful 13th-century *Stained Glass Panel with Angel* by the Protais Master of Sées and a Venetian glass ewer (*c*1500). Take a quick look at the ancient Egyptian artifacts on this floor and then head upstairs to Level 4.

On display on Level 4 are objects from both the Ancient and Islamic Middle East, as well South East Asian Art. There are lots of pots and some fine decorative Islamic tiles. The South Asian display is strong on figures of Hindu gods, but the highlights are the sculpted wood-and-copper Buddhas. The South Asian collection also has many fine 16th- to 18th-century Indian watercolors, not currently on display.

The Ahmanson Building houses a superb collection of art

Art of the Americas Building

To the west of the Ahmanson is the Art of Americas building, housing a rich variety of art from both North and South America. The Latin American collection is said to be one of the largest in the world.

Plaza level (Level 2) shows special exhibitions, so check what is currently running. Then head up to Level 3 for the American Art gallery, which focuses on artists who worked or were born in the US until around the mid-20th century. Notable works in the diverse display include John Singer Sargent's *Portrait of Mrs Edward L Davis and Her Son, Livingston Davis* (1890) Mary Cassatt's *Woman and Child,* David Hockney's *Mulholland Drive: The Road to the Studio* (1980) and F Childe Hassam's *Avenue of the Allies: Brazil, Belgium* – one of his patriotic flag series from 1918. Also on this floor are ceramics and craft exhibits.

If you like your art bold and uncompromising, be sure to visit Level 4. In Latin American Art, works by Mexican artists shine the most brightly. Look out for Diego Rivera's *Flower Day* (1925), Frida Kahlo's *Weeping Coconuts* (1951) and Rufino Tamayo's *Messengers in the Wind* (1931). There are also many religious paintings and decorative objects, which often seem emasculated by European influences. No such issues cloud the Ancient America sections, where pre-Columbian vigor holds sway. There are masks and figures, mainly from Mexico and Central America, as well as the usual pots. Take a look at the Mosaic Skull, dating from the Mixteca-Puebla period (*c*1400–1521), a human skull covered in turquoise and jadeite – perhaps the inspiration for Damien Hirst's 2007 *For the Love of God*, a £50 million diamond-encrusted skull. At the other extreme, admire the dinky *Seated Female Figure* ceramic (Teotihuacan, AD250–450).

Rembrandt's *Portrait of Martin Looten* (1632) forms part of the Ahmanson's European collection

Hammer Building

Across the plaza is the Hammer Building. This is being refurbished to show Chinese and Korean Art and is due to reopen in 2009.

Pavilion for Japanese Art

Beside the Hammer Building is the Pavilion for Japanese Art. Highlights include traditional woodblock prints, quirky sculptures and exquisite lacquerwork pieces. Don't miss Katsushika Hokusai's *South Wind, Clear Dawn* (*c*1830), with its classic view of Mount Fuji, and the beautiful 17th-century lacquered stationery box, with mother-of-pearl inlay.

Broad Contemporary Art Museum

Opened in early 2008, this three-story building designed by award-winning architect Renzo Piano is almost an artwork in itself. It connects the previously separate buildings of the museum, using natural light to great effect. The museum was created to house a collection of art spanning from 1945 to the present day.

Portrait of Mrs Edward L Davis and Her Son, Livingston Davis by John Singer Sargent

TAKING A BREAK

The **Pentimento** café on the main plaza at LACMA (tel:323/857-4761; Mon, Tue, Thu and Sat 10–8, Fri noon–8:30pm, Sun 11–6) serves Italian-style snacks, lunch and dinner as well as afternoon tea (2–5).

---

199 F3 ✉ 5905 Wilshire Boulevard, between La Brea and Fairfax (LACMA West, Southwest Museum, corner of Wilshire and Fairfax, one-half block west of main museum) ☎ 323/857-6000; www.lacma.org Mon, Tue, Thu noon–8, Fri noon–9, Sat–Sun 11–8. LACMA West closed at 5pm daily Adults moderate; pay what you wish after 5pm. Free 2nd Tue of the month

LA COUNTY MUSEUM OF ART: INSIDE INFO

Top tips The Friday evening **jazz series** (Apr–Nov Fri 6–8) is very popular; there is no reserved seating so come early for good seats.

- The museum tours provide a real insight into its collection. The 15-minute **Spotlight Talks** (most days at 1:30pm; free) focus on one work of art in the permanent collection; the 25-minute **In Focus Tours** (most days at 1pm; free) highlight an artist, style, or movement, and the **Multimedia Tours** (from welcome centers, free) provide interactive tours at your own pace, allowing users to bookmark their favorite exhibits and download them onto a 3D gallery at home.
- **Family programs** on Sundays from 12:30–3:30 offer hands-on art workshops, but check in advance as details may change. The price is included in admission.

2 La Brea Tar Pits

Right in the middle of Los Angeles, powerful saber-tooth cats once roamed, hunting woolly mammoths on Wilshire Boulevard. The proof is in their bones, thousands of which have been interred precisely where the poor animals got stuck, in the dark, primal ooze of La Brea Tar Pits, when they stopped to drink from what must have looked like a cooling pool of water. The Tar Pits is one of the world's most important documentations of now extinct plant and animal life from the Ice Age.

First, two salient notes: The name is redundant, since La Brea means "the tar" in Spanish; and it is not actually tar but asphalt that has been bubbling forth from the 100-odd pits, randomly situated in the 23-acre (10.5ha) park, for an estimated 40,000 years, through the Ice Age of the Pleistocene era.

Bare Bones

Among the 1 million or more specimens discovered here are the 9,000-year-old bones of a woman (now called La Brea Woman), thousands of bones from *Smilodon californicus*, the saber-tooth cat, along with bones from mammoths, mastodons, long-horned bison, camels, bears, giant rats, ground sloths, vultures, lizards and other species, some extinct, some still around. There are fossilized remains from

A life-size replica of a mammoth helps visitors to visualize a distant past

59 mammal species and 135 bird species and a total of 660 different species including plants and insects.

Hancock Park

You won't find the fenced-in pools pretty to look at (or to smell, for that matter), but the surrounding Hancock Park makes for pleasant walking and picnicking. Among the life-size replicas of Ice Age animals is a huge model of a trapped mammoth, which lurches out of the Lake Pit, grabbing your attention on Wilshire Boulevard.

George C Page Museum

Open since 1977, the George C Page Museum, behind La Brea Tar Pits, puts some science on the bones pulled out of the pits. Here you can view reconstructed skeletons of giant ground sloths, saber-tooth cats and similar animals. The saber-tooth cat has for long been California's official state fossil.

Educational exhibits along with a 15-minute film document the history of the digs, which have been ongoing since 1906.

For amateur and budding scientists, the opportunity to watch paleontologists in action in the Paleontology Laboratory, cleaning and classifying the uncovered bones, is a rare treat indeed.

The central courtyard of the George C Page Museum

TAKING A BREAK

Pop into cozy **Ca'Brea** for rustic Italian fare (➤ 130) or **Pinks** (➤ 132) for a perfect hotdog.

199 F3 · 5801 Wilshire Boulevard, next to LACMA between La Brea and Fairfax · 323/934-7243 (George C Page Museum); www.tarpits.org · Mon–Fri 9:30–5, Sat–Sun and public hols 10–5 · George C Page Museum: moderate; free first Tue. Tar Pits: free

LA BREA TAR PITS: INSIDE INFO

Top tips Watch scientists examine the findings from the Tar Pits and piece together a picture of the distant Ice Age at the glass-enclosed laboratory (dubbed the **"fish bowl"**) within the George C Page Museum.

- **Pit 91** is the scene of a two-month excavation project every summer, so you can watch paleontologists at work from an observation area. (Note how the pit has been divided into grids in order to keep track of the bones.)

3 Grauman's Chinese Theatre and the Walk of Fame

The fabulous Sid Grauman (1879–1950), creator of Hollywood's most delightfully vulgar movie palaces, is long gone, but his legacy lives on at Grauman's Chinese Theatre (formerly Mann's), as does the legacy of all Hollywood, in the kitschy, richly historic scene on and around Hollywood Boulevard where it crosses Highland Avenue and Vine Street. Don't let the crowds deter you; this is the heart of Old Hollywood, and well worth a good morning's walkabout. Be sure to check out the latest addition to this part of town, the highly touted mega-mall – Hollywood and Highland.

Located just west of Highland at 6925 Hollywood, **Grauman's Chinese Theatre** has been, for more than 80 years, the main event for tourists seeking the Holy Grail of Hollywood history. Designed by the architects Meyer and Holler under Grauman's direction, with a look inspired by Chinese temples, the theater's dragon reliefs, spiky roof lines and garishly enchanting forms and colors masterfully evoke the exotic East. Beginning with Cecil B DeMille's *King of Kings* in 1927, every first-night film opening of note took place here, and it has always played a significant role in Hollywood history.

The Walk of Fame

The foot-, hand- and other body-part prints left in

Grauman's Chinese Theatre, a Hollywood landmark since 1927

Famous hand- and footprints outside the Chinese Theatre

cement in the theater's sidewalk by more than 2,000 movie stars have made permanent the mystique. Legions of fans (some 2 million a year) still flock here to match their hands and feet to the prints of stars as ancient as Douglas Fairbanks Sr and Mary Pickford, the first two invited to leave their impressions, and as contemporary as Charlize Theron, Denzel Washington and Mel Gibson.

According to legend, the tradition began by accident when silent movie star Norma Talmadge serendipitously stepped in wet cement on the opening night of *King of Kings* in 1927.

The Walk of Fame provides another opportunity for star-gazing, although some of the obscure characters whose names are embedded in the Hollywood Boulevard sidewalk are far from famous. Established in 1960 by the local chamber of commerce as a way to reinvigorate the fading tourist allure of Tinseltown, the Walk of Fame has always been more gimmick than anything else. It costs the invited "star" or his/her studio or entertainment company about $25,000 to buy a star on the street – a great promotional tool to hype new movies or CDs.

The first eight names, unveiled in 1960, lend a sense of what is meant by "far from famous": Olive Borden, Ronald Colman, Louise Fazenda, Preston Foster, Burt Lancaster, Edward Sedgwick, Ernest Torrence and Joanne Woodward. Three or four bona fide stars there, but who are the others?

A Different Take

For another angle on the movies, stroll the neighborhood of **Hollywood and Vine**. Take in a few of the historic hotels, movie theaters and other Hollywood Boulevard spots that figure in the Tinseltown myth. The **Pantages Theater** (➤ 135), at 6233, has a bland exterior but an amazing interior; off the Boulevard at 1817 Ivar Avenue, you'll find the site of the boarding house where Nathanael West holed up while writing his classic Hollywood satire, *The Day of the*

Details lend the theater exotic charm

Locust. Check out the historic **El Capitan Theatre** (No 6838) and the **Egyptian Theatre** (No 6712), both of which still show movies.

The **Hollywood Roosevelt Hotel** (➤ 42) at No 7000 opened in 1927 as Hollywood's first luxury hotel, and its Cinegrill was the hang-out for W C Fields, Ernest Hemingway and F Scott Fitzgerald; the **Musso & Frank Grill** (➤ 131) at 6667 has been an industry fixture since opening in 1919. Just up from the corner of Hollywood at 1750 Vine, the 1956 **Capitol Records Tower** looks like a stack of records with a turntable on top. The rooftop beacon flashes "Hollywood" in Morse code.

Movie Stars' Homes Tour

A classic of kitschy tourism, the Movie Stars' Homes Tour remains a don't miss event. Take a bus tour and let the guide fill you in on the history and all the latest gossip. Tours leave from the Chinese Theatre or your hotel lobby. Otherwise, grab a copy of the Movie Stars' Homes Map and navigate yourself. They aren't always up to date, but they'll keep you from wandering aimlessly around the streets of Brentwood and Beverly Hills. You might see a star, you might not, but it's great fun to gaze at these huge homes and wonder who goes in and what goes on! But try to respect the privacy of the residents.

TAKING A BREAK

Tuck into all-American fare and get a taste of old-school Hollywood at **Musso & Frank Grill** (➤ 131). You may even catch a glimpse of a celebrity. Reservations recommended, even for lunch.

---

200 A3 ✉ 6925 Hollywood Boulevard ☎ 323/464-8111; www.manntheatres.com

GRAUMAN'S CHINESE THEATRE AND THE WALK OF FAME: INSIDE INFO

Top tips Look out for unusual prints outside Grauman's Chinese Theatre. Jimmy Durante left a nose-print, Betty Grable her leg-prints and Harpo Marx, of course, left a harp print.

- A **map** on the Mann Theatres' website shows the location of each of the prints, so you can easily find those made by your favorite star. Alternatively, www.hollywoodchamber.net provides a searchable directory of all the celebrities who have made their mark on the Walk of Fame with the addresses of their star.

4 Griffith Park and Observatory

Griffith Park is the country's largest city park, although the rugged Hollywood Hills that make up a good portion of it are relatively inaccessible. Named for mining millionaire Griffith J Griffith, it features 53 miles (85km) of trails, gardens, a bird sanctuary, horseback riding, bicycle rental and a swimming pool in summer. It is also home to the Los Angeles Zoo, the Autry Museum of Western Heritage and the Greek Theatre.

Since opening in 1935, the Observatory has been famous for its elegant, copper-domed Moderne design. Regally poised on the slope of Mount Hollywood, it has been used as a set in a number of films, most notably Nicholas Ray's *Rebel Without a Cause* (1955), the movie that made James Dean immortal. This bit of movie lore is memorialized on the grounds with a bronze statue of James Dean.

At the newly remodeled Observatory, the Planetarium Show tells the history of the universe with animations and state-of-the-art effects. There are eight shows daily on weekdays and ten shows on Saturdays and Sundays – tickets only available on the day. Children under 5 are only admitted to the first show each day.

Griffith Observatory
200 C4 · 2800 E Observatory Road · 213/473-0800; www.griffithobs.org · Tue–Fri noon–10, Sat–Sun 10–10 · Free

Griffith Park
200 C5 · 4730 Crystal Springs Drive · 323/913-4688; www.laparks.org · Daily 6am–10pm. Bridle trails, hiking paths and mountain roads closed at sunset · Free

From its Mount Hollywood site the Observatory commands good views

5 The Hollywood Sign

Strung across Mount Lee in the Hollywood Hills, the Hollywood sign, with its 50-foot-high (15m) letters, is possibly the most famous sign in the world. Contrary to legend, it has been the scene of just one known suicide, by 24-year-old actress Lillian "Peg" Entwhistle in 1932, who leaped to her death from the "H." The sign originally spelled "Hollywoodland" and was put up in 1923 by *Los Angeles Times* publisher Harry Chandler to promote a housing development.

This just may be the most famous sign in the world

In 1949, the "land" was dropped by the Hollywood Chamber of Commerce, which took over management of the sign with the intention of making it a landmark. By 1978 the sign was a wreck. Then celebs stepped in, with various famous folk adopting individual letters. The sign has been well-tended ever since, solidifying its position as LA's supreme pop icon.

The sign has been fenced off so that the public can't get in. The end of Beachwood Drive is as close as you'll get, and it's a long way off, with infra-red security cameras and a hefty fine waiting for transgressors, of which there are many. Along with a number of college students who've sneaked in to change the sign to their school's names (USC, Cal Tech, UCLA), quite a few pranksters have had their way with it. It has been Dollywood, Holywood, Hollyweed, even Ollywood – thanks to admirers of, respectively, Dolly Parton, evangelist Aimee Semple McPherson, marijuana and Oliver North.

Two good viewpoints of the sign are straight up Beachwood Drive and from the grounds at the Griffith Park Observatory. The best overall view is from the roof deck of the Hollywood and Highland complex.

---

200 B5
www.hollywoodsign.org

6 Universal Studios Hollywood and CityWalk

Conveniently close to Hollywood and Downtown, Universal Studios offers a great mix of amusement-park thrills and movie-making excitement. No visit to the city would be complete without a trip to Universal.

Sprawling over 415 acres (168ha), Universal Studios has been a working movie backlot since 1915. Over the decades, Universal merged with other companies, expanded and started public studio tours, all the while providing set space for many big hits and great movies: Alfred Hitchcock worked out of Universal, and both George Lucas and Steven Spielberg staged important movies here. Although Universal remains a working studio, it is as a theme park devoted to the art of movie-making that it has become a major tourist destination in the city.

Studio Tour

For film and TV fans the biggest draw continues to be the **Studio Tour**, a guided tram tour through the Universal backlot, narrated by some big-name stars. Each tram, equipped with state-of-the-art sound and video systems, takes you through 35 soundstages, giving a glimpse of what

A retro 1980s sign welcomes visitors to Universal Studios

was, what is and what will be in the world of movie-making. There's not much of a chance you'll actually get to see a movie being filmed on this tour, but you'll get a firsthand look at how it's done. Special effects, virtual-reality sets, a special presentation of "Before They Were Stars" on the tram ride, the movie set from Steven Spielberg's *War of the Worlds*. and the one and only Bates Motel from Hitchcock's *Psycho* of 1960 and 2000 are the big highlights of this tour.

The Universal Experience: Behind the Scenes of Universal Pictures, which opened in 2008, displays an eclectic range of movie memorabilia. Visitors can get up close to the props used in some movie classics – this is your chance to see the briefcase used by Gregory Peck in the 1962 film *To Kill a Mockingbird* and the costumes from the 2000 hit remake of *The Grinch Who Stole Christmas*.

Jurassic Park ® – The Ride provides realistic dinosaur encounters...

Take a Ride

For those disinclined to take the tour, take a ride instead. Several of the ones based on hit movies are lots of fun. The latest is **The Simpsons Ride™**, where visitors entering Krustyland are propelled along with Homer, Bart, and the rest of the family on a rocket-paced adventure. **Jurassic Park® – The Ride** features a boat tour through a jungle populated with animatronic dinosaurs, including a couple of *T rexs* too realistic for comfort for small children and a heart-stopping 84-foot (25.5m) drop into pitch blackness at the end. This is one of the most popular rides and once is not usually enough. Just be prepared to get wet. **Terminator 2:3D** has its admirers too, while another of the hot ones is a roller-coaster ride into an ancient Egyptian tomb in **Revenge**

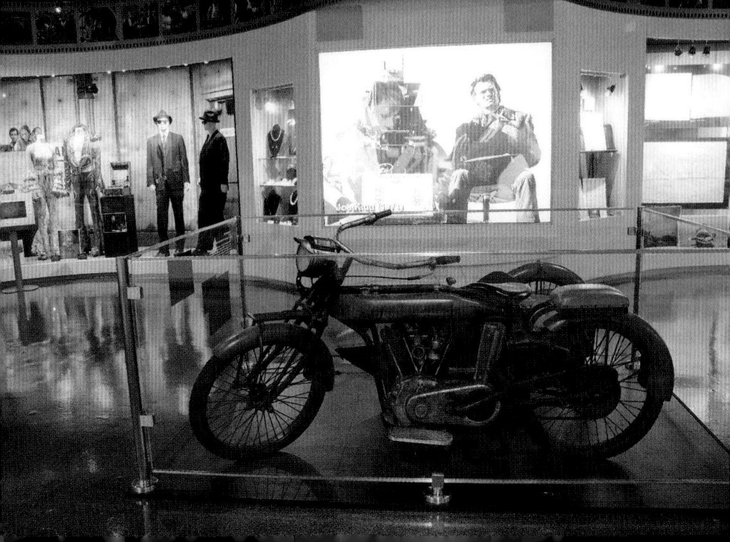

Movie memorabilia on display at The Universal Experience: Behind the Scenes of Universal Pictures

of the Mummy – the Ride, based on the *Mummy* movies. In some cases, the rides can be far more exciting than the movies, as with *Waterworld* and *Van Helsing*. **Shrek 4-D** is an original 3-D film with additional special effects, hence the "four dimensions of thrills." You'll feel the action in your seat.

The Blues Brothers perform a 20-minute concert several times daily (times vary seasonally). The place swarms with characters from TV shows, movies and cartoons. You can have your picture taken in the mouth of the *Jaws* shark, flirting with Marilyn Monroe or flexing with the Warrior Princess Xena, who's wandering around in full gladiatrix garb, trading quips with Hercules. Younger children in particular will get excited at having their photograph taken with cartoon characters like Scooby-Doo, SpongeBob SquarePants and Curious George.

The Mini used in the 2007 movie *The Bourne Ultimatum* on display at Universal

CityWalk

Universal CityWalk is the pathway that links the Universal Studios theme park (where the big shows and thrill rides live) to the Gibson Amphitheater and movie theaters (home to one of the biggest movie screens in history). CityWalk is Universal's equivalent of Disney's Downtown Disney District (➤ 169), a city "street," lined with stores and restaurants, that is completely removed from urban reality.

Here you can find specialty stores selling everything from little red wagons to big blue surfboards and high-priced memorabilia from every possible (Universal) film or TV show from *I Love Lucy* to *War of the Worlds*. It's one of the places

Stores and restaurants line Universal's bustling CityWalk

where you can still buy Hollywood trivia – the snow-globe with palm trees or the signed (but spurious) head shots of movie stars. There are bowling alleys, no less than 19 movie screens, two dozen restaurants and one of the largest IMAX® theaters. Fancy a version of indoor skydiving? Visit Ifly for one minute in a vertical wind tunnel.

All of it has been lit with hot neon, cooled with fountains and fueled by a middle-of-the-road rock soundtrack designed to let everybody know what a good time they're having. The best things are the absence of cars and the presence of street performers, who provide a pleasingly personalized counterpoint to the relentless entertainment marketeering. And the crowds of people of all ages roaming around lend the place an urban buzz in spite of its sanitized self. It's expensive and the lines are long, but you and your family can have tons of fun here. It's a good place to wind down after a concert at the Gibson Amphitheater (a vast 6,000-seat performance venue, which stages a variety of events, with headliners performing year-round) or a day at Universal Studios.

CityWalk's fantasy version of urban streetlife

TAKING A BREAK

With more than two dozen restaurants, snack bars and fast-food joints ranging from high-end gourmet to budget fries, Universal's CityWalk has something for everyone. Decide what kind of food you want and you'll almost certainly find it available somewhere in CityWalk.

---

199 F5

100 Universal City Plaza
1-800/UNIVERSAL; www.universalstudioshollywood.com
Easter, summer, Thanksgiving and Christmas daily 10–6; 8am–10pm
Expensive

Citywalk
www.citywalkhollywood.com Sun–Thu 11–9, Fri–Sat 11–11 Free

UNIVERSAL STUDIOS HOLLYWOOD AND CITYWALK: INSIDE INFO

Top tips As at all big theme parks, lines for the most popular rides can be long. A **Front of Line Pass** ($119 per person) allows you to go to the front of the line and gets you the best seats on all rides, shows and attractions. Only a limited number are sold each day.

- The **VIP Experience** ($199 per person) includes backstage tours of film sets and studio facilities in addition to priority on all rides.
- Children have to be at least 4 feet (1.2m) tall for many of the rides.

At Your Leisure

The Farmers Market is the first choice of many for fresh fruits and vegetables

7 Farmers Market

The Farmers Market first appeared during the Great Depression of the 1930s, when local farmers sold produce off the backs of their trucks. Soon stands replaced the trucks, and a ramshackle clock tower went up. Today the tower reigns over a compact warren of food stands, curiosity shops, restaurants and souvenir stands aimed chiefly at tourists.

A 6-minute ride from the Farmers Market on a glossy green streetcar lies The Grove at Farmers Market (The Grove for short), a sprawling open-air shopping complex, built in 2002 on the site of an old dairy, with a variety of chain stores and restaurants and even a dancing musical fountain that bursts into life every 30 minutes.

199 F3 6333 West Third Street, corner of Fairfax 323/933-9211; www.farmersmarketla.com Mon–Fri 9–9, Sat 9–8, Sun 10–7 Free

The Grove

189 The Grove 888/315-8883 or 323/900-8080; www.thegrovela.com Mon–Thu 10–9, Fri–Sat 10–10, Sun 11–8

8 Petersen Automotive Museum

LA's ongoing love affair with the automobile gets major treatment at the Petersen, and the results can be engrossing. Named for media mogul Robert Petersen (publisher of *Motor Trend* and *Hot Rod* magazines), the museum includes over 150 classic and rare cars as well as dioramas. The first-floor Streetscape puts visitors into historically accurate dioramas exploring LA's car-bound history.

Second-floor galleries have revolving shows: celebrity autos are everywhere; the Bruce Meyer Gallery features hot rods; and the Otis Chandler Gallery does motorcycles. The third floor offers interactive children's exhibits such as the Vroom Room.

The museum also holds special exhibits devoted to off-beat auto-related topics, for example, a tribute

Vintage vehicles on display at the Petersen Automotive Museum

to Woodies, the wood-paneled station wagons that became icons of the California surf culture.

199 F2 ✉ 6060 Wilshire Boulevard at Fairfax Avenue ☎ 323/930-2277; www.petersen.org Tue–Sun 10–6 Moderate

9 Craft and Folk Art Museum

Another treasure-filled gem on Museum Row, the Craft and Folk Art Museum stages compelling exhibitions that look in depth at the cultures that have created the objects on display. One exhibit may look at how printmaking is used to express personal identity and another at global myths through puppet making. Ensconced in a Georgian-style building, the museum's collections include contemporary, historic and ethnic arts and crafts, ranging from household objects to artworks in a variety of media from all over the world, plus a superb collection of masks.

199 F2 ✉ 5814 Wilshire Boulevard ☎ 323/937-4230; www.cafam.org Tue–Wed, Fri 11–5, Sat–Sun noon–6 Adults, seniors and students inexpensive; under 12s free; free first Wed of the month

10 Hollywood Forever

This grand old Hollywood graveyard, established in 1899, is an important stop for fans of the celebrity dead. Famous stars interred here include Rudolph Valentino, in tomb number 1205 in the Cathedral Mausoleum. In 1926 10,000 people packed into the cemetery for his funeral.

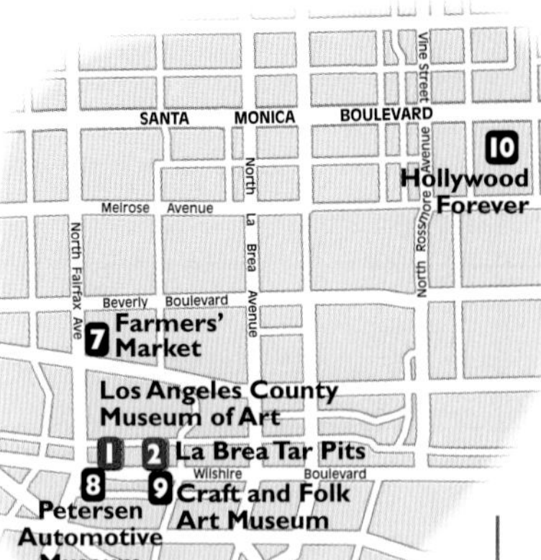

Douglas Fairbanks, Snr, Douglas Fairbanks, Jnr, and Jayne Mansfield are just some of the Hollywood greats buried here.

The new owners of Hollywood Forever have taken the still functioning cemetery firmly into the 21st century. The bereaved can pay tribute to their loved one on a wide-screen TV and even access life stories on touch screens throughout the grounds. Hollywood young bloods even employ architects to design their mausoleums. On Saturdays in summer (admission expensive), movies are projected onto mausoleums and picnics are encouraged.

200 B3 ✉ 6000 Santa Monica Boulevard between Gower and Van Ness ☎ 323/469-1181; www.hollywoodforever.com Daily 8–5 Free

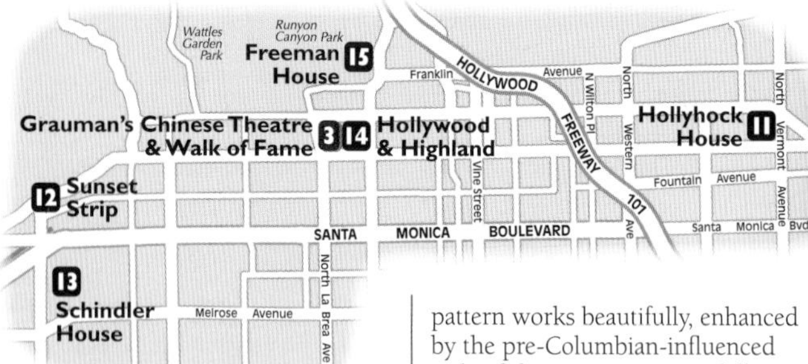

11 Hollyhock House

Millionaire oil heiress Aline Barnsdall envisioned an artists' colony or something vaguely Marxist when she arrived in LA from Chicago flush with family cash in 1915. She bought a 36-acre (14.5ha) called Olive Hill, on Hollywood's eastern edge, and called on Frank Lloyd Wright to plan the project. Wright responded with Hollyhock House, long-considered one of his greatest works and one of the most significant buildings of the 20th century, according to the American Institute of Architects. Constructed from hollow clay tile and stucco, the house has been decorated inside and out with an abstract pattern of a hollyhock, Barnsdall's favorite flower. The pattern works beautifully, enhanced by the pre-Columbian-influenced style of the structure. Barnsdall gave the property to the city in 1927. For decades, earthquakes, rain and neglect took their toll. It was designated a cultural monument in 1963. A number of ongoing restoration programs have taken place since then, which will continue until 2012. The grounds include Barnsdall Art Park, which hosts temporary exhibitions and goes some way towards realizing Barnsdall's original intention of creating a thriving center for the arts.

200 C3 ✉ 4800 Hollywood Boulevard, between Vermont and Edgemont ☎ 323/913-4157; www.hollyhockhouse.net Tours: Wed–Sun 12:30, 1:30, 2:30 and 3:30 Moderate

Hollyhock House ranks among architect Frank Lloyd Wright's greatest works

12 Sunset Strip

The Strip has been legendary for decades, and rocks on still, with giant billboards, cool nightclubs, hot comedy clubs, hip hotels and chic restaurants leading the neon-lit parade. From Crescent Heights to Doheny, Sunset reigns as one of the most famous asphalt arteries on earth. In the 1930s and 1940s, movie stars gathered at Ciro's, Mocambo, the Garden of Allah and other nightclubs. After a TV-induced nightlife lull, the late 1960s arrived in full-blown, flower-powered splendor: Whisky A Go Go, the Roxy and other rock 'n' roll venues showcased such rock icons as the Doors, the Byrds, Janis Joplin and Jimi Hendrix. The Strip has been a holy ground for the rock world ever since, spiced up by clubs like Johnny Depp's notorious Viper Room (where River Phoenix died).

Even hipper these days is the hotel scene, both old and new: Chateau Marmont, the Mondrian, the Sunset Marquis, the Argyle and others, with their celebrity bars and *haute* restaurants, are all the rage.

199 E4 ✉ Sunset Boulevard between Crescent Heights Boulevard and Doheny Drive

13 Schindler House

One of the most influential LA architects of the 20th century, Austrian immigrant Rudolph Schindler moved to California to work for Frank Lloyd Wright on the Hollyhock House, then pursued his own successful career. Many consider the studio-residence he designed for himself and his wife in 1921 to be the best of the houses he created in LA. The iconoclastic house was designed as a two-family home (Schindler and his wife lived there, separately, even after divorcing) with a single kitchen. But the real innovations were in the use of simple materials, and the complex relationships between interior and exterior space. Schindler knit concrete, redwood, glass walls and removable walls into an open plan, with all the rooms flowing into patios. The "bedrooms" were sleeping baskets on the roof, embracing the sky.

The house now serves as an outpost of Vienna's esteemed MAK (School of Applied Arts), which offers tours of LA area buildings by Schindler and other Austrian émigré architects.

199 E3 ✉ 835 N Kings Road between Melrose and Santa Monica boulevards ☎ 323/651-1510; www.makcenter.org ⏲ Wed–Sun 11–6 Moderate; free Fri 4–6pm

14 Hollywood and Highland

This would be just another intersection, lacking the historical pizzazz of nearby Hollywood and Vine, except for the huge $430 million shopping/entertainment complex. The five-floor Hollywood and Highland megamall has a variety of enticements: a luxury hotel and dozens of retail stores, nightclubs, restaurants and theaters. More alluring are the only-in-Hollywood features, including a grand staircase leading to an outdoor platform with a panoramic view of the Hollywood Sign; Babylon Court, a re-creation of the extravagant set from D W

Schindler House is an icon of LA Modernism

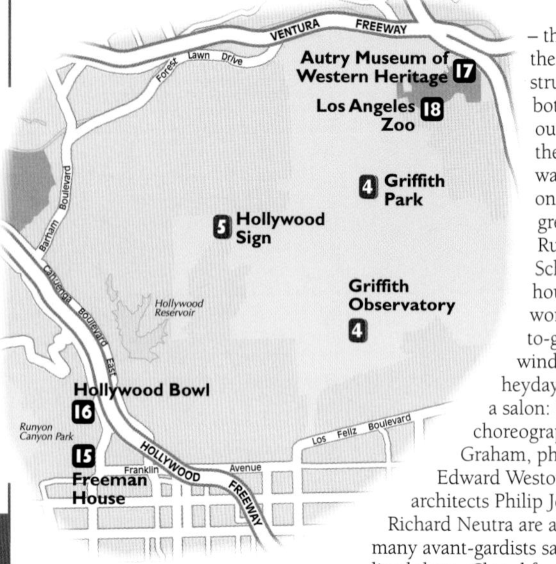

Griffith's immortal 1916 classic, *Intolerance*; a live broadcast center and the Kodak Theatre, the home for the annual Oscar telecast. The theater contains a 3,300-seat auditorium, a ballroom, a press area, a media "cockpit" and an entryway designed to bestow an even higher level of self-importance on the movie stars, as they sweep in for their Oscar evening.

200 A3 Corner of Hollywood Boulevard and Highland Avenue 323/467-6412; www.hollywood.com Mon–Sat 10–10, Sun 10–7

Kodak Theatre

323/308-6300; www.kodaktheatre.com Guided tours: Jun–Aug daily 10:30–4; Sep–May 10:30–2:30 Moderate

15 Freeman House

One of Frank Lloyd Wright's greatest LA projects is the 1924 Freeman House, created as a prototype for low-cost, mass housing. It stands out in part for its wonderful location: The views of Hollywood are spectacular. The house is also admired for the elaborate patterning – a geometric synthesis of Mayan and Islamic forms designed by Wright – that decorates the concrete structural bricks both inside and out. Much of the furniture was designed by one of LA's other great architects, Rudolph Schindler. The house features the world's first glass-to-glass corner windows. In its heyday, it was quite a salon: Dancer/choreographer Martha Graham, photographer Edward Weston, and architects Philip Johnson and Richard Neutra are among the many avant-gardists said to have lived there. Closed for renovations but tours are available through the USC School of Architecture.

200 A4 1962 Glencoe Way, Hollywood, just below the Hollywood Bowl off Hillcrest, near Highland and Franklin avenues 213/740-2723; www.usc.edu. Tours by appointment only

16 Hollywood Bowl

Listening to a well-played concert on a summer evening at the Bowl ranks among the more sublime LA experiences. The acoustics are excellent, the setting is exquisite and you won't find any but the best musicians performing on stage.

The LA Philharmonic plays its summer season here, and just about every major figure in jazz and pop has played the Bowl, from Louis Armstrong to Garth Brooks. Built in 1922 in a natural amphitheater in the Hollywood Hills, the Bowl seats 17,000, and even the budget seats are great. If you're in LA in summer, get tickets, pack a bottle of wine and a picnic and settle in for a festive evening.

Off-season or during the day, you can stroll the grounds and visit the Edmund D Edelman Hollywood Bowl Museum to see original drawings, early photos and footage of Leopold Stokowski, Judy Garland, the Beatles and other great concerts. The latest exhibit, Music for Everyone, focuses on the musical history of the Bowl.

200 A4 2301 N Highland Avenue at Odin Street, north of Whitley Heights, west of the Hollywood Freeway 323/850-2000 (Bowl), 323/850-2058 (Museum); www.hollywoodbowl.org Concert season: Jul–mid-Sep; Bowl grounds and museum: Jun–Sep Tue–Sat 10–showtime, Sun 4–showtime; Oct–May Tue–Sat 10–4 Museum: free

17 Autry Museum of Western Heritage

The singing cowboy Gene Autry contributed greatly to the Hollywood version of the Old West, and so one cannot help suspect that a museum named for him might display history rewritten to match the movies. And with Autry as the museum's major donor, there is plenty of Western movie lore here. With help from Disney's special-effects Imagineers, the museum does an entertaining job of exploring America's frontier culture. Seven themed galleries evoke the Old West of myth and reality. The Spirit of Romance, for example, examines the real hardships of life in the West while extolling the region's enchanting natural beauty. The Imagination Gallery depicts a Wild West saloon from 1880. The artifacts are fascinating: check out Billy the Kid's gun and Wyatt Earp's badge. Lively interactive scenarios thrill the kids, and a couple of galleries display special exhibitions.

200 C5 4700 Western Heritage Way, across from the LA Zoo 323/667-2000; www.autrynationalcenter.org Tue–Sun 10–5, Thu till 8 Moderate; seniors and students inexpensive. Free 2nd Tue of the month

18 Los Angeles Zoo

With 1,300 critters representing some 350 species, the LA Zoo houses enough interesting beasts to grab the fancies of most kids – and their parents. The Zoo has been upgrading lately, creating "natural" habitats for its residents. Two of them house primates: Orangutans cavort in the Red Ape Rain Forest, while chimps roam free in the Chimpanzees of the Mahale Mountains. Adventure Island offers an assortment of activities. In Koala House cute marsupials frolic in a simulated Australian forest with anteaters, rat kangaroos and flying possums. And check out the Komodo dragons – not long ago one of them took a bite out of the foot of actress Sharon Stone's husband, creating quite a furor.

It makes sense to visit the zoo and Autry Museum the same day, as they're near each other, a long way from everything else, and they share parking lots.

200 C5 5333 Zoo Drive 323/644-4200; www.lazoo.org Daily 10–5 Expensive

Gene Autry, the singing cowboy, donated many of the exhibits at the Autry Museum of Western Heritage

Where to... Eat and Drink

Restaurant Prices
Expect to pay per person for a three-course meal, excluding tax, drinks and service
$ under $30 **$$** $30–$60 **$$$** over $60

RESTAURANTS

Ago $$$
Backers including Robert de Niro and the Weinstein brothers add Hollywood cachet to this trattoria serving classic Italian fare.
199 E3 8478 Melrose Avenue 323/655-6333; www.agorestaurant.com Mon noon–2:30, 6–11:30, Sat 6–11:30, Sun 6–10:30

Boa Steakhouse $$$
This trendy, upmarket steak house within the Grafton Hotel serves up delicious Kobe beef, filet mignon and more – including lobster and fish. Sides, sauces and salads, particularly the Caesar salad, are delicious. By the time you have tucked into one of the tempting, calorie-laden desserts, you may have to roll yourself out of the place. There is a second, seafront location in Santa Monica (101 Santa Monica Boulevard).
199 E4 8462 West Sunset Boulevard, West Hollywood 323/650-8383; www.boasteak.com Sun–Thu 7am–11pm, Fri and Sat 7am–midnight

Ca'Brea $$$
Rustic Italian cooking is on the menu at this welcoming trattoria. Plenty of Hollywood film types come here to dine, but the atmosphere remains unpretentious and the food is always king. Reservations advised.
199 E3 346 S La Brea Avenue, Midtown 323/938-2863; www.cabrearestaurant.com Mon–Thu 11:30–2:30, 5–10:30, Fri 11:30–2:30, 5–11, Sat 5–11

Campanile $$$
City dwellers flock here for innovative Mediterranean cuisine. Nancy Silverton's "La Brea Bakery" breads, buns and pastries are famous, and snagging a table for a weekend brunch can be challenging. You can also buy the bakery items to go.
200 A1 624 S La Brea Avenue 323/938-1447; www.campanilerestaurant.com Mon–Thu 11:30–2:30, 6–10, Fri 11:30–2:30, 5–11, Sat–Sun 9:30–1:30, 5:30–11

Chaya Brasserie $$$
This chic Japanese/Mediterranean restaurant serves superbly presented East–West fusion dishes. Move from sushi appetizers to the tuna tartare starters and on to a main course from a lengthy menu of seafood, steak and vegetarian entrees. The wine list is excellent and cocktails also pour forth from the full bar.
199 E3 8741 Alden Drive 310/859-8833; www.thechaya.com Mon–Fri 11:30–2:30; 6–10:30, Sat 6–11, Sun 6–10

Dan Tana's $$–$$$
For more than 40 years this traditional Hollywood establishment has been serving up classic Italian fare to celebrities, locals and tourists. The extensive menu includes all the old Italian favorites, as well as melt-in-the-mouth clams, superb lobster and super-size cocktails
199 E3 9071 Santa Monica Boulevard, West Hollywood 310/275-9444; www.dantanasrestaurant.com/

Dar Maghreb $$$

Cross the threshold into an exotic re-creation of a Moroccan palace, where you'll recline on cushions, watch belly dancers and sup on a traditional seven-course feast. After a ceremonial washing, your hands become utensils for picking through lemon chicken, pigeon pie, couscous and other delights.

199 F4 7651 Sunset Boulevard 323/876-7651; www.darmaghrebrestaurant.com Mon–Fri 6–11, Sat 5:30–11, Sun 5:30–10:30

Lucques $$$

For all the raves it receives in the press, Lucques is surprisingly understated, with faded brick, a lovely fireplace and a covered patio that create a comforting atmosphere. Tempting dishes include Alaskan black cod with vanilla potatoes or slow roasted rabbit with sausage stuffing. Three-course prix-fixe meals on Sunday nights are $45.

199 E3 8474 Melrose Avenue 323/655-6277; www.lucques.com Mon 6–10pm, Tue noon–2:30, 6–10, Wed–Sat noon–2:30, 6–11, Sun 5–10pm

Musso & Frank Grill $$

For the ultimate Hollywood-noir experience, ask for a seat in the original side of this, the oldest restaurant in town, and order from a menu that features traditional American dishes such as liver and onions, juicy steaks, mashed potatoes and creamed spinach. Cocktails are perfectly mixed and the waiters display a befittingly crusty attitude while tending to your every need.

200 A3 6667 Hollywood Boulevard 323/467-7788 Tue–Sat 11–11

Sona $$$

It is pretty much agreed among LA foodies that this modern restaurant is currently one of the city's best. The French cuisine, prepared with seasonal produce, has won fistfuls of awards. The courses offered – described as firsts, seconds and thirds – manage to be both uncomplicated and yet mouthwatering. Revel in the wonderfully attentive service and do consider the degustation menus.

199 E3 401 N La Cienega Boulevard 310/659-770; www.sonarestaurant.com Tue–Thu 6–10pm; Fri–Sat 6–11pm

Sonora Café $$

If you fancy Southwestern cuisine, head to this eatery that dishes up incredibly nouvelle pleasures in an industrial-chic setting. Feast on innovative recipes incorporating smoked salmon, corn pudding, cowboy steak or south Texas antelope. The signature dish is Texas-style barbeque pork chops. As an alternative to red meat, try the ahi or one of the other seafood dishes.

200 A1 180 S La Brea Avenue 323/857-1800; www.sonoracafe.com Mon 11:30–9, Tue–Thu 11:30–10, Fri 11:30–11, Sat 5–11pm, Sun 5–9pm

Yamashiro $$

In a historic 1911 pagoda set high above Hollywood Boulevard, Yamashiro boasts incredible views. The menu includes traditional sushi and sashimi along with Cal-Asian dishes such as miso salmon, Asian BBQ baby back pork ribs, filet mignon carpaccio and curry coconut shrimp.

200 A4 1999 North Sycamore Avenue 323/466-5125; www.yaashirorestaurant.com Sun–Thu 5:30–10, Fri–Sat 5:30–11 (bar open nightly till midnight)

CAFÉS

Fred 62 $

This retro-cool Los Feliz destination serves diner fare with a gourmet spin and playful menu items like "Hunka Burnin' Love" (pancakes stuffed with peanut butter and chocolate). Expect the requisite vinyl and an alternative wait staff.

200 C3 1850 N Vermont 323/667-0062; www.fred62.com 24 hours

Insomnia Café $
Entertainment industry moguls and those who want to be their best friends inhabit this café where the coffee's strong and the patrons are enthusiastic.
199 F3 7286 Beverly Boulevard 323/931-4943 Daily 10am–1:30am

Pink's Famous Chili Dogs $
This family-run business has been in this location since 1930. It may look like just a funky hot dog stand, but Pink's is famous with everyone from movie stars to the hapless homeless for its wondrous, luscious, messy-as-can-be chili dogs.
199 F3 709 N La Brea Avenue 323/931-4223 www.pinkshollywood.com Sun–Thu 9:30am–2am, Fri–Sat 9:30am–3am

BARS

B B King's Blues Club
Universal CityWalk sets the stage for the legendary guitarist's local franchise, where blues fans and curious visitors clamor in for hot tunes to go with cool drinks. There is decent Southern food, but more importantly, musical talent that lives up to its namesake.
199 F5 100 Universal City Drive 818/622-5464; www.bbkingblues.com Daily 6pm–2am

Bar Marmont
Attached to the celebrity-hideaway Chateau Marmont Hotel, Bar Marmont offers a deliciously dark, elegant and intimate environment to sip on a cocktail amid some of the coolest characters in Hollywood. This bar is far less pretentious than any of the others along the Sunset Strip.
199 E4 8171 Sunset Boulevard 323/650-0575 Daily 6pm–2am

Barney's Beanery
Legend has it that Jim Morrison and Janis Joplin got into a brawl at this unassuming local joint where bikers, 1960s hippies and authentic rednecks gather for brews, beans and roadhouse fare, while a jukebox belts out rock 'n' roll tunes.
199 E3 8447 Santa Monica Boulevard 323/654-2287; www.barneysbeanery.com Daily 11am–2am

Cat & Fiddle
The outside patio of this pub is filled with comedians and sitcom stars who mingle with other customers and locals over a pint, a game of darts, live jazz or some authentic English pub grub.
200 A3 6530 Sunset Boulevard 323/468-3800; www.thecatandthefiddle.com Daily 11:30am–2am

The Derby
This superbly glamorous club reeks with swankiness, retro glamour and swing dancers. Locals dress up to drink, then sashay on the dance floor.
200 C4 4500 Los Feliz Boulevard 323/663-8979; www.clubderby.com Daily 4pm–2am

Formosa Café
Step back into Hollywood's film-noir days in this wonderful 1930s café/bar across the street from Warner Bros. Hollywood Studios. It was once a favorite spot for such stars as Marilyn Monroe and Humphrey Bogart. More recently the Formosa was the set for a scene in the movie *LA Confidential* (1997). For a more private evening, sip on a *mai tai* or other exotic concoctions in a dark booth or under the stars on the rooftop patio.
199 F4 7156 Santa Monica Boulevard 323/850-9050; www.formosacafe.com Mon–Fri 4pm–2am, Sat–Sun 6pm–2am

Purple Lounge at the Standard
The bar at The Standard Hotel in Hollywood is cool, dark and – as its name suggests – purple, catering to a cosmopolitan crowd. When the bar shuts down at 2am, the action moves next door to the 24-hour diner.
199 E4 8300 Sunset Boulevard 323/650-9090 Daily 10pm–2am

Where to... Shop

Shopping in Hollywood and its environs must rank as one of the unique experiences in the world. Although the Hollywood and Highland complex has taken center stage, there are still plenty of other interesting choices.

HOLLYWOOD BOULEVARD

The **Hollywood and Highland** retail and entertainment complex (➤ 127–128), which opened in 2001, has brought shoppers back to an area that in past years had become little more than a strip of tawdry souvenir shops.

You'll find hundreds of stores, the **Kodak Theater** (➤ 128), home to the Academy Awards ceremonies, and plenty of bright lights/big city within this uniquely designed complex centered around the showpiece Babylon Court. There are no large department stores, but major retailers include Gap, Victoria's Secret, Banana Republic, Ann Taylor Loft, bebe and Express.

The huge two-level **DFS Galleria** showcases both "duty free" and taxable merchandise and includes such chic lines as Celine, Fendi, Polo Ralph Lauren, Louis Vuitton, Coach and Sephora. M-A-C Cosmetics features private makeup areas and moveable stations where customers can try out a new face. For fine jewelry, scout out classy Dejaun Jewelers.

The rest of **Hollywood Boulevard** pales for local shoppers, but souvenir hunters will find bargain stores selling T-shirts, baseball caps, shot glasses and other "been there" merchandise.

You can't miss the purple-and-pink **Frederick's of Hollywood** (No 6751; tel: 323/957-5953; Mon–Sat 10–9, Sun 11–7), famous for its kinky lingerie, feather boas, frou-frou stilettos and other accessories – many in hard-to-find sizes.

Hollywood Toys & Costume (No 6600; tel: 800/554-3444; daily 10–6) offers a boggling assortment of costumes, masks and makeup for both adults and children, as well as stuffed animals, toys and models.

You'll find big pink hair and sparkling tiaras at **Hollywood Wigs** (No 6311), where dress-up and disguise are de rigeur.

Larry Edmund's Cinema and Theater Bookshop (No 6644; tel: 323/463-3273; daily 10–5:30) is another Hollywood mainstay, with one of the world's largest collections of books on the entertainment industry.

MELROSE AVENUE AREA

Melrose Avenue continues to be a favorite shopping street. Trinkets and vintage apparel now dominate the area between Citrus and La Brea avenues, while smart home decor and design houses are grouped around La Cienega and Robertson avenues, close to Beverly Center and the Pacific Design Center.

For cutting-edge furnishings, housewares and boutiques head to La Brea Avenue and Beverly Boulevard (the major intersection south of Melrose Avenue).

Aardvark's Odd Ark (No 7579; tel: 323/655-6769; Mon–Thu noon–8, Fri–Sat 11–9, Sun noon–7) is filled with racks of reasonably priced vintage clothing, including Hawaiian shirts, beaded sweaters, men's suits, women's gowns, hippie wear and tons of accessories.

Try on some of the designer and collectible eyewear at **l.a. Eyeworks** (No 7407; tel: 323/931-7795; Mon–Fri 10–7, Sat 10–5).

Vintage Americana is the specialty at kitsch-filled **Off the Wall** (No 7325; tel: 323/930-1185).

Find a different variety of wind-ups at **Wanna Buy a Watch** (No 8465; tel: 323/653-0467; Tue–Sat 11–6) with everything from antique pocket watches and cuckoo clocks to costly Rolexes.

New and used heavy metal and indie rock is the focus at **Melrose Music** (No 7714).

Hard-to-find 1930s–1960s designer furniture, lighting and artwork are highlighted at **Fat Chance** (162 N La Brea Avenue; tel: 323/930-1960; daily 11–6).

American Rag at 150 S La Brea Avenue (tel 323/935-3154; Mon–Sat 10–9, Sun noon–7) is noted for fine vintage clothing as well as new edgy styles, and it's all pretty expensive.

Nibble on complimentary cupcakes while you browse the merchandise at **Sugar** (633 N La Brea Avenue), which sells clothes and accessories from top designers (tel: 323/965-0359; Mon–Thu 11–6, Fri–Sat 11–7, Sun noon–5).

Excellent Modernist furnishings, including one of the largest collections of Eames bucket chairs, are showcased at **Modernica** (7366 Beverly Boulevard; tel: 323/933-0383; daily 9–6).

NEAR BEVERLY CENTER

The **Beverly Center** (Beverly and La Cienega boulevards; tel: 310/854-0071; www.berverlycenter.com; Mon–Fri 10–9, Sat 10–8, Sun 11–6) houses three levels of high-caliber brand-name retailers, along with branches of department stores Macy's and Bloomingdale's.

You can visit more than 200 showrooms in the vast **Pacific Design Center** (8687 Melrose Avenue; tel: 310/657-0800; Mon–Fri 9–5) – the West Coast's largest interior-design marketplace – but you'll need to employ the services of a designer (many are nearby) to make purchases.

Fabulous shoes can be yours – if you're willing to pay the price at **Sigerson Morrison** (8307 W Third Street; tel: 323/655-6133; Mon–Sat 10–6, Sun noon–5). They give Manolo a run for his money.

The Bodhi Tree (8585 Melrose Avenue; tel: 310/659-1733; daily 10–11), Los Angeles's favorite New Age bookstore, offers good vibes to go with a really vast selection of books on meditation, healing and all things spiritual, as well as music.

Every trendsetter in town, and many a celebrity, eventually waltzes into the original **Fred Segal** (8118 Melrose Avenue; tel: 323/651-3698; Mon–Sat 10–6, Sun noon–5), a block-large complex with designer wear, kid's clothes, gadgets, luggage, shoes and other necessities of life in Los Angeles.

SUNSET STRIP

Along Sunset Strip, you'll find designer boutiques in and around **Sunset Plaza** (tel:310/652-2622; Mon–Sat 10–6:30, Sun noon–5) near the corner of Doheny Drive.

Book Soup (8818 Sunset Boulevard; tel:310/659-3110; daily 9–10) is a top shop for entertainment-related titles, classics, literature and international newspapers and magazines.

OTHER AREAS

The landmark **Farmers Market** (Third Street and Fairfax Avenue), despite the addition of **The Grove at Farmers Market** complex, still provides plenty of nostalgia where you can buy fresh produce, meat, poultry, handmade candies and other tasty treats (➤ 124).

Don't overlook the museum stores on **Museum Row** (Fairfax Avenue and Wilshire Boulevard) for high-quality art prints, books, cards and unique gift items.

Universal CityWalk (➤ 122–123) offers an architecturally striking stretch filled with eateries, clubs and dozens of retailers.

Where to... Be Entertained

THEATER

Henry Fonda Music Box Theater

Touring shows and musicals are the main offerings in this fine theater, named for the great actor.
200 B3 6126 Hollywood Boulevard 323/464-0808; www.henryfondatheater.com

Fountain Theatre

An intimate theater with only 78 seats, the Fountain has still managed to win more than 160 awards for excellence since it opened in 1990. The theater stages both new works and established plays.
200 C3 5060 Fountain Avenue
323/663-1525; www.fountaintheatre.com

Matrix Theatre Company

This intimate Melrose Avenue venue has won numerous accolades for its off-Broadway-caliber productions of works by such playwrights as Samuel Beckett and Harold Pinter.
199 E3 7657 Melrose Avenue
323/852-1445; www.matrixtheatre.com

Pantages Theater

You can see lavish Broadway spectacles and concerts in this landmark 2,600-seat art-deco performance hall on Hollywood Boulevard. Its unassuming exterior belies the theater's grandiose interior.
200 A3 6233 Hollywood Boulevard
323/468-1770; www.pantages-theatre.com

COMEDY AND CABARET

Comedy Store

This top comedy club presents well-received comics; legends such as Jerry Seinfeld sometimes make appearances.
199 E4 8433 Sunset Boulevard
323/656-6268; www.thecomedystore.com

Groundlings Theatre

Few can keep a straight face during the groundbreaking stand-up acts that appear here. Making his debut to the stage at the Groundlings Theatre launched the career of stars such as Pee Wee Herman.
199 F3 7307 Melrose Avenue
323/ 934-4747; www.groundlings.com

The Improvisation

This branch of New York's famous Improv venue brings established big names as well as hot newbies to the stage.
199 E3 8162 Melrose Avenue
323/651-2583; www.improv2.com

MUSIC AND DANCE

The Baked Potato

If jazz is your thing, this is the place to go, with performances by jazz greats and jam sessions.
199 F5 3787 W Cahuenga Boulevard
818/980-1615; www.thebakedpotato.com
Daily 7pm–2am

Catalina Bar and Grill

Top jazz legends perform at this intimate club with superior acoustics.
200 A3 6725 W Sunset Boulevard
323/466-2210; www.catalinajazzclub.com Daily 7pm–midnight

Deep at the Vanguard

If you are big on style, keen to show off your latest dance moves and are not afraid to wait in line, head to Deep on Sundays and swirl around the swanky dance floor.
200 B3 1707 Vine Street
323/455-6734; www.deep-la.com
Sun 9pm–2am

El Rey Theatre
Hipsters groove to the live tunes of cutting-edge bands at this snazzy art-deco former movie theater with sunken dance floor.
199 F2 ✉ 5515 Wilshire Boulevard
☎ 323/936-4790; www.theelrey.com

Greek Theatre
Located in Griffith Park, this out-door Greek-style amphitheater offers a summer schedule of big-name artists, with everything from reggae to rock and pop to classical music.
200 C4 ✉ 2700 N Vermont Avenue
☎ 323-665-5857; www.greektheatre.com
Hours vary according to shows

Key Club
A large multi-level club on Sunset Strip, the Key Club entertains with top rock and other bands, plus DJs.
199 D3 ✉ 9039 Sunset Boulevard
☎ 310/274-5800; www.keyclub.com
Daily 7pm–2am

Roxy
Roxy is one of the hottest clubs on the Strip, hosting national touring acts as well as lesser-known wannabes.
199 D3 ✉ 9009 W Sunset Boulevard
☎ 310/278-9457; www.theroxyonsunset.com Daily 7pm–2am

The Troubadour
This famous, all-ages venue has been in business for over 50 years. Although it has changed with the times, rock 'n' roll still shares the line-up with an assemblage of raunchier bands.
199 D3 ✉ 9081 Santa Monica Boulevard
☎ 310/276-6168; www.troubadour.com
Daily 6pm–2am

Viper Room
The Viper Room, popular with Hollywood A-listers, is owned by Johnny Depp. The venue hosts big-name musicians, local bands and impromptu acts (such as Neil Young). Intimate and low-lit, it is more focused on disco than high profile rock musicians. The death of actor River Pheonix of an overdose on the sidewalk outside in 1993 has ensured the venue's notoriety.
199 D3 B8852 Sunset Boulevard
☎ 310/358-1881; www.viperroom.com
Daily 9pm–2am

Whisky A Go Go
This legendary 1960s club still thrills music fans who come to see the current era's prime rock and alternative bands.
199 D3 ✉ 8901 Sunset Boulevard
☎ 310/652-4202; www.whiskyagogo.com
Daily 8pm–2am

MOVIE THEATERS

El Capitan Theatre
This spectacular art-deco movie theater on Hollywood Boulevard showcases Disney features.
199 F4 ✉ 6838 Hollywood Boulevard
☎ 323/467-7674; www.disney.go.com

Egyptian Theatre
The American Cinemateque presents art films, foreign entries and experimental works at this historic movie theater.
200 A3 ✉ 6712 Hollywood Boulevard
☎ 323/461-2020; www.egyptiantheatre.com

Grauman's Chinese Theatre
(➤ 115–117).

New Beverly Cinema
The New Beverly presents the rare double bill, with the chance to see such nostalgic combinations as the 1955 film classics *Rebel Without a Cause* and *The Blackboard Jungle*.
199 F3 ✉ 7165 Beverly Boulevard
☎ 323/938-4038; www.newbevcinema.com

Silent Movie Theatre
The silent-film era is alive and well in this unpretentious movie house.
199 E3 ✉ 611 N Fairfax Avenue
☎ 323/655-2520; 323/655-2510; www.silentmovietheatre.com

Downtown and Pasadena

Getting Your Bearings

The face of the city's downtown is changing before our very eyes. With a new skyline and a new metro, this part of the city is now home to the sparkling – and oh so Los Angeles – LA LIVE. Here, swanky international hotels such as the Marriott and Ritz Carlton sit alongside sports and entertainment facilities. But let's not forget the downtown of old with its historic and acclaimed arts venues.

A few miles north by freeway, once-sleepy Pasadena and its San Gabriel Valley neighbors have gone along quietly for decades, it seems, without getting much attention from travelers (other than football and Rose Parade fans). That has all changed. The heart of Old Pasadena has emerged as a shopping, dining and cultural mecca without losing its historic soul, while the region's museums, gardens and period houses enchant visitors.

★ Don't Miss

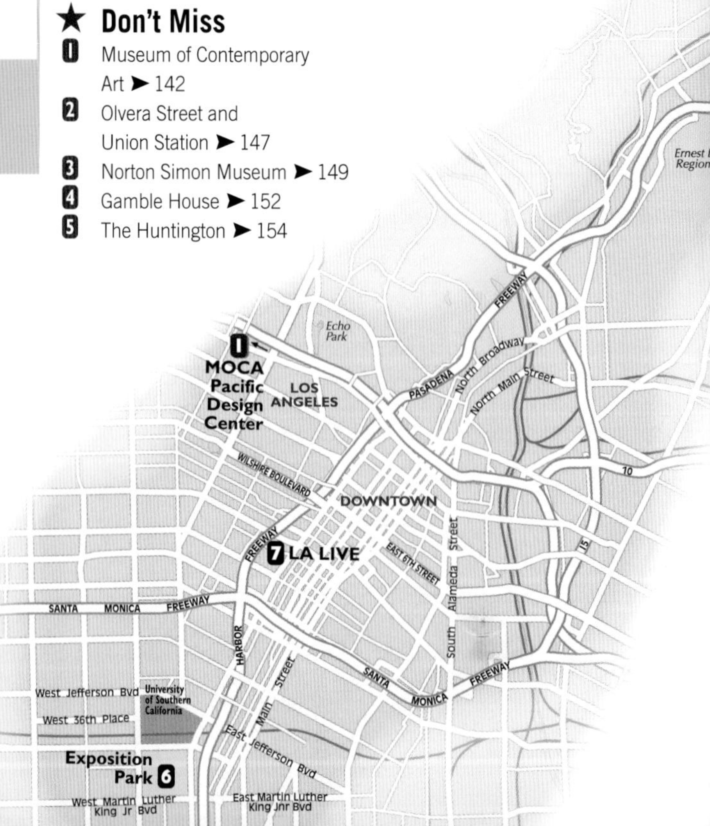

At Your Leisure

Page 137: Cathedral of Our Lady of the Angels

In Two Days

If you're not quite sure where to begin your travels, this itinerary recommends a practical and enjoyable two days in downtown and Pasadena, taking in some of the best places to see using the Getting Your Bearings map on the previous page. For more information see the main entries.

Day One

Morning

Take a pre-breakfast walk through the fragrant stalls of the 8 **Flower Markets** (➤ 156) and breakfast at one of downtown's classic eateries. Then visit the downtown sights on foot, perhaps taking in the colorful 10 **Grand Central Market** (➤ 157). Take a trip down to 2 **Olvera Street and Union Station** (➤ 147–148) before popping into 14 **Chinatown** (➤ 158) for a wander and some lunch.

Afternoon

Spend the afternoon at the 1 **Museum of Contemporary Art** (MOCA, ➤ 142–146) for a leisurely immersion in contemporary art.

Evening

Ease into the evening with a superb cocktail at the swanky Millennium Biltmore (➤ 43), followed by dinner in a Downtown restaurant. Then step out to an acoustic extravaganza at the 11 **Walt Disney Concert Hall** (lobby below, ➤ 157), Frank Gehry's architectural *tour de force*, or a show in one of the Downtown theaters (➤ 164).

Day Two

Morning

Allow half an hour to get from your hotel to 15 **Old Pasadena** (➤ 159). To reach Old Pasadena from Downtown, take the Pasadena Freeway (110) north from Downtown until it changes into Arroyo Parkway and follow it until it ends at Colorado Boulevard. Turn right and you are there. Spend two hours on breakfast, shopping and seeing the sights along Colorado Boulevard and the other streets of Old Pasadena. Take time to drive down to Arroyo Seco and have a look at the Rose Bowl, then head up and park at the 4 **Gamble House** (above, ➤ 152–153). While waiting for it to open at noon (sign up for the first tour), take a walk to see the several splendid **Greene & Greene houses** on Arroyo Terrace near by. Take the one-hour Gamble House tour. Explore the nearby 3 **Norton Simon Museum** (➤ 149–151), taking time to have lunch in the gardens.

Afternoon

Drive to 5 **The Huntington** (➤ 154–155). Tour the gardens and library. Have tea in the Rose Garden Tea Room (➤ 162). If you're not dining or staying at the **Langham, Huntington Hotel and Spa** (➤ 43), at least drive by to have a look and a quick tour. The award-winning restaurant, peaceful gardens and sublime spa all deserve a look.

Evening

Alternatively, go for cocktails in one of the lively bistros in Old Pasadena, followed by dinner in the Playhouse District (➤ 163). Enjoy showtime at the **Pasadena Playhouse** (➤ 164), one of LA's finest traditional theaters.

0 Museum of Contemporary Art

The Museum of Contemporary Art (MOCA), the only LA museum to focus solely on contemporary art, is perhaps the best of its kind in the country. More than 6,000 post-1940 works in all kinds of visual media are housed in three separate locations: MOCA Grand Avenue, Geffen Contemporary at MOCA and MOCA Pacific Design Center.

MOCA Grand Avenue

When seen from outside, this low-rise 1980s building, designed by Japanese architect Arata Isozaki, offers an understated yet powerful geometric assemblage of pyramids, cylinders and cubes clad in rough red sandstone, flanking a copper-sheathed barrel vault. The structure, located on Bunker Hill, gracefully holds its own against the Downtown skyline. Bathed in rich washes of natural light from rooftop skylights, the galleries have a serene, sanctuary-like quality – an ambience attained, in part, by placing them "underground," away from the business of the street.

The warehouse home of the Geffen Contemporary

Opening on to a spacious courtyard, the barrel vault looks as if it should be the museum entrance, but instead, here you'll find offices, a ticket booth and museum store. The entrance to the galleries is downstairs, off a sunken courtyard that also shelters the museum café, Patinette (▶ 146).

Geffen Contemporary at MOCA

The Geffen Contemporary was an old warehouse structure converted by architect Frank Gehry into a temporary museum space to house the growing MOCA collections during its construction phase in the 1980s. Gehry did a masterful job of utilizing the structure's inherent strengths – massive doors, redwood ceilings, steel columns, trusses and beams and a vast, open floor space – and the Temporary Contemporary, as it was dubbed, proved enormously popular, staking a claim for itself as a permanent part of the LA art scene. After closing for a couple of years in the early 1990s when MOCA Grand Avenue opened, it reopened with an endowment from entertainment mogul David Geffen, whose name now graces the building.

The plaza at MOCA Grand Avenue, encircled by graceful structures

MOCA Pacific Design Center

Finally, in what appears to be an effort to have a presence farther west, where most of LA's new money is and where LACMA and the Getty rule, in 2001 MOCA opened a third outpost, devoted to temporary exhibitions of art, architecture and design, on the grounds of the Pacific Design Center in West Hollywood.

Temporary and Permanent

MOCA's curators host about 20 temporary shows every year, highlighting the work of artists ranging from the internationally famous to relative unknowns in the formative stages of their careers.

There is plenty of outstanding work on permanent display – enough to engage even the most demanding connoisseur of post-1940 art. The permanent collections include over 5,000 pieces, beginning with the Abstract Expressionists and ending with the latest art stars of the new millennium. Some of the famous names whose works have been collected at MOCA include Diane Arbus, Willem de Kooning, Sam Francis, Arshile Gorky, Robert Irwin, Jasper Johns, Roy Lichtenstein, Joan Miró, Louise Nevelson, Claes Oldenburg, Jackson Pollock, Robert Rauschenberg, Mark Rothko, Cy Twombly and Andy Warhol.

Not surprisingly, the collections are particularly strong on LA artists and collectors. The original MOCA board of trustees, formed in the late 1970s, included artist Sam Francis, who gave ten major pieces to the collections. (Francis was also instrumental in commissioning Arata Isozaki to design the California Plaza building.) Artist Ed Moses contributed 11 paintings and drawings, while trustee Marcia Simon Weisman honored the museum with a collection of 83 drawings and prints, including major pieces by de Kooning, Gorky and Johns. The museum

BY DESIGN

MOCA has also achieved a real reputation for its architecture and design shows, offering one-man exhibitions that explore the work of stellar designers like Louis Kahn and Frank Gehry and focusing attention on lesser-known architects like Rudolph Schindler and other early LA Modernists.

purchased a major collection of 80 abstract expressionist and pop art pieces from the Italian count Giuseppe Panza; later, Panza gave the museum another 70 pieces, and bequests from assorted LA media millionaires have deepened the collections of contemporary work over the past three decades.

MOCA opened a third gallery at the Pacific Design Center in West Hollywood in 2001

Collection of Collections

MOCA's acclaimed permanent exhibits have been amassed thanks to the generosity of individual collectors and artists. Recognition of this came in 2008 with the staging of Collecting Collections: Highlights from the Permanent Collection of The Museum of Contemporary Art, at MOCA

Grand Avenue. Exhibits included masterpieces, one-off installations, minimalist art and work of both local and international artists.

Highlights

Amid all the riches to be found in both Downtown MOCAs, a number of works should not be missed: Jackson Pollock's powerful *Number 1* (1949) and *Number 3* (1948) show the master of over-scale splatter painting at his best. Robert Rauschenberg's *Coca Cola Plan* is an amusing item, a battered cabinet with old bottles and wings. Jasper Johns' *Map* (1962) is a layered and textured map of the US that has become an icon of the Abstract Expressionist movement; Warhol's *Telephone* is a pop art stand out.

Several of the New York art stars of the postmodern, post-pop 1980s – Julian Schnabel, David Salle, Eric Fischl and Barbara Kruger among them – also have artwork in the collections, so you can see for yourself what all that 1980s art hype was about. Schnabel's monumental *Owl* (1980), illustrates his powerful way with paint and other materials and the Salle piece, named *View the Author Through Long Telescopes* (1981), is representative of his mocking, ironically charged work.

Also in that 1980s vein, don't miss Cindy Sherman's bizarre photographic self-portraits, or the six pieces by the tragically short-lived Jean Michel Basquiat.

TAKING A BREAK

Patinette at MOCA Grand Avenue (Mon–Fri 11–5, Wed–Thu 11–8, Sat–Sun 11–6; $$) is a convenient, although not very enticing, place to get a snack when visiting the museum. Be warned: prices are somewhat over the odds.

MOCA Grand Avenue (on Bunker Hill)
197 D5 250 S Grand Avenue 213/626-6222; www.moca.org Mon, Thu–Fri 11–5 (also 5–8 Thu), Sat–Sun 11–6 Adults moderate; students and seniors inexpensive; children free; Thu 5–8 free

Geffen Contemporary at MOCA (in Little Tokyo)
197 E4 152 N Central Avenue 213/626-6222; www.moca.org See MOCA (Bunker Hill) above Adults moderate; students and seniors inexpensive; children free; Thu 5–8 free

MOCA Pacific Design Center (in West Hollywood)
199 E3 8687 Melrose Avenue 310/289-5223; www.moca.org Tue–Fri 11–5, Sat–Sun 11–6 Free

MUSEUM OF CONTEMPORARY ART: INSIDE INFO

Top tip To get a real insight into the exhibits, join one of the free, 45-minute conversational **tours** led by MOCA professionals at MOCA Grand Avenue and the Geffen Contemporary at MOCA. Tours operate Thursday to Monday at noon, 1pm and 2pm, with additional tours Thursday at 5pm, 6pm and 7pm and Saturday at 3pm.

2 Olvera Street and Union Station

Those curious about the early history of Los Angeles need go no farther than El Pueblo de Los Angeles State Historic Park. This collection of 27 historic buildings, including the city's oldest church and its first building, on a 44-acre (18ha) site (known as Olvera Street) just north of Downtown encapsulates LA's Hispanic roots and its transformation from dusty Spanish *pueblo* to thriving Anglo-Mexican town.

Birthplace of the City

It's best to see El Pueblo on foot. Whichever route you take, or if you take one of the free tours, there are several must-sees. Start with the **Pobladores (Founders) Plaque** in the old plaza. It lists the names of the 44 settlers who came from Mexico in 1781 to bolster the Spanish claim to California by settling El Pueblo. The original village is long gone; the oldest building on Olvera is the 1818 **Avila Adobe**, now a museum on the Hispanic lifestyle of 1840s California. Other pre-Anglo sites include the **Plaza Catholic Church** (1818–22), across North Main Street from the plaza and the adjacent **Campo Santo**, site of the pueblo's first cemetery.

During the 1840s California changed from Mexican to American rule – a change reflected in the buildings in the historic district, as brick and wood replaced adobe. Several fine examples of late 19th-century architecture have been restored and transformed into museums. LA's first firehouse, from 1884, across the plaza from Olvera Street, is now a museum about 19th-century firefighting. The 1870 **Pico House** was originally a hotel belonging to Pio Pico, the last governor of Alta (upper) California. Today it houses a museum devoted to the history of his family.

The Pelanconi Building on Olvera Street is the oldest brick-built house in the city

Olvera Street

Run-down and surrounded by decrepit buildings, Olvera Street was scheduled to be razed in the 1920s, until Christine Sterling, a local preservationist, convinced the powers-that-be to save the street. Lined with restored old buildings (dating from 1818 to 1926) that now house restaurants, curio shops, museums and historic sites, Olvera Street is a lively pedestrian arcade. Don't miss the Avila Adobe, Sepulveda House, the Biscailuz Building and the Pelanconi Building, which now contains the historic La Golondrina Café (► below).

Union Station

Slip across Alameda Street for a tour of Union Station, a grand 1930s terminal worth a walk-through even if you're not headed for the Metro (via a tunnel to the Gateway Transit Center east of the station) or dining at Traxx, the chic in-station restaurant (► 162). Anchored by a Mediterranean-style clock tower, the station gracefully mixes Mission, Streamline Moderne and Moorish design elements. Its lobby ceilings soar overhead, supported on massive wooden beams, and great swatches of original tilework display patterns inspired by everything from art deco to Navajo.

Union Station's soaring interior: Dig those comfy chairs

TAKING A BREAK

Enjoy LA's Mexican heritage at **La Golondrina Café** (17 Olvera Street; tel: 213/628-4349; Mon–Fri 9–9, Sat, Sun 9am–10pm; $$). Alternatively, stop at **Philippe the Original** (1001 Alameda Street at Ord Street, tel: 213/628-3781; daily 6am–10pm), one of the city's first fast-food stands.

Olvera Street
197 F5 ✉ 125 Paseo de la Plaza (bordered by Alameda Street, Spring Street, Sunset Boulevard ☎ 213/485-6855; www.ci.la.ca.us/ELP; www.olvera-street.com

Visitor Center
197 F5 ✉ First Floor, Sepulveda House, 662 N Main Street ☎ 213/628-1274 ⌚ Daily 11–11 (restaurants), 11–7 (retail)

Union Station
197 F5 ✉ 800 N Alameda Street ⌚ Daily 24 hours

OLVERA STREET AND UNION STATION: INSIDE INFO

Top tip Union Station has "starred" in several movies, among them *The Way We Were* (1973), *Blade Runner* (1982) and *To Live and Die in LA* (1985).

Hidden gem As you're strolling Olvera Street, you may see a series of marked bricks that trace the course of the centuries-old *zanja madre*, or mother ditch, which ran from the original Los Angeles River along what is now Olvera Street. The original settlement of Los Angeles grew up around this man-made canal.

3 Norton Simon Museum

This museum is home to the superb collection of art amassed by the great 20th-century industrialist Norton Simon (1907–1993), with treasures from both Asian and Western art spanning more than 2,000 years. Visitors can delight in sculptures, photography, etchings and graphics, with works by Kandinsky and Klee as well as Rembrandt and Picasso. The serene garden is one of the highlights.

Simon began acquiring European art in the 1950s, starting with 19th and early 20th centuries works by Degas, Cézanne, Renoir and Gauguin. In the 1960s he added a large number of Old Master paintings from the 16th to the 18th centuries. The collection grew to include hundreds of artworks from the last 700 years of European painting and sculpture.

Simon also began to acquire artworks from south Asia. He put his collection on tour, lending it to a number of museums prior to settling in Pasadena in 1974, where he took over the financially troubled Pasadena Museum of Modern Art (built in 1969) and transformed it into a home for his 12,000 pieces.

Works are displayed with style in the galleries of the Norton Simon

Artist's Architect

Simon's passionate commitment to his museum left everyone uncertain as to what would happen when he died in 1993. Fortunately, his widow, actress Jennifer Jones Simon,

announced in the mid-1990s a $3 million plan to renovate the building and gardens. Architect Frank Gehry masterminded the work, completed in 1999, which turned out surprisingly subdued and elegant, given his radical reputation. In fact, Gehry has always been an artists' architect and here, with one of the world's great collections of Old Masters to inspire him, he worked quiet wonders. The galleries have been made more intimate, the lighting vastly improved and the flow of spaces matches the stylistic and chronological flow of the artworks. Outside the building, landscape architect Nancy Goslee Powers redesigned the museum's formal sculpture gardens to evoke the spirit of Monet's gardens at Giverny.

Van Gogh's *Portrait of a Peasant* (1888) is one of several of his works in the museum's collection

Making a Grand Entrance

The greatness of Norton Simon's collection lies in its extensive European art holdings. Rodin's magnificent *The Burghers of Calais* greets visitors outside the entry. From the entrance lobby, the 19th- and 20th-century galleries lie to the left.

Tahitian Woman and Boy **(1899) a Post-Impressionist masterpiece by Gauguin**

Here, you'll find more than 100 pieces by Edgar Degas, including a complete set of bronze sculptures cast from the artist's waxes found in his studio after his death, and dozens of paintings and drawings of his elegant dancers, such as *Dancers in the Wings* (1880). Don't miss Manet's *The Ragpicker*; Cézanne's *Portrait of Uncle Dominique, Vase of Flowers and Tulips in a Vase*; Monet's *The Artist's Garden at Vetheuil*; and Renoir's fascinating group portrait, *The Artist's Studio*.

Great Works

Van Gogh is represented by several works, including *Portrait of the Artist's Mother* (1888) and the striking *Mulberry Tree* (1889). Gauguin's *Tahitian Woman and Boy* (1899), Rousseau's *Exotic Landscape* (1910) and dozens of other great artists' works are here, including some by Picasso and Matisse, with a generous selection of outstanding pieces.

After the Impressionists and Post-Impressionists, head across the hall and immerse yourself in an earlier Europe, when the artists concentrated on painting religious figures – along with portraits of the wealthy and scenes from Testaments Old and New. Don't miss Botticelli's *Madonna and Child with Adoring Angel*, Raphael's *Madonna and Child with a Book* and Lucas Cranach's *Adam and Eve*.

There are masterpieces everywhere; one of the most captivating paintings in the collection is the *Self-Portrait* by Rembrandt (1636–38). Canaletto's views of Venice in the 18th century are exquisite.

TAKING A BREAK

The Norton Simon's sculpture gardens, ponds and plantings gracefully evoke Monet's gardens at Giverny; the small outdoor café ($–$$) makes a wonderful setting for a snack (Wed–Mon noon–5:45, Fri noon–7)

---

201 D5 411 W Colorado Boulevard, corner of Colorado and Orange Grove boulevards, intersection of Foothill (210) and Ventura (134) freeways, a few blocks west of Old Pasadena 626/449-6840; www.nortonsimon.org Wed–Mon noon–6, Fri till 9 Adults moderate; seniors inexpensive; students and children under 18 free; free first Fri of the month 6–9pm

NORTON SIMON MUSEUM: INSIDE INFO

Top tips There are numerous famous sculptures to the rear, artfully placed around the ponds and plantings. Downstairs, be sure to see the museum's enthralling collection of South Asian sculptures.

- Free family guides, with fun information and activities for children, as well as children's audio tours are available at the information desk.

4 Gamble House

The architectural side of the Arts and Crafts movement doesn't get any better than this. Brothers Charles and Henry Greene put all their considerable skills to work in creating the gorgeously detailed Gamble House, built in 1908 as a winter getaway for midwestern millionaires David and Mary Gamble, of Procter and Gamble money and fame.

Rather than imitate the other wealthy Pasadena snowbirds, who built their *beaux-arts* winter palaces along Orange Grove Boulevard (nicknamed Millionaires' Row), the Gambles chose nearby Westmoreland Terrace and hired the Greenes to make their vacation home. The Greenes already had a reputation for their brilliant interpretations of the English-originated Arts and Crafts style. Swiss and Japanese influences are lovingly integrated into this bungalow.

Museum Masterpiece

The 100-year-old building unquestionably ranks among the finest house museums in America. The obvious exterior elements that define the Arts and Crafts style include broad, deep overhanging eaves and generously proportioned porches. However, the real allure lies inside, behind the beautiful front door, which features an image of a stylized tree with spreading branches and leaves executed in leaded glass. The built-in cabinetry, walls, floors, doors, indeed every last bit of wood and hardware, were created by craftsmen employed by Peter and John Hall in their Pasadena workshop. Woods include everything from teak and redwood to maple, mahogany and oak, all meticulously finished and impeccably preserved. The interior is rich, dark, flooded with warm light streaming through leaded glass windows and marvelously detailed.

Magnificent leaded glass sets the front door glowing

Guided Tours

Visitors can arrive at the Gamble House from 10am and sign up for one of the one-hour guided tours of the house (no unguided tours are permitted) that

The California bungalow at its Arts and Crafts best

start at noon, before exploring the landscaped gardens and browsing the well-stocked gift shop.

The Greenes created a number of smaller but equally well-crafted houses in the neighborhood. Take a walking tour on your own of the other Greene & Greene houses on Arroyo Terrace, near Westmoreland Place. Along with the Cole House next door on Westmoreland (now a Unitarian Community House), the following privately owned houses on Arroyo Terrace are all Greene & Greene designs: Nos 440, 424, 408, 400, 370 and 368; also, Nos 210, 240 and 235 Grand Avenue, around the corner.

To the north lies **Prospect Park**, another residential enclave and in the distance, the **Rose Bowl**. At Prospect Park is **Millard House**, another Frank Lloyd Wright design. Known as La Miniatura, it was the first of his concrete block houses and looks something like a Mayan ruin buried in the jungle.

TAKING A BREAK

Drive to **Leonidas** (49 W Colorado Boulevard, Old Pasadena; $) for an espresso pick-me-up.

---

201 D5 · 4 Westmoreland Place, Pasadena · 626/793-3334; www.gamblehouse.org · Thu–Sun noon–3 · Moderate. Guided tours only

GAMBLE HOUSE: INSIDE INFO

Top tip Only a limited number of places are available on the 1-hour **guided tours** (tel: 626/793-3334; Thu–Sun noon–3; admission: moderate). Tickets, which can be bought only on day of the tour, go on sale in the bookstore at 10am, 11:30am on Sundays. Reservations can be made a week in advance for the 2pm tour each tour day.

5 The Huntington

Reigning over a 207-acre (84ha) hilltop site, the Huntington Library, Art Collections and Botanical Gardens bring together in one place three distinct attractions, each of which is unmissable. Among them are a completely renovated Huntington Art Gallery and a spectacular new Chinese garden, which opened to the public in 2008.

The Huntington is a magnificent gift from a magnanimous millionaire, Henry Edwards Huntington (1850–1927). He came west, established LA's once-great transit system, made a large fortune larger and retired in 1908 to his San Marino ranch to pursue his real passion: collecting English and American books, manuscripts and paintings.

The Library

Today the Library possesses more than 4 million pieces. While most of the books, manuscripts, maps, photographs and other items are in storage, available primarily to scholars, the **Exhibition Hall** on the ground level houses a fascinating selection. Here you'll find the Ellesmere Chaucer, an illuminated manuscript of the *Canterbury Tales* from 1405; a *Gutenberg Bible* from 1455 is displayed in a permanent exhibition devoted to the transition from handwritten to printed books.

The **Shakespeare collection** is one of the best in the world. You might also see works by Copernicus, Charles Dickens, James Joyce and hundreds of other writers, artists and printmakers. One of the most famous books on display is William Blake's *Songs of Innocence and Experience*, with its illustrated version of his great poem *The Tyger*. The library also has an original 1778 copy of *The Federalist Papers* and 400 documents written by George Washington, several of which are on display.

The Terrace of the Jade Mirror, in the spectacular Liu Fang Yuan (Garden of Flowing Fragrance)

The Blue Boy **(*c*1770) by Thomas Gainsborough**

The Art Collections

Displayed in a palatial *beaux-arts* building, the **European art collection** focuses primarily on English paintings of the 18th and early 19th centuries. Some galleries are resplendent with Louis XIV-style carpets, chairs, tables and statuary. One of Gilbert Stuart's famed George Washington portraits hangs in the dining room. In the main **portrait gallery**, highlights include *The Blue Boy* by Thomas Gainsborough, *Pinkie* by Thomas Lawrence and Sir Joshua Reynolds' *Mrs Siddons as the Tragic Muse*.

The **Virginia Steele Scott Galleries of American Art** (closed until June 2009) features works from every period of American history. Look for Mary Cassatt's *Breakfast in Bed* (1897) and Edward Hopper's evocative *The Long Leg* (1935). Surrounded by the **Dorothy Collins Brown Gardens**, the **Boone Gallery** hosts changing exhibitions. It stands near the Scott Gallery in the northwestern part of the grounds. The mausoleum, designed by John Russell Pope, is a short stroll to the north.

Botanical Gardens

Many visitors come just for the Botanical Gardens. Pick up a brochure with a map at the entrance or take one of the tours (➤ Inside Info). The **North Vista**, a grand allée flanked by rows of 17th-century statuary, features a formal sweep of lawn that shapes a view of the San Gabriel Mountains. The **Shakespeare Garden** displays plants mentioned in his works. In the **Rose Garden**, take in 1,000 years of rose history told through some 1,200 cultivars. The compelling **Desert Garden** is home to the world's largest outdoor collection of desert plants. The spectacular Chinese garden, which opened in 2008, is almost a work of art in itself. **Liu Fang Yuan** (Garden of Flowing Fragrance) includes scholarly elements, as well as a lake, pavilions and a teahouse.

TAKING A BREAK

Tea in the **Rose Garden Tea Room** (➤ 162) is a lovely event (tel: 626/683-8131).

---

201 F4 ✉ 1151 Oxford Road, San Marino (second entrance on Orlando Road at Allen Avenue) ☎ 626/405-2100; www.huntington.org ⌚ Summer Wed–Mon 10:30–4:30; winter Mon, Wed–Fri noon–4:30, Sat–Sun 10:30–4:30 ⓢ Expensive; moderate for students and youths; free for children under 5; free first Thu every month with advance reservations only

THE HUNTINGTON: INSIDE INFO

Top tips Free garden tours are available with paid admission. Times may vary; see posted schedule at the information desk. Free audio tours are available for selected exhibitions.

- The Japanese garden complex includes an authentic, reconstructed Japanese house, a traditional landscape with a moon bridge and an extensive bonsai garden.

At Your Leisure

6 Exposition Park

In 1932, the Memorial Coliseum, now a national historic landmark, hosted the Olympic Games. With the Coliseum, the Rose Garden and several fine museums, including the California Science Museum, the park remains a major draw.

The California African-American Museum has an impressive sculpture court. The permanent collection offers paintings, sculptures, photographs and works in other media by African-American artists from the 19th century to the present. An excellent long-term exhibit on the life of singer Ella Fitzgerald has been mounted in the form of a backstage dressing room. It also stages fascinating temporary exhibitions.

The Natural History Museum serves as one of the nation's most comprehensive collections of artifacts relating to the history of the earth. There is so much to choose from, you might want to focus on just one of the four main departments. Life Sciences features birds, mammals, reptiles, fish and the like. The highlight here is the Insect Zoo. Earth Sciences covers dinosaur bones, fossils, gems and minerals. Two impressive Dinosaur Halls are due to open in 2011. Archaeological Treasures from Ancient Latin America, with exhibits from the mighty Aztec, Maya and Inca civilisations opened in early 2009.

196 A1 ✉ 700 Exposition Park Drive ☎ 213/744-7458; www.exposition.org Free

California African-American Museum

✉ 600 State Drive, off Figueroa Street ☎ 213/744-7432; www.caamuseum.org Tue–Sat 10–5, Sun 11–5, tours available, reservations at least 3 weeks in advance

Natural History Museum

✉ 900 Exposition Boulevard ☎ 213/763-3466; www.nhm.org Mon–Fri 9:30–5, Sat–Sun 10–5 Moderate; free 1st Tue of the month

7 LA LIVE

This entertainment complex vows to do things better and louder than ever before. It incorporates bowling facilities and numerous movie screens with the Nokia Theatre LA, Nokia Plaza, and is the new host of both the American Music Awards and the EMMYs. At the GRAMMY Museum four levels of interactive and educational exhibits explore different types of music, but particularly relate to the history of the GRAMMYs.

196 C4 ✉ 777 Chick Hearn Court ☎ 213/763-5483 or toll free 866/548-3452; www.lalive.com Admission, opening and telephone contact varies depending on event and venue

GRAMMY Museum

☎ 213/765-6800; www.grammymuseum.org Daily 10–6 Expensive

8 Flower Markets

A pre-breakfast trip to the Flower Markets, an aromatic, bustling and stunningly colorful place, is a great

The distinctive 1926 Los Angeles Central Library is a city landmark

way to start the day. Since these markets supply most of the flower shops in LA, the stalls sell out fast: Arrive early if you want to see it in full bloom and have your pick. They've got every flower imaginable, from gerbera daisies to long-stem roses. The two markets (across the street from each other) are near LA's Skid Row sleaze, so park as close as possible.

197 D3 766 Wall Street 213/627-3696; www.laflowerdistrict.com Mon, Wed, Fri 8am–noon, Tue, Thu, Sat 6am–noon, closed Sun Inexpensive

9 Los Angeles Central Library

The Central Library has a wealth of engrossing architectural details, highlighted by a series of interior wall murals on California's history. The original building is a vision of LA eclecticism. The exterior has a Moderne look, with Egyptian detailing. Inside are more classical forms: a dome, arches and vaults. Don't miss the limestone figures of literary greats on the exterior, or the awesome sweep of the central rotunda ceiling with its 1933 murals. In the west garden you'll find Jud Fine's intriguing sculpted entryway, *Spine*. The opening of the Annenberg Gallery in 2003 created an exhibition space within the Library in which some of its hidden treasures could be displayed. Changing exhibits now showcase its collections of photographs, illustrations, posters and maps.

197 D4 630 W Fifth Street 213/228-7000; www.lapl.org Mon–Thu 10–8, Fri–Sat 10–6, Sun 1–5 Free; tours daily

10 Grand Central Market

Since 1917 the Grand Central Market has served LA as an indoor market for fresh produce. The exotic range of food on sale reflects the city's multicultural population: expect color and flavor. Unless you are looking to stock up on groceries, the best way to experience this market is by tucking in at its food court. Look for handmade tortillas, mango ice-cream cones and fresh juice. Mariachi bands often play by the Hill Street entrance on weekends.

197 E4 317 S Broadway, second entrance on Hill Street 213/624-2378; www.grandcentralsquare.com Daily 9–6 Free

11 Walt Disney Concert Hall

Until the Walt Disney Concert Hall began rising on the Downtown skyline, Frank Gehry had never

WATTS TOWERS

Watts Towers (1765 E 107th Street, 6 miles (10km) south of Downtown) is one of the great folk-art monuments in the country. Allow an hour's travel time, roundtrip (take the Metro Blue Line, or drive), and half an hour to view. Italian immigrant Simon Rodia spent 33 years, from 1921 to 1954, on the eight 100-foot (30m) towers. He worked alone, building the openwork iron frames with salvaged steel rods, pipes and assorted debris, and then embellishing them with 70,000 crushed sea-shells and bits of broken glass and ceramics. Call Watts Towers Art Center (tel: 213/847-4646). Tours (suggested donation) run every half hour Friday 11–3, Saturday 10:30–3, Sun 12:30–3pm. Admission is moderate.

Architect Frank Gehry's stainless steel sails at the Walt Disney Concert Hall

had a truly major LA commission. With the sculpted elegance of the surrealistically swooping steel frame, rising on its Bunker Hill site, the new Concert Hall is spectacular. Voluptuous sails of stainless steel encircle the auditorium, reception areas, lobby and rehearsal halls. It took 16 years and close to US$300 million to create this concert hall and it ranks among the world's finest venues. Try to get tickets for a concert or at the very least take one of the self-guiding tours.

197 D5 111 South Grand Avenue 323/850-2000; www.laphil.com Audio self-guiding tours (excluding auditorium): most non-matinee days 10–2, matinee days 10–11 Free

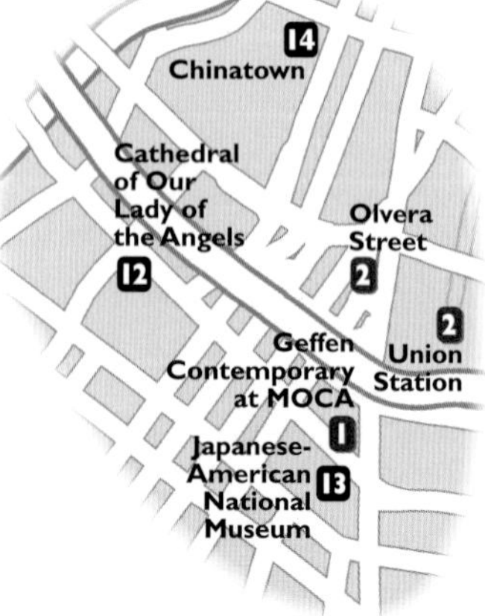

12 Cathedral of Our Lady of the Angels

It took just three years to construct the cathedral, an exposed concrete structure designed by José Rafael Moneo. It is a contemporary place of worship – a construction with few right angles – although there are traditional plazas, colonnades and a pair of heavy bronze doors. Worshippers flock here, and for the city's Roman Catholics it is an expression of their vibrant faith.

On Sundays Mass is celebrated in English at 8am and 10am, and in Spanish at 12:30pm.

197 E5 555 W Temple Street 213/680-5200; www.olacathedral.org Mon–Fri 6:30–6, Sat 9–6, Sun 7–6

13 Japanese-American National Museum

This striking contemporary museum in the Little Tokyo district gives an insight into Japanese-American history and culture. The innovative exhibitions change frequently and focus on the lives and contributions of Japanese-Americans and on the tragedy of forced internment of some 100,000 Japanese-American citizens during World War II. Permanent displays include more than 60,000 artifacts making up significant artistic and photographic collections.

197 F4 369 E First Street at Central Avenue 213/625-0414; www.janm.org Tue–Sun 11–5 (also 5–8 Thu) Adults moderate; seniors and students inexpensive; free third Thu of every month and Thu after 5

14 Chinatown

The original Old Chinatown evolved in the 1870s when the city's Chinese were forced out of a downtown area by discriminatory housing laws. They formed their own community, which was razed in the late 1930s to make way for Union Station. Thus was born "New Chinatown," the first such enclave in the country to be owned and financed by Chinese. The main street is North Broadway, where the buildings are embellished with the ornamental facades and rooflines that lend the district its Chinese identity. Between Broadway and Hill Street, Gin Ling Way offers a pedestrians-only strip of stores and restaurants. Try dim sum at Ocean Seafood (747 N Broadway, tel: 213/687-3088; daily 9am–10pm) or spicy Szechuan at Yang Chow (819 N Broadway, tel: 213/625-0811; Sun–Thu 11:30–9:45, Fri, Sat 11:30–10:45). There are several funky art galleries on Chung King Road. There is a lively calendar of events in Central Plaza (see website for details). Consider the 2.5-hour Undiscovered Chinatown Tour, which runs on the first Saturday of the month (10:30–1).

www.chinatown.com

197 F5 Bordered by N Broadway, N Hill Street, Bernard Street and Cesar Chavez (Sunset) Boulevard

15 Old Pasadena

More than 200 buildings dating from the 1880s and 1890s, trendy boutiques, neighborhood coffee shops and antique dealers make up the historic district of Old Pasadena. Lined with vintage buildings, Colorado Boulevard may be the district's liveliest retail axis, but also try to see the Venetian Revival Building (17 S Raymond), the impressive Castle Green (99 S Raymond), the Santa Fe Railroad Station (222 S Raymond) and the White Block (Fair Oaks Avenue). Farther down Colorado, stroll over to see the Pasadena Civic Auditorium (300 E Green Street), the 1925 Pasadena City Hall (100 N Garfield) and the Central Library (285 E Walnut).

201 D5 Pasadena Heritage, 651 South St John Avenue 626/441-6333; www.oldpasadena.org

16 Pacific Asia Museum

Grace Nicholson built her Chinese Treasure House in 1924 and willed the building to Pasadena on her death in 1948. It served as the Pasadena Art Museum, then in 1971 it became home to the Pacific Asia Museum's 17,000 pieces. Collections include Chinese textiles, Ming and Ching Dynasty porcelain, carved jade and Japanese Edo paintings. The museum's temporary exhibitions and programs range from workshops in *mah-jongg* (an ancient Chinese tile game) and *ikebana* (flower-arranging) to displays of works by contemporary Asian and Asian-American artists. Even if you don't visit the exhibitions, you should see the building.

201 E5 46 N Los Robles Avenue, Pasadena 626/449-2742; www.pacificasiamuseum.org Wed–Sun 10–5 (also Fri 5–8pm) Moderate; concessions: inexpensive; free fourth Fri of month

Where to... Eat and Drink

Restaurant Prices
Expect to pay per person for a three-course meal, excluding tax, drinks and service
$ under $30 **$$** $30–$60 **$$$** over $60

RESTAURANTS

A Thousand Cranes Restaurant $$$

Set inside the Kyoto Hotel in Little Tokyo, this Japanese dining spot offers an oasis of calm with views of a waterfall and Japanese garden. Diners relax over traditional Japanese dishes such as sukiyaki, or make delectable selections at the sushi and tempura bars. The festive Sunday brunch is a crowd pleaser, with both Japanese and Western selections.

197 E4 120 S Los Angeles Street 213/253-9255 Mon–Fri 11:30–3, 5–10, Sat 5–10, Sun 11–3, 5–10

Arroyo Chop House $$$

This serious steakhouse is a bastion of dark woods and clubby atmosphere, Craftsman-style decor and live piano music. The tab is quite easily racked up by an a la carte menu consisting of stylish steaks and chops with rich cream sauces, substantial starters, hearty side dishes and straightforward desserts.

201 D4 536 S Arroyo Parkway, Pasadena 626/577-7463; www.arroyochophouse.com Sun–Thu 5–9:30pm, Fri–Sat 5–10pm

Bistro 45 $$

California-French cuisine, with a hint of Pacific Rim, is showcased in this restored art-deco building – a favorite haunt for romantic-minded locals who duck into the several intimate rooms. Dishes are prepared with high-quality seasonal seafood, game and veal, with scintillating reduction sauces and expertly woven flavors. Cassoulet and lighter fare are also offered and all are complemented by a fine wine list.

201 E4 45 S Mentor Avenue, Pasadena 626/795-2478; www.bistro45.com Tue–Thu 11:30–2, 6–9, Fri 11:30–2, 6–9:30, Sat 6–9:30, Sun 5–9

Checkers $$

In the Hilton Hotel, Checkers offers delicacies such as pâté de foie gras terrine, veal- and duck-filled ravioli and some truly succulent salads. The cuisine has French, Californian, and Asian influences and the wine list offers fine California chardonnays and cabernets.

197 D4 535 S Grand Avenue 213/624-0000 Mon–Sat 7 am–10:30 pm, Sun 11–2:30, 5–10:30

Ciudad $$

Latin cuisine from Havana to Lisbon is represented at this Downtown urban space. On Sunday night it's an all-tapas menu paired with Spanish wines and Tuesday is Paella on the Patio night

197 D4 445 S Figueroa Street 213/486-5171; www.ciudad-la.com Mon–Tue 11:30–9, Wed–Thu 11:30–11, Fri 11:30–midnight, Sat 5–midnight, Sun 5–9pm

Empress Pavilion $

You'll be hard-pressed to find better Hong Kong-style dim sum or a more impressive just-like-China environment than this landmark restaurant in Chinatown's Bamboo Plaza. There seems to be a perpetual throng

of diners at this 500-seat restaurant waiting for some of the hundreds of steaming, sizzling morsels. You'll be dazzled by the staff's well-tuned choreography and efficient service.
201 E2 988 N Hill Street 213/617-9898 Mon–Thu 10–3, 5–9, Fri 10–3, 5–9:30, Sat 9–3, 5–10, Sun 8:30–3:30, 5–10

Mi Piace $
This busy Italian place on bustling Colorado Boulevard will have you tucking into traditional Italian pastas and entrees, as well as New York-style pizzas with such no-nonsense toppings as pepperoni, sausage and anchovies. The dessert case, filled with fine French cakes and pastries, is a welcome treat.
201 D5 25 E Colorado Boulevard, Pasadena 626/795-3131 Mon–Thu 7:30am–11:30pm, Fri–Sat 7:30am–12:30am, Sat 8am–12:30, Sun 8am–11:30pm

Noe Restaurant & Bar $$
Across the street from the Walt Disney Concert Hall in the Omni Hotel, this award-winning restaurant attracts everyone from theatergoers to business travelers to food-loving Angelenos. The creative fusion fare, drawing on Japanese and French influences, may include three preparations of foie gras, hazelnut-crusted tuna, or duck with prosciutto-wrapped fennel. Candles and glowing images of the Eiffel Tower contribute to the romantic setting.
201 E1 251 South Olive Street 213/356-4100; www.noerestaurant.com Sun–Thu 5–10, Fri–Sat 5–11 (bar open 3pm–2am daily)

Parkway Grill $$
Often referred to as Pasadena's "Spago," the 1980s Parkway Grill was indeed at the forefront of the local food scene. This popular restaurant is perpetually crowded with die-hard diners who feast on creative California cuisine prepared on an open mesquite-fired grill. The black bean soup and brick-oven pizzas are favorites.
201 D4 510 S Arroyo Parkway, Pasadena 626/795-1001; www.theparkwaygrill.com Mon–Fri 11:30–2:30, 5:30–10, Sat–Sun 5–10

Raymond Restaurant $$$
While the ambience is decidedly early-Pasadena in this beautifully restored Craftsman bungalow, the cuisine at Raymond's is a blend of California and Continental flavors. The limited menu is nonetheless compiled of carefully prepared dishes such as fig-wrapped pancetta and rack of lamb. An extravagant afternoon tea is served Friday to Sunday 1:30–2:30pm.
201 D4 1250 S Fair Oaks Avenue, Pasadena 616/441-3136; www.theraymond.com Tue–Fri 5:30–10, Sat 10–2:30, 5:30–10, Sun 10–2:30, 5–9

Saladang Song $$
Some insist that this stylish spot ranks as the best Thai restaurant in Greater LA. Classic Thai favorites are presented like fine works of art. Ginger-and-chicken pearly rice soup might be on the breakfast menu, while noodle soups and heavier meat, fish, seafood and vegetarian dishes progress into lunch and dinner. Not to be mistaken for its sister restaurant, Saladang, a block away.
201 D4 383 S Fair Oaks Avenue, Pasadena 626/793-8123 Daily 10–10

Water Grill $$$
It may not be close to the ocean but the Water Grill is known around town as one of the finest seafood restaurants in the city. The atmosphere is sophisticated and clubby. Raves go to the heavenly clam chowder, the incredibly fresh seafood selections, seasonal oysters and plucked-from-the-tank Maine lobsters and Dungeness crabs. But leave room for the equally mouth-watering choice of desserts.
197 D4 544 S Grand Avenue 213/891-0900; www.watergrill.com Mon–Fri 11:30–9:30

Yujean Kang's $

Prepare yourself for Chinese dishes with a modern twist, infused with wunderkind chef Yujean Kang's uncanny and now revered flavor combinations and exquisite presentation. Beijing duck, a masterwork, must be ordered two days ahead.

201 D5 67 N Raymond Avenue, Pasadena 626/585-0855; www.yujeankangs.com Mon–Thu, Sun 11:30–2, 5–9, Fri–Sat 11:30–2, 5–10

CAFÉS

Downtown cafés are sprinkled about the business district and located inside most hotels and some cultural attractions. There are numerous cafés and bakeries throughout Pasadena.

Rose Garden Tea Room $

Enjoy traditional high tea in the Huntington's tea room. The buffet-style treats include scones, sandwiches, dainty pastries and – of course – the Huntington's well-known blends of tea. Reservations for tea are required at least two weeks in advance.

201 F4 1151 Oxford Road, San Marino 616/683-8131 Mon, Wed, Thu, Fri noon–4:30, Sat–Sun 10:45–4:30

Luigi Ortega's Café $

This friendly spot attracts a mixed crowd of students, sports fans (there are lots of TV screens) and those wanting to plug into the free WiFi. The Italian and Mexican food is inexpensive and hearty.

200 F5 1655 East Colorado Boulevard, Pasadena 626/396-9669; www.luigiortegas.com Daily 8am–11pm

BARS

Fox Sports Sky Box

Sports fanatics can cheer the action from right inside the Staples Center (► 164). Huge screens and crowd-pleaser appetizers are right on the mark, but the drinks are on the costly side. Adjacent to the VIP entrance, this is as close to the glitz as you can get without a ticket.

197 D5 1111 S Figueroa Street 213/742-7345 Daily 11–11

McMurphy's Tavern

This energetic Old Pasadena hang-out with live music, dancing, sports screens and a young crowd has a near nightly program of events.

201 D5 72 N Fair Oaks Avenue, Pasadena 626/666-1445 Daily 11am–1:30am

Millennium Biltmore Hotel

This is one of LA's most enjoyable hotel bars. Any drinking experience here is sublime whether you're ordering cognac, champagne or cocktails. Live jazz at weekends.

197 D4 506 S Grand Avenue Daily 4pm–2am

Rooftop Bar at the Standard Downtown

You'll find a 360-degree view of Downtown and a well-heeled crowd at this funky bar in the Standard Downtown hotel (► 43). This is the perfect place to enjoy a cocktail or an appetizer.

197 D4 550 S Flower Street 213/892-8080 Daily noon–1:30am

Traxx

Union Station's old telephone room has been transformed into a chic, art deco bar and restaurant, where it feels like the 1920s.

197 F5 800 N Alameda Street 213/625-1999; www.traxxrestaurant.com Mon–Thu 11:30–2:30, 5:30–9, Fri 11:30–2:30, 5:30–9:30, Sat 5–9pm (bar 1:30–8pm)

Twin Palms

On weekend nights, dance the night away under the tent-covered starry night. Enjoy dance music Friday and Saturday and lunchtime jazz on Sundays. It's a popular choice for special events so check it is open in advance.

201 D4 101 W Green Street 626/577-2567; www.twinpalms.com Mon–Thu 11:30–11, Fri–Sat 5pm–1am, Sun 10:30am–11pm

Where to... Shop

DOWNTOWN

Locals go to the **LA City Mall** (201 N Los Angeles Street) near City Hall for break-from-work shopping and dining. Both **City National Plaza** (505 S Flower Street) and **Broadway Plaza** (Seventh and Flower streets) have stores and restaurants (opening times vary).

Bound by 7th, Spring, Main and San Pedro streets, the Fashion District (www.fashiondistrict.org) draws bargain hunters who sort through the heavily discounted designer- and brand-name clothing and accessories. Most of the action is centered around the **California Mart** (910 S Los Angeles Street), **Cooper Building** (860 S Los Angeles Street) and Santee Alley.

Stands at the **Grand Central Market** (➤ 157) sell fresh produce, meat and poultry, fish, baked goods, Latin American staples, fresh tortillas and fruit milkshakes.

Casa de Sousa (19 Olvera Street; Mon–Fri 10–7, Sat 10–9, Sun 11–6) is famed for its imported Mexican and Central American folk arts, particularly the Oaxacan vases. Also for sale are specialty coffee and chocolate "potions."

Those more inclined toward pen and ink will delight in the handmade papers at **McManus and Morgan** (2506 W Seventh Street; tel: 213/387-4433; Mon–Fri 9–5, Sat 10–2).

Cirrus Gallery (542 S Alameda Street; tel: 213/680-3473; Tue–Sat 10–5), one of the first (and last) art dealers in the Downtown area, offers fine art prints by many big-name California artists.

PASADENA

Pasadena is full of stores, compartmentalized in three areas.

South Lake Avenue is the major district, where hundreds of stores and department stores stretch the 10 tree-lined blocks between California and Colorado boulevards.

The 20-block **Old Pasadena historic enclave** (bound by Colorado Boulevard, Fair Oaks Avenue, De Lacey Avenue and Union Street) is anchored by the One Colorado building and offers many national retailers as well as specialty stores and boutiques. Shop opening hours vary.

Antiques dealers, bookstores and eclectic merchants surround the **Pasadena Playhouse District** (Colorado Boulevard and El Molino Avenue). The three-block, open-air **Paseo Colorado** complex (Colorado Boulevard, between Los Robles and Marengo) re-creates an urban village with stores, outdoor cafés, a gourmet market and 14-screen Cineplex movie theater.

Bookworms need go no farther than **Vroman's** (695 E Colorado Boulevard; tel: 626/449-5320; Mon–Thu 9–9, Fri 9–10, Sat 10–9, Sun 10–7), a century-old icon with a huge selection.

Distant Lands (56 S Raymond Avenue; Mon–Thu 10:30–8, Fri, Sat 10:30–9, Sun 11–6) is well-known for travel guides and literature.

Canterbury Records (805 E Colorado Boulevard; tel: 626/792-7184; Mon–Thu 9–9, Fri 9–10, Sat 9–9, Sun 10–7) specializes in big band, jazz, classical and world music CDs and albums.

Try the luscious baked goods at **EuroPane** (950 E Colorado Boulevard; tel: 626/577-1828; Mon–Sat 7–5:30, Sun 7–3:30) or the wines at **Mission Wines** (1114 Mission Street tel: 626/403-9463; Mon–Sat 10–7, Sun noon–5).

Where to... Be Entertained

THEATER

Actors' Gang Theater
Classics, musicals and alternative works are performed in this theater co-founded by actor Tim Robbins.
200 A3 9070 Venice Boulevard
310/838-4264; www.theactorsgang.com

Ahmanson Theatre
LA's top theater, with 2,000 seats, is the setting for huge Broadway musicals and other spectacles.
197 E5 135 N Grand Avenue
213/972-7401

Mark Taper Forum
The Performing Arts Center offers classics and contemporary works.
197 E5 135 N Grand Avenue
213/972-7211

Pasadena Playhouse
Pasadena's landmark theater has been the jumping-off point for many celebrated actors.
201 E4 39 S El Molino Avenue
626/356-7529; www.pasadenaplayhouse.org

MUSIC AND DANCE

Dorothy Chandler Pavilion
This 3,200-seat auditorium is home to the Los Angeles Opera and Dance at the Music Center, which presents a full program of ballet.
197 E5 135 N Grand Avenue
213/972-8001

The Mayan
Prepare for a high-energy dance club, inside one of LA's historic theaters, where dancers move to salsa and merengue (downstairs), or DJ-spun house, hip-hop and oldies (upstairs).
197 D3 1038 S Hill Street
213/746-4674

Pasadena Civic Auditorium
This large complex hosts the Pasadena Symphony Orchestra as well as many other performing groups.
201 D4 300 E Green Street, Pasadena 626/584-8833; www.thepasadenacivic.com

Shrine Auditorium
Choral gospel groups, as well as such prominent dance companies as the Bolshoi and Kirov, are the highlights here.
196 B2 665 W Jefferson Boulevard
213/748-5116; www.shrineauditorium.com

Staples Center
Downtown's fabulous sports venue also hosts high-profile rock concerts that reel in crowds of pre-teens to baby boomers.
196 C3 1111 S Figueroa Street
213/742-7340; www.staplescenter.com

COMEDY AND CABARET

The Ice House Comedy Club
This famous club, located in a former 1920s ice factory, features established comedians, newcomers and improv acts. Theme-oriented sketch comedy is also staged here.
201 E5 24 N Mentor Avenue, Pasadena 626/577-1894; www.icehousecomedy.com

MOVIE THEATERS

The Paseo Colorado (➤ 163) retail complex houses a 14-screen movie theater with first-run movies.

USC, CalTech and California State University at Los Angeles often screen student works and interesting film fests. Check the Sunday *Los Angeles Times* "Calendar" section for listings.

Excursions

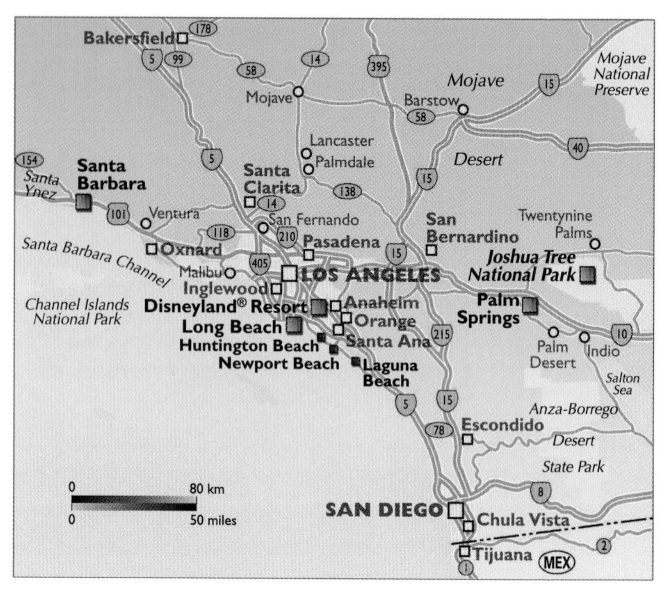

Disneyland Resort

Thirty miles (48km) by freeway from Downtown LA, Disneyland reigns as the most famous theme park in the world, a monumental construct of pop cultural fantasy that remains unmatched – except by its bigger sister park in Florida. With the opening of Disney's California Adventure Park next door to the Disneyland Park, visitors can enjoy shows and rides that celebrate the history of the Golden State.

Disneyland Park

Disneyland opened in 1955, brainchild of the late, great animator, movie-maker and dream-weaver Walt Disney. Carved out of orange groves in the sleepy Orange County town of Anaheim, it quickly became a world-famous destination, much-admired, much-copied and packed with entertaining attractions and characters drawn from comic books and fairy tales, outer space, culture and history.

The original Disneyland was renamed Disneyland Park in 1998 to distinguish it from the Disneyland Resort, created with the addition of Disneyland's California Adventure Park (➤ 168) and Downtown Disney District (➤ 169).

Aside from bringing Tomorrowland's retro vision of the future up to contemporary speed, the changes have not altered the essence of the park. Some of the parades and

Page 165: A secluded cove at Laguna Beach

shows scheduled throughout the park all day are now more directly linked to hit movies than in the past; the same goes for many of the newer rides and attractions.

You enter the park at **Main Street, USA**, a Norman Rockwell-style fantasy replica of small-town America at the beginning of the 20th century. From here you can head off on foot or jump on the Disneyland Railroad trains that circle the park, climbing off at any one of the themed "lands," which surround the Central Plaza.

Tomorrowland offers, along with its classic Space Mountain, draws including the 3-D "Honey, I Shrunk the Audience" (where special effects make you feel really tiny) and Buzz Lightyear Astro Blasters (where you pilot a spacecraft and save the universe) and the Finding Nemo Submarine Voyage.

The old standards of **Fantasyland** still delight the little ones: They'll love the Mad Tea Party, Peter Pan's Flight, It's a Small World, the King Arthur Carrousel and Sleeping Beauty Castle. The Matterhorn Bobsleds ride can be found here and it's well worth waiting for.

Mickey's Toontown, drawn from the 1988 *Who Framed Roger Rabbit* movie, offers rides and attractions geared toward the kindergarten set. Here, kids can meet and greet cartoon characters like Mickey Mouse, Goofy, Donald Duck and Roger Rabbit, but the most fun is simply to walk around – the whole off-kilter place is designed to put you inside a cartoon.

Adventureland's Tarzan's Treehouse (based on the 1999 animated film) is a good climb-around. Walt Disney's Enchanted Tiki Room will transport you to tropical Hawaii with its colorful music show featuring more than 225 singing

Join Buzz and his friends in their fight against the Evil Emperor Zurg at the Buzz Lightyear Astro Blasters in Tomorrowland

and dancing parrots and plants. The popular and exciting Indiana Jones™ Adventure takes you right into Indy's harrowing escape from the Temple of the Forbidden Eye.

Frontierland's Big Thunder Mountain Railroad rockets through an abandoned gold mine. The kids will like the nighttime Fantasmic! show and the Mark Twain Riverboat.

New Orleans Square features an amazing Haunted Mansion with high-tech ghost activity. As you float through an underground cave in a boat, treasure-hunting while a scruffy lot of pirates put on a show, you'll see why the Pirates of the Caribbean has emerged as a favorite attraction.

Finally, **Critter Country** offers Splash Mountain, one of the largest water-flume rides around.

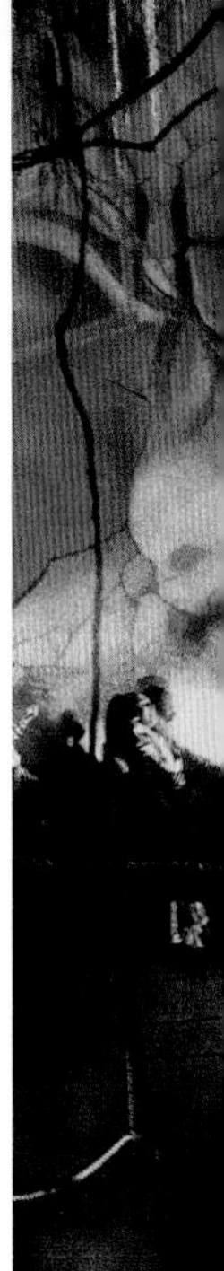

© Disney / Lucasfilm

Disney's California Adventure Park

The thrill rides attract a late teen and young adult market, but there is still much to interest visitors of other ages. A US$1.4 billion project due to be completed in 2012 will see re-theming of existing lands, the creation of a new "land," inspired by the film *Cars*, as well as other new attractions.

You enter the 55-acre (22ha) park by passing under a scaled-down version of the Golden Gate Bridge of San Francisco. And this pretty much summarizes what the park is all about – a collection of Californiana transformed into an amusement park. There are four main "lands": **a bug's land**, where little guests can roam a farm area, watch a 3-D movie and explore an oversize playground inspired by the movie *A Bug's Life*; **Paradise Pier**, an authentic-looking but high-tech version of a California waterfront; **Hollywood Pictures Backlot**, a fantasy vision of Hollywood, focusing on Hollywood Boulevard; and **Golden State**, which is divided into six districts representing different aspects of California: Grizzly Peak Recreation Area, Bountiful Valley Farm, Pacific Wharf, Condor Flats, The Bay Area and The Golden Vine Winery. Over 30 attractions have been concocted around these icons of California.

At Paradise Pier you can loop-the-loop on California Screamin' and be catapulted at speed into the air on the Maliboomer, a modern version of an old fairground attraction, where you reach a height of 180 feet (55m) and can experience zero gravity.

Hollywood Pictures Backlot gives an insight into animation and film-making and at the Golden State you can fly over the Sunshine State on the **Soarin' Over California**, a simulated hang-glider ride over the whole shebang or hang on tight at the **Grizzly River Run**, a white-water thrill ride.

HOW TO GET THE MOST OUT OF A VISIT

Waits for some rides can be 90 minutes or more, so **start early**.

A **Park Hopper pass** allows admission to both Disneyland Park and Disney's California Adventure, a convenient and cost-effective choice if you intend to visit both parks. Passes range from one to as many as five days (or more) depending on visitors' requirements.

The free **FASTPASS** system allows you to reserve a specific ride at a specific time via computer; instead of waiting, you can do something else and come back when it's time for the ride. Look for FASTPASS machines near the major attractions at Disneyland and Disney's California Adventure.

Downtown Disney District

You can eat well in Disney's California Adventure, or head over to Downtown Disney District, which is connected to Tomorrowland by monorail. This lively strip of restaurants (that serve alcohol), nightclubs, movie theaters and stores is conveniently located between the two parks, and you can choose from 12 dining spots ranging from Tortilla Jo's Mexican cuisine to the Rainforest Café, followed by entertainment at such stalwarts of nightlife as The House of Blues and Ralph Brennan's Jazz Kitchen.

Away from the lines and noise of the rides in the parks, a visit to the pretty streets and stores of Downtown Disney District can provide a pleasant interlude, adding even more enjoyment to your trip.

TAKING A BREAK

If you want something a little bit special, head to **Napa Rose** at Disney's Grand Californian Hotel (tel: 714/300-7170; daily 11:30–10:30; $$) to enjoy elegant Napa Valley cuisine in what is widely agreed to be the best restaurant in the resort. As with most theme parks, there are endless places to eat around the Disney parks. Whatever you feel like eating, you should be able to get it here.

Head to Adventureland in Disneyland Park for the thrilling Indiana Jones™ Adventure

---

201 F1 ✉ 1313 Harbor Boulevard at Katella Avenue, Anaheim, off the Santa Ana Freeway ☎ 714/781-4565; www.disneyland.com Disneyland: daily 10–10; Disney's California Adventure: daily 10–9 (subject to seasonal change); Downtown Disney District: daily 7am–2am Expensive; free under 3

DISNEYLAND RESORT: INSIDE INFO

Top tips If you're doing both parks over two or more days, Disney's **Grand Californian Hotel**, in the center of Disneyland Resort, is probably the most convenient place to stay.

- If it's possible, avoid summer, holidays and weekends, when crowds are heaviest. Mid-week from mid-September to mid-November and mid-January to mid-March are the quietest times.
- Food within the resort is often expensive and the lines can be very long.

Getting there If you're not driving, you can get there by **train** from Downtown LA via Fullerton, or take the **MTA bus** No 460 for a 90-minute trip from Downtown. A **GrayLine** does the same trip in half the time, 16 times daily; buses also go to Disneyland from LAX, Long Beach, Pasadena and Hollywood.

Santa Barbara

Roughly 90 minutes' drive northwest of Los Angeles up the California coast, Santa Barbara, the community for well-off Angelenos, remains a tranquil, Spanish-tinged coastal small city. The rugged Santa Ynez Mountains rise to the east; the Pacific stretches away to the west, bedecked with its Channel Islands jewels. In between, Santa Barbara's Mediterranean-style downtown and waterfront parks and streets offer visitors a low-key yet rich assortment of attractions, ranging from white sand beaches to sophisticated galleries and museums.

Santa Barbara's mission and its splendid little natural history museum lie in the hills east of downtown, as do many of the city's most desirable residential areas. You'll find most of Santa Barbara's attractions relatively close to the waterfront.

European Enclave

Santa Barbara was leveled by an earthquake in 1925. During reconstruction, the town planners decreed that all buildings would be Spanish Mediterranean in style. As a result, the city's commercial district features lovely structures with adobe-textured walls, rounded archways, glazed tilework and terra-cotta-tile rooftops. Take a self-guided **Red Tile Tour** (maps and video podcasts are available from the Visitor Information Center and from their website). Among the finer buildings are the **County Courthouse** (1929) and the **Museum of Art**, an outstanding regional museum with a surprisingly deep collection, including works by Matisse, Chagall, O'Keefe and Monet, and an exquisite assortment of Chinese ceramics. Wining, dining and strolling the stores and galleries of State Street and surrounding streets down to the waterfront is a wonderful way to spend an afternoon.

Santa Barbara is lucky to have miles of white sand beaches

A brown pelican at Stearns Wharf

The Waterfront

Here you can roam out onto historic **Stearns Wharf**, with its shops, restaurants and sweeping views, or stroll along Chase Palm Park and the waterfront to the **Zoological Gardens**, a nifty little zoo that can be toured in less than an hour. If you've had enough walking, take the waterfront shuttle back to State Street or take a break on **East Beach**, which stretches north from the zoo back to Stearns Wharf. The beach is clean and pretty, with volleyball courts, picnic areas with barbecue grills and the **Cabrillo Pavilion**, a bathhouse and recreation and arts center in a landmark 1925 building. There are many beaches within walking or cycling distance where you can lounge, swim, surf, sail, sunset cruise, whale watch…whatever. And the nearby hills shelter a number of lovely wineries producing some fine California vintages. Consult www.sbcountywines.com for more information.

TAKING A BREAK

Esau's Coffee Shop (721 Chapala Street, tel: 805/965-4416; Mon–Thu 6:30am–10pm, Fri 6:30am–11pm, Sat 7am–11pm, Sun 7am–10pm; $), serves great homemade food.

Santa Barbara Visitor Information Center
113 Harbor Way, Waterfront Center 4th Floor 805/884-1475; www.santabarbaraca.com Daily 8:30–5

Santa Barbara County Courthouse
1100 Anacapa Street 805/962-6464; www.santabarbaracourthouse.org Mon–Fri 8–5, Sat–Sun and holidays 10–4:30 Free; tours daily 2pm (also Mon, Tue and Fri 10:30am)

Santa Barbara Museum of Art
1130 State Street 805/963-4364; www.sbma.net Tue–Sun 11–5 Moderate; under 6 free every Sun

Santa Barbara Zoological Gardens
500 Niños Drive 805/963-5695; www.santabarbarazoo.org Daily 10–5, last admission 4; closed Christmas and Thanksgiving Moderate, free under 2

Santa Barbara Mission
Laguna and Los Olivos streets 805/682-4713; http://santabarbaramission.org Daily 9–4:30 Inexpensive; free under 6. Self-guided tours with admission

Santa Barbara's "Queen of the Missions" dates from 1786

Santa Barbara Museum of Natural History
✉ 2559 Puesta del Sol Road ☎ 805/682-4711; www.sbnature.org ⊙ Daily 10–5 Adults moderate; children 3–12 years inexpensive, under 3 free

Cabrillo Pavillion
✉ 1118 E Cabrillo Boulevard ☎ 805/897-1983 ⊙ Irregular hours Free

SANTA BARBARA: INSIDE INFO

Top tips Don't miss the graceful **Santa Barbara Mission**, established in 1786 by Father Serra and built by the Chumash (➤ 12–14). Known as "The Queen of the Missions," it overlooks the city, the Pacific and the Channel Islands.

- The **Santa Barbara Museum of Natural History**, a small gem alongside Mission Creek in the hilly east side of town, has several fabulous collections, including a wonderful selection of artifacts from the Chumash and other Native Californians. It's close to the mission, so plan to do them both on the same trip.
- A four-wheel **surrey cycle** is a great way for families to tour Santa Barbara's 2 miles (3km) of level waterfront cycle paths. You can rent these along with cycles at various locations in Santa Barbara (www.stb.he.org has details of rentals and rates).

Getting there To do Santa Barbara in a single day, rise at the crack of dawn and get on to the Ventura Freeway (101), then head north from LA. If you're planning on spending the night, a drive along the coast through Malibu and Oxnard on Highway 1, before you pick up the freeway in Ventura, is much prettier but a bit slower. Either way, you'll arrive in Santa Barbara's Downtown via 101 (Pacific Coast Highway).

Long Beach

Devotees of maritime lore come to Long Beach to visit the magnificent *Queen Mary*, purchased by Long Beach's city managers and converted into a floating hotel/museum in 1967. She remains a world-class attraction, with lavish art-deco and Moderne interiors maintained in perfect condition. Yet there's more to Long Beach than the *Queen Mary*: a brilliantly designed aquarium and a significant art museum are other crowd pleasers.

Long Beach is California's fifth largest city and for a century served as a major shipping port and an active Navy town until the Cold War ended, leading to the economically devastating closure in 1991 of the city's naval station and shipyard. In the years since, Long Beach has been hard at work replacing the sailors with tourists. The city hosts a world-class grand prix auto race in April (► 193), a Bayou music festival in June, and an impressive blues festival in September. But travelers need not wait for a special event.

Long Beach's pride and joy, the *Queen Mary*

With 5.5 miles (9km) of beaches, the *Queen Mary*, the stores of Shoreline Village and the Aquarium of the Pacific, Long Beach's attractions are distinctly maritime, although the **Long Beach Museum of Art** and the **Museum of Latin American Art**, the only museum in the LA area devoted entirely to contemporary Hispanic art, provide entertainment with a more cultural emphasis.

Queen Mary

You could easily spend two days in Long Beach, with a night aboard the opulent *Queen Mary*. Elegantly detailed staterooms constructed of tropical hardwoods, miles of bakelite hand-rails, teak decks and memorabilia-filled exhibits everywhere – including one devoted to sister ship the *Titanic* – make time spent onboard the *Queen* utterly fascinating. Visitors can even explore and then descend in the Cold-War era Soviet submarine *Scorpion*, which is docked nearby.

Aquarium of the Pacific

Housed in a glass structure with undulating walls and roof designed to echo the look and movement of water, the 120,000-square-foot (11,150sq m) aquarium contains more than 12,000 sea creatures. It examines in immaculate detail the ecology of the Pacific Ocean.

Divided into three sections, covering Southern California/ Baja, the Tropical Pacific and the Northern Pacific, the aquarium includes some amazing exhibits, such as an underwater tunnel that puts you inside a seal and sea lion habitat and a 35,000-gallon (159,000-litre) Deep Reef exhibit populated with armadas of vividly colored tropical fish.

Take to the Water

If aquariums aren't your thing, go outside: Watch whales, ride in a gondola, sail in a tall ship or explore a submarine. These attractions and more can be found on or near the Long

A balmy seaside scene at Shoreline Village

Beach waterfront. San Pedro and the LA Harbor are right next door, and the Catalina Express boats to Santa Catalina Island (➤ 21) dock a few yards from the *Queen Mary*.

Overlooking the harbor, the **Long Beach Museum of Art** resides in a 1912 Craftsman-style house and an adjacent pavilion; the focus here is primarily on contemporary work by Southern California artists. The collections are fine, but the real highlight is video: The museum owns more than 3,000 artists' videos, one of the country's largest collections, on revolving display in the video annex.

Often overlooked along the waterfront, Long Beach's old **downtown** has a rich selection of thrift shops, antiques outlets and used bookstores, many housed in vintage buildings.

TAKING A BREAK

Barbecue, burgers and sandwiches are on the menu at **Lucille's Smokehouse BarBQue** (4828 E Second Street, tel: 562/434-7427; www.lucillesbbq.com; Sun–Thu 11–10, Fri–Sat 11–11; $$).

---

www.visitlongbeach.com

Museum of Latin American Art
628 Alamitos Avenue · 562/437-1689; www.molaa.com · Tue–Fri 11:30–7, Sat 11–7, Sun 11–6 · Adults moderate; students and seniors inexpensive; free Fri and for under 12s

Colorful architecture at the Museum of Latin American Art

Queen Mary
1126 Queens Highway (at the end of the 710 freeway, across the Queensway Bridge from the Aquarium) · 562/435-3511 or 800/437-2934; www.queenmary.com · Daily 10–6; extended summer hours · Expensive; combination ticket with Aquarium of the Pacific available

Aquarium of the Pacific
100 Aquarium Way · 562/590-3100; www.aquariumofpacific.org · Daily 9–6 · Expensive; combination ticket with *Queen Mary* available

Long Beach Museum of Art
2300 East Ocean Boulevard · 562/439-2119; www.lbma.org · Tue–Sun 11–5 · Moderate; free Fri and for under 12s

LONG BEACH: INSIDE INFO

Top tip A **combined ticket** provides access to both the Aquarium and the *Queen Mary* on the same day with a complimentary shuttle.

Getting there Take the Harbor Freeway (110) to the San Diego Freeway (405) to the Long Beach Freeway (710), or take 405 to 710 from the West Side. Or take the Metro Blue Line; the last four stops are in Long Beach.

Orange Coast Beaches

A number of small cities are strung out along Orange County's Pacific coastline, from the south end of Long Beach to the north end of San Diego County. This excursion focuses on three of them: Huntington Beach, the birthplace of California's surf scene; Newport Beach, home to the world's largest yacht harbor; and Laguna Beach, famed for its art scene, shopping and secluded beaches.

Surf City

You'll know you're in **Huntington Beach** when you've passed Bolsa Chica State Beach and the **Bolsa Chica Ecological Preserve**, a bird sanctuary across the highway. The once-scruffy oil town has been growing inland for years, but the beach remains the focus, especially where Main Street meets the Coast Highway. Watch the surfing from the pier, check out the **Surfers Walk of Fame** and the **International Surfing Museum** to get a historical perspective on the sport. It really did have its California start here, in 1907, when Henry Huntington brought surfers over from Hawaii to encourage visitors to come to the beach on his Pacific Electric Railroad.

Newport Beach

Ten miles (16km) south, you move into one of the more expensive precincts of Southern California – Newport Beach, home to 10 yacht clubs and over 10,000 yachts. Wrapped around a natural bay, Newport includes the Balboa Peninsula along the ocean side, pricey Lido and Balboa Islands in the

For yachtsmen, Newport Harbor can't be beat

bay and waterfront homes, piers, stores and boats around the bay. Among them, the **Lovell Beach House** (viewed only from the outside), at W Ocean Front and 13th Street, survives as one of architect Rudolph Schindler's most famous works. The **Orange County Museum of Art** displays contemporary Californians like Ed Ruscha, Ed Kienholz and video artist Bill Viola. At the east end of the bay lies the **Upper Newport Bay Ecological Reserve and Regional Park**, with 10 miles (16km) of trails winding through a sanctuary that shelters up to 30,000 birds from 160 different species.

Laguna Beach

South of Newport you pass through Corona del Mar, then along the 3 miles (5km) of pristine coastline that forms **Crystal Cove State Park**. After Crystal Cove comes Laguna Beach. Laguna has clung to its artsy tradition as much as possible, given the pressures of mega-bucks real-estate realities. The Pacific Coast Highway passes through the middle of town, just a few steps from the unpretentious Main Beach. Laguna shelters dozens of smaller, more secluded beaches. If this town beach is overcrowded, head down to the Aliso Pier, a couple of miles south. In "the Village," you'll find a colorful assortment of stores, cafés and pubs and more than 60 art galleries displaying innumerable Laguna beachscapes and landscapes, the primary inspiration for the town's artists since the late 19th century. The best of the genre can be found in the **Laguna Art Museum**.

Bolsa Chica Ecological Preserve
Pacific Coast Highway at Warner Avenue 714/846-1114 (Bolsa Chica Conservancy); www.bolsachica.org Daily sunrise–sunset Free

International Surfing Museum
411 Olive Avenue, Huntington Beach 714/960-3483; www.surfingmuseum.org Mon–Fri noon–5, Sat–Sun 11–6 Inexpensive; free under 6

Orange County Museum of Art
850 San Clemente Drive, Newport Beach 949/759-1122; www.ocma.net Wed–Sun 11–5 (Thu also 5–8pm) Moderate; free 3rd Thu of the month

Upper Newport Bay Ecological Reserve and Regional Park
Newport Bay Naturalists (for information, maps), 600 Shellmaker Drive (off Backbay Drive) 949/640-6746; www.newportbay.org Free

Crystal Cove State Park
8471 PCH, just north of Laguna Beach 949/494-3539 ; www.crystalcovestatepark.com (information on camping and recreational activities) Day-parking moderate

Laguna Art Museum
307 Cliff Drive, Laguna Beach 949/494-8971; www.lagunaartmuseum.org Daily 11–5 Moderate; tours available

ORANGE COAST BEACHES: INSIDE INFO

Getting there From Long Beach or from the 405 Freeway, make your way to Seal Beach, Orange County's most northerly town. Head south on Highway 1, the Pacific Coast Highway (PCH).

Palm Springs and Joshua Tree National Park

When the Rat Pack came here to play in the 1950s, Palm Springs was the epitome of cool. Today, "America's Desert Playground" is swinging again. It offers fabulous opportunities to hit the links, but if you don't play golf, there are plenty of other activities to keep you here for a few days. And if you like your nature a little wilder, head up into one of the Indian Canyons for a hike. Better still, make the one-hour drive to Joshua Tree National Park, east of Palm Springs.

There are spectacular views from the Palm Springs Aerial Tramway

Palm Springs

The best bet for (well-heeled) visitors is to stay in a golf resort, such as the Marriott Desert Springs Resort, Rancho Las Palmas or La Quinta Resort and Club – for convenience and a taste of the high life, club style. Alternatively, check out one of the funky boutique hotels, housed in 1950s-style buildings.

If you don't play golf, you can hike wild canyons, ride trams into snowcapped mountain ranges, trek through a desert national park, go shopping, sunbathe, swim, play tennis, cycle or tour a compelling collection of architect-designed homes from the golden era of Modernism.

One of the best family options is the **Knott's Soak City Water Park**. With 12 waterslides, a wave pool for board and body surfing, an inner-tube ride and "beaches" with private cabanas and food service, this facility offers a complete oceanfront package, 125 miles (200km) from the ocean.

Don't miss the **Palm Springs Aerial Tramway**, rising from the desert floor to the top of 8,516-foot (2,595m) Mount San Jacinto, where you'll find snowshoeing and cross-country skiing trails in winter and great hiking in summer. The cars rotate during the 14-minute, 2.5-mile (4km) ascent to give spectacular panoramic views. Take an extra sweater; the summit can be very cold, even in summer. Once on top, you can grab a bite in a snack bar or have a meal at Elevations restaurant.

Architecture buffs will find a good selection of Modernist buildings in "The Springs." As well as the Tramway Valley Station, noted architect Albert Frey designed the Palm Springs City Hall, the Tramway gas station and his own house off Tahquitz Canyon Way. John Lautner's home for Bob Hope is another standout.

Lovers of the wild desert have options near and far. Close at hand is the **Living Desert Wildlife and Botanical Park**, a 1,200-acre (485ha) destination in nearby Palm Desert, complete with 400 species of desert animals (some, like bighorn sheep and coyotes, native; others, like cheetahs and zebras, not so native), botanical gardens, a spectacle called the Wildlife Wonders Animal Show and some fine hiking trails.

Joshua Tree National Park

The striking Joshua tree, *Yucca brevifolia*, is so-called because of its outstretched limbs, which reminded early Mormon settlers of the biblical Joshua leading wanderers through the desert. They also called it the "praying plant." In the

PALM SPRINGS AND JOSHUA TREE NATIONAL PARK: INSIDE INFO

Getting there Palm Springs lies about 120 miles (193km) east of LA via Interstate 10. Leave the freeway at the Palm Springs exit and take California 111 onto North Palm Canyon Drive and into town. The drive takes roughly two hours. Airlines serving LAX to Palm Springs include United (tel: 800/241-6522), American, US Airlines and Delta.

Where to stay Among the best places to stay in Palm Springs are the Marriott Desert Springs Resort (tel: 760/341-2211), Rancho Las Palmas (tel: 760/568-2727) and La Quinta Resort and Club (tel: 800/598-3828).

Top tip For animal lovers, dawn or dusk is the best time for spotting any of the primarily **nocturnal creatures** that inhabit the park, including bighorn sheep, coyotes, black-tailed jackrabbits and kangaroo rats.

national park are two very different deserts: the **Colorado Desert**, to the east, dominated by the creosote bush; and the higher, cooler **Mojave Desert**, to the west, with great stands of Joshua trees. Miles of hiking and cycling trails lace through the park, allowing visitors a chance to delve deeply into the ecology of the desert.

Wild desert at its best: the Living Desert Wildlife and Botanical Park

TAKING A BREAK

With three different types of Mexican food on the menu – Mayan, Huasteco and Aztec – a meal at **Edgardo's Café Veracruz** is an eye-opening, delicious experience (494 N Palm Canyon Road, tel: 760/320-3558, daily 11–10).

---

www.palm-springs.org
www.nps.gov/jotr

Palm Springs Official Visitors Center
2901 North Palm Canyon Drive (former Tramway gas station)
760/778-8418 or 1-800/347-7746
Daily 8–5

Knott's Soak City Water Park
1500 Gene Autry Trail (off I-10) between Ramon Road, E Palm Canyon Drive
760/327-0499; www.knotts.com/soakcity Mid-Mar to Labor Day daily 1–6; Sep–Oct Sat–Sun 11–6 Expensive

Palm Springs Aerial Tramway
Tramway Road (off Highway 111) 760/325-1391; www.pstramway.com
Mon–Fri 10–8, Sat–Sun 8–8 Expensive

Living Desert Wildlife and Botanical Park
47-900 Portola Avenue, Palm Desert 760/346-5694; www.livingdesert.org Sep–Jun 15 daily 9–5; Jun 16–Aug 8–1:30
Adults/seniors expensive; children 3–12 moderate

Indian Canyons (Andreas, Murray and Palm Canyons)
760/323-6018; www.indian-canyons.com Oct–Jul daily 8–5; Jul–Sep Fri–Sun 8–5 Moderate

Joshua Tree National Park
74485 National Park Drive, Twentynine Palms 760/367-5500; www.nps.gov/jotr All year daily Day-use moderate per car; inexpensive per person; camping expensive per day

SPIRALGUIDE Questionnaire

Dear Traveller

Your comments, opinions and recommendations are very important to us. Please help us to improve our travel guides by taking a few minutes to complete this simple questionnaire.

You do not need a stamp (unless posted outside the UK). If you do not want to remove this page from your guide, then photocopy it or write your answers on a plain sheet of paper.

Send to: The Editor, Spiral Guides, AA World Travel Guides, FREEPOST SCE 4598, Basingstoke RG21 4GY.

Your recommendations...

We always encourage readers' recommendations for restaurants, night-life or shopping – if your recommendation is used in the next edition of the guide, we will send you a FREE AA Spiral Guide of your choice. Please state below the establishment name, location and your reasons for recommending it.

____

____

____

____

____

Please send me AA Spiral ______________________________

(see list of titles inside the back cover)

About this guide...

Which title did you buy?

______________________________ **AA Spiral**

Where did you buy it? ______________________________

When? m m / y y

Why did you choose an AA Spiral Guide? ______________________________

____

____

____

____

Did this guide meet your expectations?

Exceeded ☐ **Met all** ☐ **Met most** ☐ **Fell below** ☐

Please give your reasons ______________________________

____

____

____

____

continued on next page...

Were there any aspects of this guide that you particularly liked?

____

____

____

____

____

Is there anything we could have done better?

____

____

____

____

About you...

Name (Mr/Mrs/Ms) ______________________________

Address ______________________________

____

______________________________ **Postcode** ______________

Daytime tel no ______________________ **email** ______________________

Please *only* give us your email address and mobile phone number if you wish to hear from us about other products and services from the AA and partners by email or text or mms.

Which age group are you in?

Under 25 ☐ **25–34** ☐ **35–44** ☐ **45–54** ☐ **55–64** ☐ **65+** ☐

How many trips do you make a year?

Less than one ☐ **One** ☐ **Two** ☐ **Three or more** ☐

Are you an AA member? Yes ☐ **No** ☐

About your trip...

When did you book? m m / y y **When did you travel?** m m / y y

How long did you stay? ______________________________

Was it for business or leisure? ______________________________

Did you buy any other travel guides for your trip? ☐ Yes ☐ No

If yes, which ones? ______________________________

____

Thank you for taking the time to complete this questionnaire. Please send it to us as soon as possible, and remember, you do not need a stamp (unless posted outside the UK).

The information we hold about you will be used to provide the products and services requested and for identification, account administration, analysis, and fraud/loss prevention purposes. More details about how that information is used is in our privacy statement, which you'll find under the heading "Personal Information" in our terms and conditions and on our website: www.theAA.com. Copies are also available from us by post, by contacting the Data Protection Manager at AA, Fanum House, Basing View, Basingstoke, RG21 4EA.
We may want to contact you about other products and services provided by us, or our partners (by mail, telephone) but please tick the box if you DO NOT wish to hear about such products and services from us by mail or telephone. ☐

Acknowledgments

The Automobile Association wishes to thank the following photographers and organisations for their assistance in the preparation of this book.

Abbreviations for the picture credits are as follows – (t) top; (b) bottom; (l) left; (r) right; (c) centre; (AA) AA World Travel Library

Front Cover: Sunset Boulevard, AA/M Jourdan
Back Cover top: Venice Beach, AA/M Jourdan
Back Cover centre: Dogs, AA/M Jourdan
Spine: Signpost, AA/M Jourdan

2t AA/A Mockford & N Bonetti; **2c** AA/A Mockford & N Bonetti; **2c** AA/A Mockford & N Bonetti; **2b** AA/A Mockford & N Bonetti; **3t** AA/A Mockford & N Bonetti; **3c** AA/A Mockford & N Bonetti; **3c** AA/A Mockford & N Bonetti; **3b** AA/A Mockford & N Bonetti; **5l** AA/A Mockford & N Bonetti; **5cb** AA/A Mockford & N Bonetti; **5br** AA/A Mockford & N Bonetti; **6–7** AA/A Mockford & N Bonetti; **8** Hulton Archive/Getty Images; **10** Douglas C. Pizac/AP/PA Photos; **11** Bettmann/Corbis; **12** David Muench/Corbis; **13** Nik Wheeler/Corbis; **14** Marilyn Angel Wynn/Nativestock Pictures/Corbis; **15** Warner Bros/The Kobal Collection/Marshak, Bob; **16-17** David Crausby/Alamy; **16b** Universal/The Kobal Collection; **18-19** AA/A Mockford & N Bonetti; **20bl** Rich Reid/National Geographic RF/Getty Images; **20br** Ian Shive/Aurora Creative/Getty Images; **21** John Elk III/Lonely Planet Images/Getty Images; **22** AA/A Mockford & N Bonetti; **23** AA/A Mockford & N Bonetti; **24** AA/A Mockford & N Bonetti; **25** AA/A Mockford & N Bonetti; **26** AA/A Mockford & N Bonetti; **27** AA/A Mockford & N Bonetti; **29tr** AA/A Mockford & N Bonetti; **29cr** AA/A Mockford & N Bonetti; **29br** AA/A Mockford & N Bonetti; **30** AA/A Mockford & N Bonetti; **31** AA/A Mockford & N Bonetti; **32** AA/A Mockford & N Bonetti; **33l** AA/A Mockford & N Bonetti; **33bc** AA/A Mockford & N Bonetti; **33br** AA/A Mockford & N Bonetti; **49l** AA/A Mockford & N Bonetti; **49bc** AA/A Mockford & N Bonetti; **49br** AA/A Mockford & N Bonetti; **52** AA/A Mockford & N Bonetti; **53** AA/A Mockford & N Bonetti; **54** AA/A Mockford & N Bonetti; **55** AA/A Mockford & N Bonetti; **56** AA/A Mockford & N Bonetti; **57** AA/A Mockford & N Bonetti; **58** AA/A Mockford & N Bonetti; **59** AA/A Mockford & N Bonetti; **60** AA/A Mockford & N Bonetti; **61** AA/A Mockford & N Bonetti; **62** AA/A Mockford & N Bonetti; **63** AA/A Mockford & N Bonetti; **64t** AA/A Mockford & N Bonetti; **64b** AA/A Mockford & N Bonetti; **66** AA/A Mockford & N Bonetti; **67** AA/A Mockford & N Bonetti; **69** AA/A Mockford & N Bonetti; **75l** AA/A Mockford & N Bonetti; **75bc** AA/A Mockford & N Bonetti; **75br** AA/A Mockford & N Bonetti; **76** AA/A Mockford & N Bonetti; **78** AA/A Mockford & N Bonetti; **79** AA/A Mockford & N Bonetti; **80** AA/A Mockford & N Bonetti; **81** AA/A Mockford & N Bonetti; **82-83** AA/A Mockford & N Bonetti; **84** AA/A Mockford & N Bonetti; **85** AA/A Mockford & N Bonetti; **86t** AA/A Mockford & N Bonetti; **86b** AA/A Mockford & N Bonetti; **87** AA/A Mockford & N Bonetti; **88** AA/A Mockford & N Bonetti; **89** AA/A Mockford & N Bonetti; **90t** AA/A Mockford & N Bonetti; **90b** AA/A Mockford & N Bonetti; **91** AA/A Mockford & N Bonetti; **92** AA/A Mockford & N Bonetti; **93** AA/A Mockford & N Bonetti; **94** AA/A Mockford & N Bonetti; **95** AA/A Mockford & N Bonetti; **96** AA/A Mockford & N Bonetti; **103l** AA/A Mockford & N Bonetti; **103bc** AA/A Mockford & N Bonetti; **103br** AA/A Mockford & N Bonetti; **104** AA/A Mockford & N Bonetti; **106** AA/A Mockford & N Bonetti; **107t** AA/A Mockford & N Bonetti; **107b** AA/A Mockford & N Bonetti; **108** AA/A Mockford & N Bonetti; **109** AA/A Mockford & N Bonetti; **110** AA/A Mockford & N Bonetti; **111** AA/A Mockford & N Bonetti; **112** AA/A Mockford & N Bonetti; **113** AA/A Mockford & N Bonetti; **114** AA/A Mockford & N Bonetti; **115** AA/A Mockford & N Bonetti; **116** AA/A Mockford & N Bonetti; **117** AA/A Mockford & N Bonetti; **118** AA/A Mockford & N Bonetti; **119** AA/A Mockford & N Bonetti; **120** AA/A Mockford & N Bonetti; **121t** AA/A Mockford & N Bonetti; **121b** AA/A Mockford & N Bonetti; **122t** AA/A Mockford & N Bonetti; **122b** AA/A Mockford & N Bonetti; **123** AA/A Mockford & N Bonetti; **124** AA/A Mockford & N Bonetti; **125** AA/A Mockford & N Bonetti; **126** AA/A Mockford & N Bonetti; **127** AA/A Mockford & N Bonetti; **129** AA/A Mockford & N Bonetti; **137l** AA/A Mockford & N Bonetti; **137bc** AA/A Mockford & N Bonetti; **137br** AA/A Mockford & N Bonetti; **140** AA/A Mockford & N Bonetti; **141** AA/A Mockford & N Bonetti; **142** AA/A Mockford & N Bonetti; **143** AA/A Mockford & N Bonetti; **144-145** Mark A Johnson/Alamy; **147** AA/A Mockford & N Bonetti; **148** AA/A Mockford & N Bonetti; **149** AA/A Mockford & N Bonetti; **150** AA/A Mockford & N Bonetti; **151** AA/A Mockford & N Bonetti; **152** AA/A Mockford & N Bonetti; **153** AA/A Mockford & N Bonetti; **154** AA/A Mockford & N Bonetti; **155** The Huntington; **157** AA/A Mockford & N Bonetti; **158** AA/A Mockford & N Bonetti; **165** AA/A Mockford & N Bonetti; **165bc** AA/A Mockford & N Bonetti; **165br** AA/A Mockford & N Bonetti; **167** © Disney Enterprises, Inc./Pixar; **168-169** © Disney/Lucasfilm Ltd; **170** AA/A Mockford & N Bonetti; **171** AA/A Mockford & N Bonetti; **172** AA/A Mockford & N Bonetti; **173** AA/A Mockford & N Bonetti; **174** AA/A Mockford & N Bonetti; **175** AA/A Mockford & N Bonetti; **176** AA/A Mockford & N Bonetti; **178** AA/A Mockford & N Bonetti; **180** AA/A Mockford & N Bonetti; **181l** AA/A Mockford & N Bonetti; **181bc** AA/A Mockford & N Bonetti; **181br** AA/A Mockford & N Bonetti; **182** AA/A Mockford & N Bonetti; **183** AA/A Mockford & N Bonetti; **184** AA/A Mockford & N Bonetti; **186** AA/A Mockford & N Bonetti; **187l** AA/A Mockford & N Bonetti; **187bc** AA/A Mockford & N Bonetti; **187br** AA/A Mockford & N Bonetti; **191t** AA/A Mockford & N Bonetti; **191cl** AA/A Mockford & N Bonetti; **191cr** AA/A Mockford & N Bonetti.

Every effort has been made to trace the copyright holders, and we apologise in advance for any accidental errors. We would be happy to apply any corrections in the following edition of this publication.

Walks and Tours

1 SANTA MONICA

Walk

DISTANCE 4 miles/6.5km (round trip) **TIME** 1.5 hours round trip, allow longer for stops
START/END POINT South end of Palisades Park at Santa Monica Pier 202 D2

This walk encompasses great sea views, an option for strenuous stair-climbing and a look at one of Santa Monica's pleasant residential neighborhoods. Finally, it takes you to Third Street Promenade, a stroller's haven. You'll find plenty to enjoy along the way.

1–2

Start at the south end of **Palisades Park**, where Colorado Boulevard meets the **Santa Monica Pier** (➤ 57–58). Head north through Palisades Park, the grassy, palm-shady strip that runs along the top of the cliffs. Stop to take a look at **Santa Monica Pier and Beach** (➤ 57–59) below, and Santa Monica Bay and the Pacific. On a clear day you can see Santa Catalina Island (➤ 21) off in the distance near the peninsula of Palos Verdes. To the right of Point Dume in Malibu, the **Santa Monica Mountains** form a bumpy northern horizon.

2–3

As you stroll parallel to **Ocean Avenue**, you'll pass boulevards that run all the way from here to Downtown Los Angeles and beyond, including Santa Monica Boulevard and Wilshire Boulevard. The foot of Santa Monica Boulevard here is the end of the fabled **Route 66**. You'll also pass a couple of fabulous hotels – the **Fairmont Miramar** (101 Wilshire Boulevard) and the Streamline Moderne **Shangri-La** (1301 Ocean Avenue).

0 500 m
0 500 yds
Palisades Beach
3
Adelaide Steps
4
San Vicente Boulevard
Georgina Avenue
Alta
4th

The Santa Monica Pier conjures that old-time seaside carnival atmosphere – a great place to end a walk or begin a cycle ride

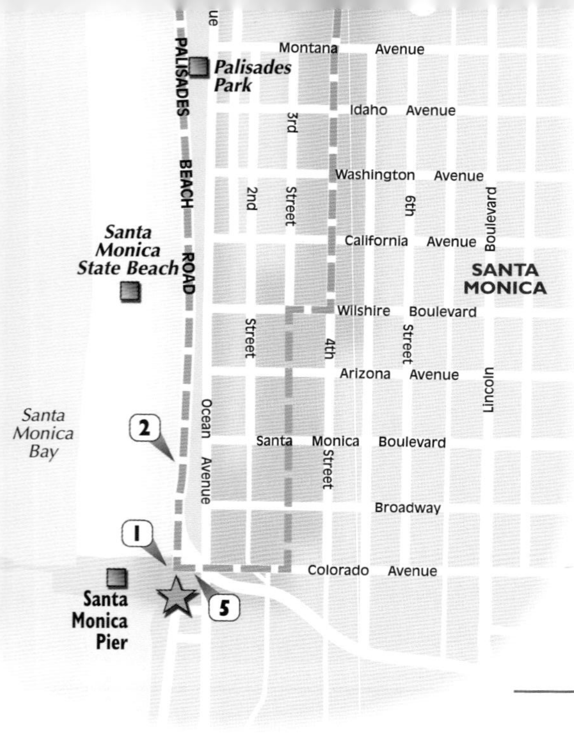

3–4
When you reach the north end of Palisades Park, head east on Adelaide Drive. At **Fourth Street**, make a choice: If you're feeling energetic, head down the **Adelaide Steps** with the rest of the fitness buffs and then back up. If you're not feeling so fit, enjoy the views over **Santa Monica Canyon** and watch the stair-climbers do their thing.

4–5
To get to the **Third Street Promenade** (➤ 72), go south along Fourth Street to Wilshire, then after around ten blocks right on Third Street and you're on this bustling three-block stretch of cafés, movie theaters, shops, fountains, topiary dinosaurs and a good mix of locals for people-watching. At the south end of the Promenade, go right down Colorado Avenue, cross Ocean Avenue, and you're back at Santa Monica Pier. Call in to the Lobster (➤ 70) for some superb seafood and a strong cocktail.

Topiary dinosaurs on Third Street Promenade

2 SOUTH BAY

Cycle ride

DISTANCE 22 miles (35km) **TIME** 2 hours **START POINT** Will Rogers State Beach 202 D2
END POINT Torrance Beach 202 off E1

This spin along the South Bay beachfront is one of the city's great pleasures. There are numerous cycle rental places between the Santa Monica and Venice piers, as well as on or near the boardwalk north of Santa Monica Pier and near the foot of Pier Avenue in Hermosa Beach. Most cyclists will probably want to enjoy a leisurely experience along one section, so here it is divided into manageable sections that can be entered or left at any point (or completed in reverse). Dockweiler Beach is about half way. It's a good idea to start early as the path can get busy, especially on summer weekends.

1–2

Start at **Will Rogers State Beach** (➤ 67) in Pacific Palisades. As you head south, the sands beckon on your right, and there you have it: the Pacific! The ocean here can range from quite rough to completely placid, depending on the weather, the wind, the time

Cyclists on a stretch of the 22-mile (35km) beachfront cycle path

of year and the swell. South of Santa Monica Canyon, the path drops down on to the beach, which is now **Santa Monica State Beach** (you've crossed from Pacific Palisades, part of LA, into the sovereign city of Santa Monica). Now you're closer to the ocean; look for dolphins, whales and other marine life – and watch out for high-speed cyclists and inline skaters, especially on busy summer afternoons. On your left are beach clubs, chic homes, a couple of restaurants, including **Patrick's Roadhouse** (106 Entrada Drive; tel 310/459-4544; Mon–Fri 7–3, Sat–Sun 8–4,) a funky breakfast and lunch spot serving hearty American fare, and bicycle rental places; beyond the highway, the cliffs rise to Santa Monica's Ocean Park. At **Santa Monica Pier** you've traveled about 3 miles (5km).

2–3

About a mile (1.5km) south of the pier you leave Santa Monica and reenter LA. From here to the next section at Marina del Rey is another 4 miles (6km). There's great people-watching on the beach and boardwalk, restaurants, bars, shops and vendors along the boardwalk (the cycle path is distinct

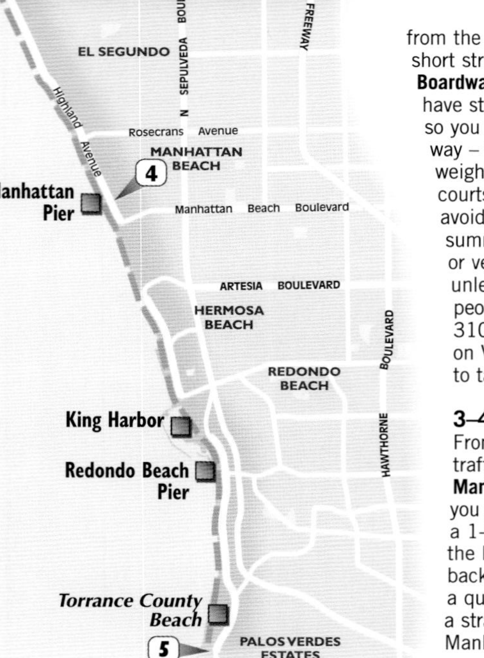

from the boardwalk, but parallels it for short stretches here and there). **Venice Boardwalk** and **Venice Beach** (➤ 54–56) have starred in hundreds of movies, so you may recognize spots along the way – Venice Pier, the Muscle Beach weightlifting pens and the basketball courts). It's a popular spot, and to avoid the worst of the crowds in the summer it's best to go on weekdays or very early in the morning – unless of course you're in it for the people. Try the **Sidewalk Café** (tel: 310/399-5547; daily 8am–11pm) on Venice Boardwalk if you're ready to take a break.

3–4

From **Venice Pier** start with a traffic-dodging detour through **Marina del Rey** (➤ 63–64). Once you get around the marina – about a 1-mile (1.5km) side trip through the land of luxury boats – you're back on the beach at **Playa del Rey**, a quiet little town. From here it is a straight shot down the coast to Manhattan Beach.

Along the way you pass Dockweiler Beach, El Segundo and El Porto, home to water-treatment plants, refineries and the LA airport flight path. But the surroundings get more pleasant again as you cross **Rosecrans Avenue** to enter the increasingly pricey beachfront enclave of **Manhattan Beach** (➤ 63).

On the 900-foot (275m) Manhattan Pier, about 12.5 miles (20km) south of the Santa Monica Pier, is an **aquarium** (tel: 310/379-8117, open Mon–Fri 3pm–sunset, Sat–Sun 10am–sunset, free), where you can see crabs, lobsters, eels and "touchable" anemones and starfish.

4–5

The last section of the path is about 6 miles (10km) from **Manhattan Pier** to Torrance Beach. Around **Hermosa Beach Pier** you'll find surfers, surf shops and other evidence of the urban surf culture that is integral to the South Bay, and if there's a good swell, you can watch them riding the waves. At the foot of Pier Avenue in Hermosa Beach is **Hennessy's Tavern** (8 Pier Avenue; tel: 310/372-5759; daily 8–11pm), a bar and rooftop deck with a fine view of Hermosa Beach and much of Santa Monica Bay. To the east, Manhattan, Hermosa and Redondo are dense, low-rise, residential neighborhoods, once solidly working-class but now increasingly pricey and exclusive.

Where cycling and pedestrian zones converge cyclists must dismount or face a high fine

You have to navigate your way along some busy streets in King Harbor, but once you get round it you're back on the beach for another mile before passing through a parking garage and pedestrian walkway at **Redondo Beach Pier** – a fun, on-foot side-trip. Be sure to take heed of the signs and dismount and walk your bike on the pedestrian section as you can get ticketed and there is a high fine if you do not. Stop for a walk on Redondo Wharf to see the Great White Shark, taken off the coast of Washington State years ago, on display in one of the curio shops. Continue on the 2-mile (3km) stretch of **Torrance Beach** – a lovely, uncrowded beach that ends at the northern edge of Palos Verdes.

Practicalities

BEFORE YOU GO

WHAT YOU NEED

● Required
○ Suggested
▲ Not required

Check with embassies, consulates and other sources for information on visa, passport and other entry requirements as well as new airport and airplane security requirements.

	UK	Germany	USA	Canada	Australia	Ireland	Netherlands	Spain
Passport/National Identity Card	●	●	▲	○	●	●	●	●
Visa	▲	▲	▲	▲	▲	▲	▲	▲
Onward or Round-Trip Ticket	●	●	▲	▲	●	●	●	●
Health Inoculations (tetanus and polio)	▲	▲	▲	▲	▲	▲	▲	▲
Health Documentation (► 192, Health)	▲	▲	▲	▲	▲	▲	▲	▲
Travel Insurance	●	●	▲	○	●	●	●	●
Driver's License (national)	●	●	●	●	●	●	●	●
Car Insurance Certificate	n/a	n/a	●	●	n/a	n/a	n/a	n/a
Car Registration Document	n/a	n/a	●	●	n/a	n/a	n/a	n/a

WHEN TO GO

Peak season — Off-season

JAN	FEB	MAR	APR	MAY	JUN	JUL	AUG	SEP	OCT	NOV	DEC
65°F	66°F	67°F	69°F	72°F	77°F	83°F	81°F	81°F	77°F	73°F	69°F
19°C	19°C	19.5°C	20.5°C	22°C	25°C	28°C	27°C	27°C	25°C	23°C	20.5°C

Very wet — Wet — Cloud — Sun — Sun/ Showers

While summer remains the most popular time to visit the city, the heat and crowds do not necessarily make it the best time to go – especially when winter temperatures can range from the mid-60s Fahrenheit up into the 80s. Winter also means less smog, although beach-lovers will find the ocean temperatures colder. Fall can be a very pleasant time of year to visit LA, except when the winds off the desert – the notorious "Santa Anas" – push the temperatures into the 80s and even 90s (over 30 degrees Celsius). Spring can be beautiful, although the "June gloom" – marine fog that rolls in off the sea – can linger along the coast. Rain usually comes in late fall and winter, occasionally in torrential bouts, which cause mudslides.

GETTING ADVANCE INFORMATION

Websites

- LA Convention and Visitors Bureau: www.lacvb.com www.visitcalifornia.com
- Los Angeles Times weekly entertainment magazine http://theguide.latimes.com

In the US

Los Angeles Convention and Visitors Bureau
www.discoverlosangeles.com

GETTING THERE

By Air All international flights to LA arrive at Los Angeles International Airport (LAX) or Ontario International Airport. Check online at www.lawa.org for further information.
From the UK and Ireland: The following offer daily non-stop direct flights to LA from London: Air New Zealand, British Airways, United Airlines, Virgin Atlantic, American, United Airlines. The following offer one-stop direct flights to LA from Gatwick: Continental, Delta, Northwest. Direct flights from regional airports to the US (but not direct to LA): American Airlines and British Airways from Manchester and Glasgow, Northwest from Glasgow, Delta from Manchester. Delta and Aer Lingus both fly direct from Ireland to LA.
From Australia and New Zealand: There are direct flights on United Airlines and Qantas out of Sydney, although fares are better on flights originating in Auckland, New Zealand, with stops in Hawaii or the South Pacific.
Within the US: All major US carriers serve LAX and John Wayne; other regional airports (Ontario, Long Beach, Santa Barbara, Burbank) offer excellent service and (often) less expensive round-trip fares. Non-stop, direct or stopover flights are readily available from practically every large city in the US and Canada. Check travel agents, flight brokers, travel sections in newspapers and the Internet for the best deals and special offers.

By Rail and Bus Amtrak operates national and regional train lines into LA from the north and east. The *Southwest Chief* originates in Chicago; the *Sunset Limited* starts in Florida. The Coast *Starlight* runs along the Pacific Coast from Seattle to San Diego via LA. For information on Amtrak routing and scheduling tel: 800/872-7245; www.amtrak.com. Riding a bus is not the greatest way to see the country. The main operator is **Greyhound** (tel: 800/231-2222; www.gryehound.com), but be prepared for bus stations in the dingier parts of towns, often frustratingly slow travel and more expensive than you expect.

TIME

Los Angeles is on Pacific Standard Time (PST), eight hours behind Greenwich Meantime (GMT -8). Daylight Savings Time, from April through November, moves the clocks up one hour to GMT -7.

CURRENCY AND FOREIGN EXCHANGE

Currency The basic unit of currency in the United States is the dollar ($1). One dollar is 100 cents. **Bills** come in denominations of $1, $5, $10, $20, $50 and $100. **Coins** come in 1 cent (penny), 5 cents (nickel), 10 cents (dime) and 25 cents (quarter). There are also one-dollar coins, but these are comparatively rare. An **unlimited amount** of US dollars can be imported or exported.
ATMs available throughout the city are by far the easiest way to obtain cash. US dollar **travelers' checks** are accepted as cash in most places (not taxis), as are **credit cards** (Amex, VISA, MasterCard, Diners Card). **Debit cards** may be accepted at retail outlets that are validated for international access.

Exchange There are foreign exchange bureaus in the major terminals at LAX, but it might be easier to buy American dollars or travelers' checks at your own bank before you depart.

In the UK
www.usembassy.org.uk
for visa information only

In Canada
Embassy of the USA
490 Sussex Drive, Ottawa, Ontario
K1N 1G8
☎ (613) 238-5335;
www.ottawa.usembassy.gov

In Australia
US Embassy Canberra
Moonah Place,
Yarralumla, ACT 2600
☎ (02) 6214 5600;
http://canberra.usembassy.gov/

WHEN YOU ARE THERE

CLOTHING SIZES

UK	Rest of Europe	USA	
36	46	36	Suits (men)
38	48	38	
40	50	40	
42	52	42	
44	54	44	
46	56	46	
7	41	8	Shoes (men)
7.5	42	8.5	
8.5	43	9.5	
9.5	44	10.5	
10.5	45	11.5	
11	46	12	
14.5	37	14.5	Shirts (men)
15	38	15	
15.5	39/40	15.5	
16	41	16	
16.5	42	16.5	
17	43	17	
8	34	6	Dresses (women)
10	36	8	
12	38	10	
14	40	12	
16	42	14	
18	44	16	
4.5	38	6	Shoes (women)
5	38	6.5	
5.5	39	7	
6	39	7.5	
6.5	40	8	
7	41	8.5	

NATIONAL HOLIDAYS

Jan 1	New Year's Day
Third Mon Jan	Martin Luther King Jr Day
Third Mon Feb	Presidents' Day
Mar/Apr	Easter (half day Good Friday, whole day Easter Monday)
Last Mon May	Memorial Day
Jul 4	Independence Day
First Mon Sep	Labor Day
Second Mon Oct	Columbus Day
Nov 11	Veterans' Day
Fourth Thu Nov	Thanksgiving
Dec 25	Christmas Day

Some stores open for business on national holidays, but most are closed for Thanksgiving and Christmas.

OPENING HOURS

Stores · Offices · Banks · Post Offices · Museums/Monuments · Pharmacies

8am 9am 10am noon 1pm 2pm 4pm 5pm 7pm

Day · Midday · Evening

Stores Hours vary greatly, but most open till 9pm on one day. Some open Sun noon–5.
Banks Some banks open till 4pm, or Fri 6pm. Most are closed Sat; all are closed Sun.
Post Offices Open Mon–Fri 9–5, till 1pm Sat. Smaller offices keep shorter hours.
Museums Hours vary. Most open 9:30 or 10am to 5 or 6pm. Some keep longer hours Thu, Fri or Sat. Many are closed one day a week.
Places of Worship See the *Yellow Pages*.

TIME DIFFERENCES

GMT/UK 12 noon

Los Angeles 4am

New York 7am

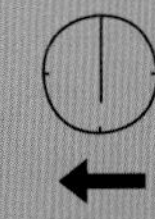
Chicago 6am

Spain 1pm

Australia 10pm

PERSONAL SAFETY

Crime levels in Los Angeles have fallen sharply over recent years, but it is still wise to take sensible precautions:

- Avoid the notorious South-Central district and East LA.
- Don't walk alone in quiet streets or Venice Beach after dark.
- Carry only the cash you need; leave other cash and valuables in the hotel safe.
- Report theft or mugging to the police to provide a reference in case of an insurance claim.

Police assistance:
911 from any phone

TELEPHONES

There are payphones on some street corners and most are coin operated. From public phones dial 0 for the operator and give the name of the country, city and number you are calling. You will need at least $5.50 in quarters for an overseas call. Some phones take prepaid phone cards, available at drugstores and newsstands, and some take credit cards. Dial 1 plus the area code for numbers within the US and Canada. Dial 411 to find US and Canadian numbers.

International Dialing Codes
Dial 011 followed by

UK:	44
Ireland:	353
Australia:	61
Germany:	49
Netherlands:	31
Spain:	34

POST OFFICES

LA's main branch post office: 7101 S Central Avenue. For location of nearest branch, tel: 800/ASK-USPS. The LAX branch is located at 9029 Airport Boulevard, Inglewood. Some branches are open on Saturday mornings.

ELECTRICITY

The power supply is 110/120 volts AC (60 cycles). Sockets take two-prong,

flat-pin plugs. An adaptor is needed for appliances with two-round-pin and three-pin plugs. European appliances also need a voltage transformer.

TIPS/GRATUITIES

Tipping is expected for all services. As a general guide:

Restaurants (service not included)	15–20%
Bar service	15%
Tour guides	discretion
Hairdressers	15%
Taxis	15%
Chambermaids	$2 per day
Porters	$2–$5 per bag

POLICE 911

FIRE 911

AMBULANCE 911

HEALTH

Insurance Charges for health care in the US are exorbitant. Some kind of travel health insurance coverage is highly recommended. If you are involved in an accident, you will be taken care of, but you will be charged high fees later.

Dental Services Dental treatment in the US is very expensive. Travelers are advised to make sure that their medical insurance policy also includes adequate dental coverage. You may have to pay up front at the time of service, so save all bills for later compensation from your provider.

Weather Los Angeles is nearly always warm and sunny. Sunscreen is highly recommended, especially if you're going to the beach. Evenings in spring, fall and winter can be chilly, so it's a good idea to take an extra sweater if you go out at night.

Drugs Like most large American cities, LA seems to have huge drugstores on every other block. Most of them are chains, like Rite-Aid, and many stay open 24 hours a day, dispensing prescription and non-prescription drugs as well as everything from shampoo to dog food. Consult the phone book's *Yellow Pages* for a drugstore near to your hotel.

Safe Water LA's tap water is clean and safe to drink. Bottled water or seltzer is available in supermarkets, drugstores, convenience stores and most restaurants and bars.

CONCESSIONS

Students Holders of an International Student Identity Card are entitled to discounts on many attractions. Contact tourist information for details.

Senior Citizens Senior citizens (seniors) will find discounts on many services and attractions. Qualifying age varies from 55 to 65. You need to request a discount up front and may be asked to show proof of age. Contact AARP on 800/687-2277; www.aarp.org for more information.

TRAVELING WITH A DISABILITY

Most LA facilities provide access for people with disabilities. This includes accessible toilets, and buses equipped with lifts and space inside for wheelchair users. Amtrak trains provide sleeping and seating areas for passengers with disabilities. Many car-rental companies offer cars with special hand controls. Call the LA County Commission on Disabilities for more specific local information, tel: 213/974-1053; http://laccod.org.

CHILDREN

LA is generally very child-friendly, with the exception of some of the very upscale or trendy restaurants. Look for listings in the *Los Angeles Times* and other local sources for children's activities.

RESTROOMS

There are good public restroom facilities at all public beaches along the LA coast. Otherwise, try in hotel lobby areas for the best options.

CUSTOMS

The import of wildlife souvenirs from rare or endangered species may be illegal or require a special permit. Before buying, check your home country's regulations.

EMBASSIES AND CONSULATES

UK
09042 450100 or
0207 894 0563

Ireland
028 9038 6100

Canada
800/375-5283

Australia
(02) 6214 5600

New Zealand
0900 878 472

What's On

For details on what's happening in the city contact the LA Convention and Visitors Bureau's multilingual events hotline (tel: 213/689-8822; www.lacvb.com). The "Calendar" section in the Los Angeles Times every Sunday also has listings for all events in the city each week (www.latimes.com).

JANUARY

- 1st – **Tournament of Roses Parade**: Hugely popular parade in Pasadena with marching bands and floats adorned with thousands of blooms. Every four or five years the Rose Parade is followed by the final of the inter-collegiate football championship in the Rose Bowl Stadium (www.tournamentofroses.com).

FEBRUARY

- Dates vary – **Chinese New Year Festival**: A colorful carnival and parade feature dragon dancers and fireworks in LA's Chinatown.

FEBRUARY/MARCH

- 1st Sunday – **Los Angeles Marathon**: The city is host to 20,000 runners in this annual event (www.lamarathon.com).
- Early March – **Academy Awards (Oscars)**: LA's most famous celebration of the movie industry takes place in the purpose-built the Kodak Theatre in the Hollywood and Highland complex.

APRIL

- Mid-April – **Toyota Long Beach Grand Prix**: The streets of Long Beach are the setting for this world-class auto race. A pro/celebrity race features many famous faces (www.longbeachyp.com).

MAY

- 5th – **Cinco de Mayo**: A celebration of Hispanic heritage and culture with music and dancing. A huge Cinco de Mayo fiesta is also held on the last Sunday in April along Broadway, Hill and Spring streets in Downtown.
- Late May – **Old Pasadena Summerfest**: A lively festival with music, arts, crafts, food and sports events (www.oldpasadenasummerfest.com).

JUNE

- Mid-June – **Sunset Series Sailboat Races**: A race from the marina to the California Yacht Club in Marina del Rey.
- Mid- to late June – **Lesbian and Gay Pride Celebration**: A weekend festival in West Hollywood Park. The Sunday-morning parade winds its way to the park along Santa Monica Boulevard.
- Third weekend – **Mariachi USA Festival**: Celebrate mariachi music with more than 200 world-class performers. Also features ballet folklorico and fireworks (www.mariachiusa.com).
- June to August, Sundays – **Woodland Hills Concerts in the Park**: Enjoy a varied series of outdoor concerts at Warner Ranch Park.

JULY

- 4th – **Independence Day**: Fireworks displays (most spectacular at Marina del Rey), parades and festivities.
- July to mid-September – **Hollywood Bowl Concert Season**: Bring a picnic and enjoy the music on a balmy evening at this renowned concert theater.

- Second Weekend – **Lotus Festival**: A celebration of Asian-Pacific culture at Echo Park Lake with music, dance, food, flowers and dragon boat races (www.laparks.org/calendar/lotus/lotus.htm).
- Late July/early August – **Central Avenue Jazz Festival**: A weekend of jazz performances in and around the legendary Dunbar Hotel.

AUGUST

- Early August – **Festival of the Chariots Parade**: Venice Beach is the setting for this parade of giant chariots (www.festivalofchariots.com).
- Early August – **Watts Summer Festival**: An African-American festival of arts and culture with a carnival, a parade and a great deal of live music (www.wattsfestival.org).
- Early August – **Nisei Week Japanese Festival**: Japanese arts and culture in LA's Little Tokyo.
- Early August – **International Surf Festival**: The Hermosa, Redondo and Manhattan beaches host championship surfing competitions over a week.
- Mid-August – **Venice Beach Showcase Celebrations**: This Boardwalk festival has plenty of children's activities, music, power-lifting demonstrations and skating and skateboarding competitions.
- Last three weekends – **African Marketplace and Cultural Fair**: A celebration of African-American communities in the US, with arts and crafts, concerts, exhibitions, traditional food, a film festival and a soccer tournament (www.africanmarketplace.org).
- Late August – **Sunset Junction Street Fair**: A weekend of live music on three stages, carnival rides and more than 200 craft, artisan and food stands (www.sunsetjunction.org).

SEPTEMBER

- Mid-September – **Los Angeles County Fair**: The world's largest county fair, held annually in Pomona, west of Los Angeles. Livestock, old-style side-shows and horse races are among the attractions (www.lacountyfair.com).
- Late September – **Lobster Festival**: Head to Redondo Beach for lobsters, local seafood, ethnic cuisine, crafts and kids' rides (www.lobsterfestival.com).

OCTOBER

- Mid-October – **AFI-LA International Film Festival**: A major film festival screening international films.

NOVEMBER

- 2nd – **Dia de los Muertos (Day of the Dead):** Music, art exhibitions and other festivities in LA's El Pueblo district (www.olvera-street.com).
- Sunday before Thanksgiving – **Doo Dah Parade**: A parody of Pasadena's Rose Parade takes place in the same town with local people lampooning just about anything of a topical nature.

DECEMBER

- Sunday after Thanksgiving – **Hollywood Christmas Parade**: Hundreds of celebrities and flamboyant floats parade along Hollywood and Sunset boulevards during this popular event.
- First week – **Downtown Tree Lighting Ceremony**: Once lit, the fir tree in the Citicorp Plaza is the focus for carol singing and other seasonal events.
- Mid-December – **Las Posadas**: Candlelit processions accompany a nine-day reenactment of the journey to Bethlehem, which takes place at Olvera Street, Downtown LA. Traditional Mexican Christmas music and children's parties complete the celebrations.

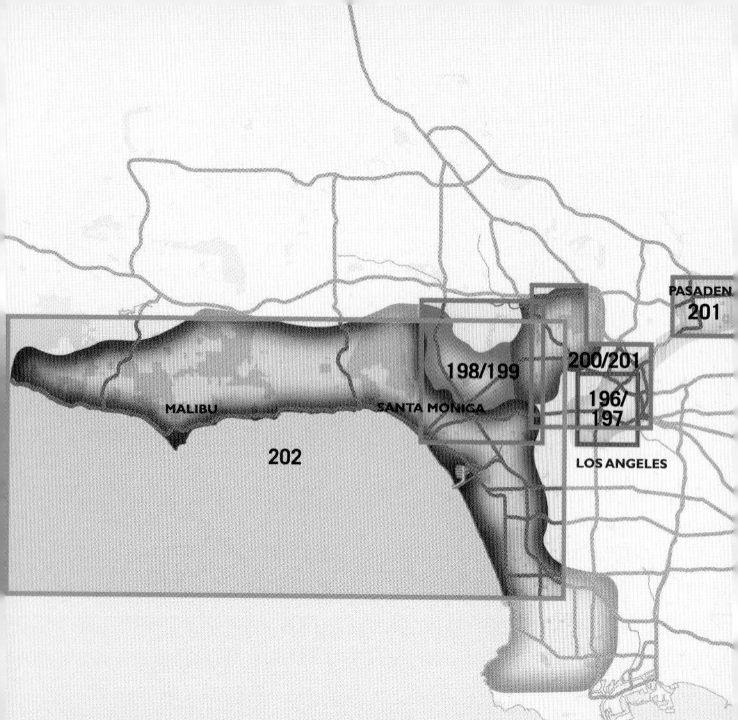

PASADENA
201
198/199
200/201
196/
197
MALIBU
SANTA MONICA
202
LOS ANGELES

To identify the regions, see the map on the inside of the front cover

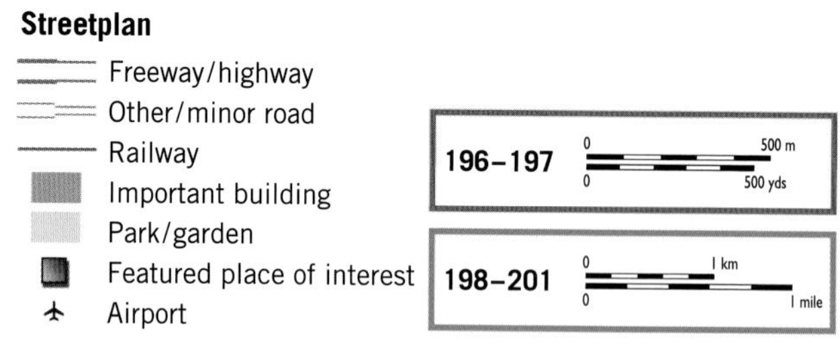

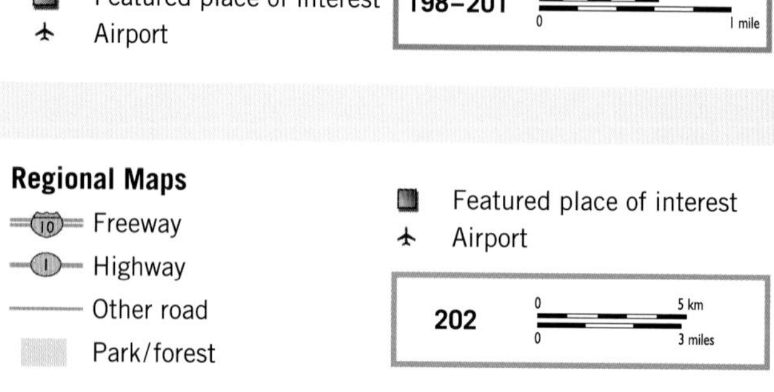

Streetplan

Downtown Los Angeles

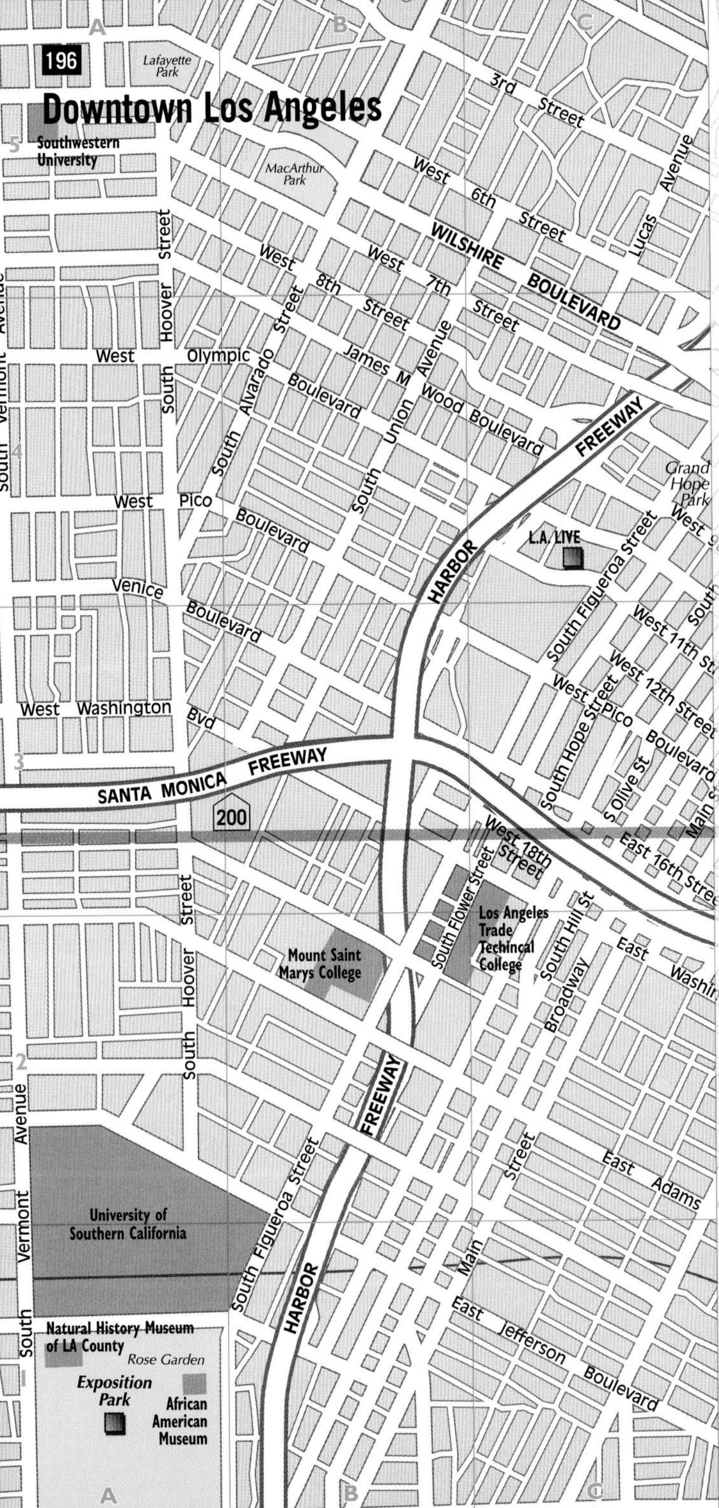

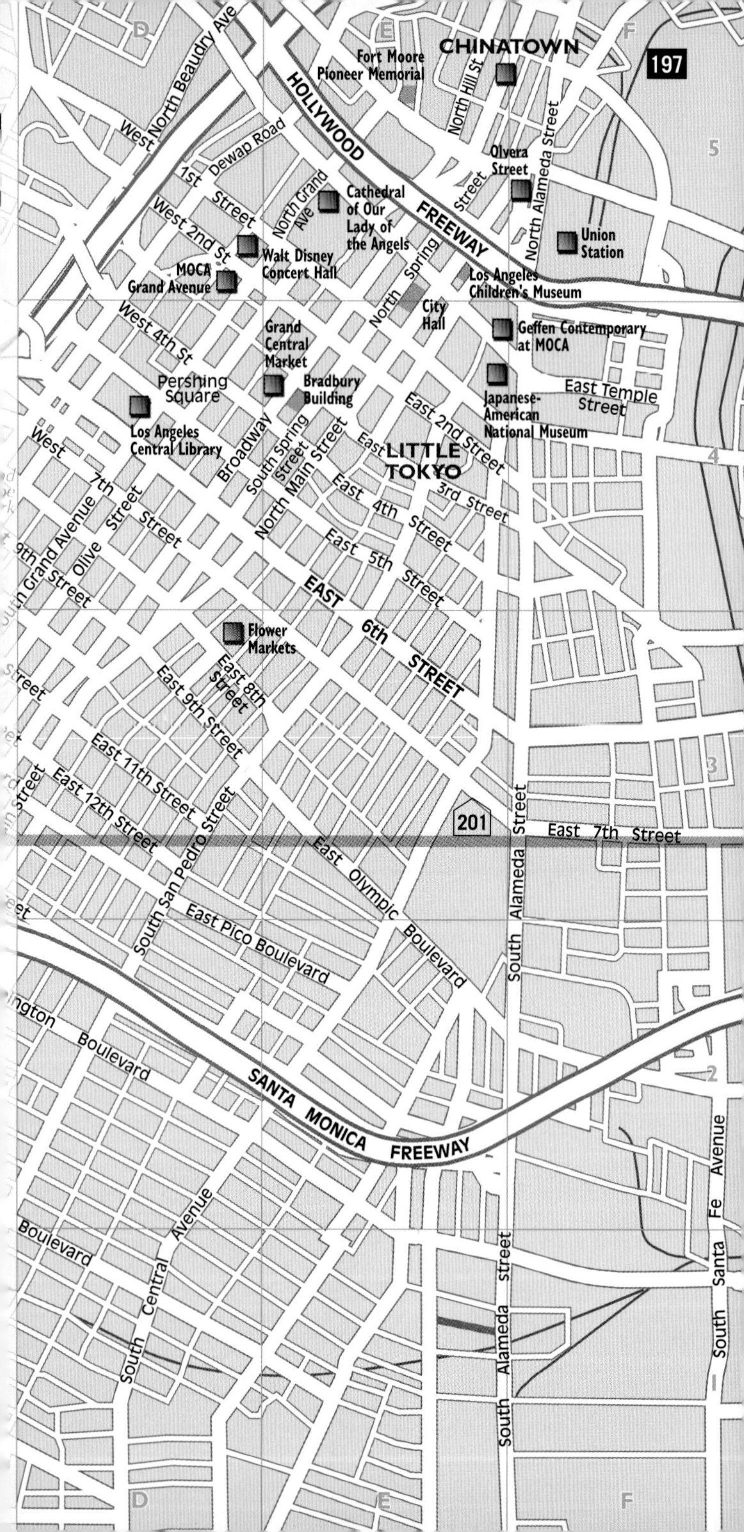

197
CHINATOWN
Fort Moore Pioneer Memorial
HOLLYWOOD FREEWAY
North Beaudry Ave
West
1st Street
Dewap Road
West 2nd St
North Grand Ave
Cathedral of Our Lady of the Angels
North Hill St
Street
Olvera Street
North Alameda Street
Union Station
Walt Disney Concert Hall
MOCA Grand Avenue
North Spring
Los Angeles Children's Museum
City Hall
West 4th St
Grand Central Market
Geffen Contemporary at MOCA
Pershing Square
Bradbury Building
Japanese-American National Museum
East Temple Street
Los Angeles Central Library
East 2nd Street
West 7th Street
Broadway
South Spring Street
North Main Street
LITTLE TOKYO
East 3rd Street
East 4th Street
South Grand Avenue
Olive Street
9th Street
East 5th Street
EAST 6th STREET
Flower Markets
East 8th Street
East 9th Street
East 11th Street
East 12th Street
South San Pedro Street
201
South Alameda Street
East 7th Street
East Olympic Boulevard
East Pico Boulevard
Boulevard
SANTA MONICA FREEWAY
Avenue
South Central Avenue
Boulevard
South Alameda Street
South Santa Fe Avenue

Westside

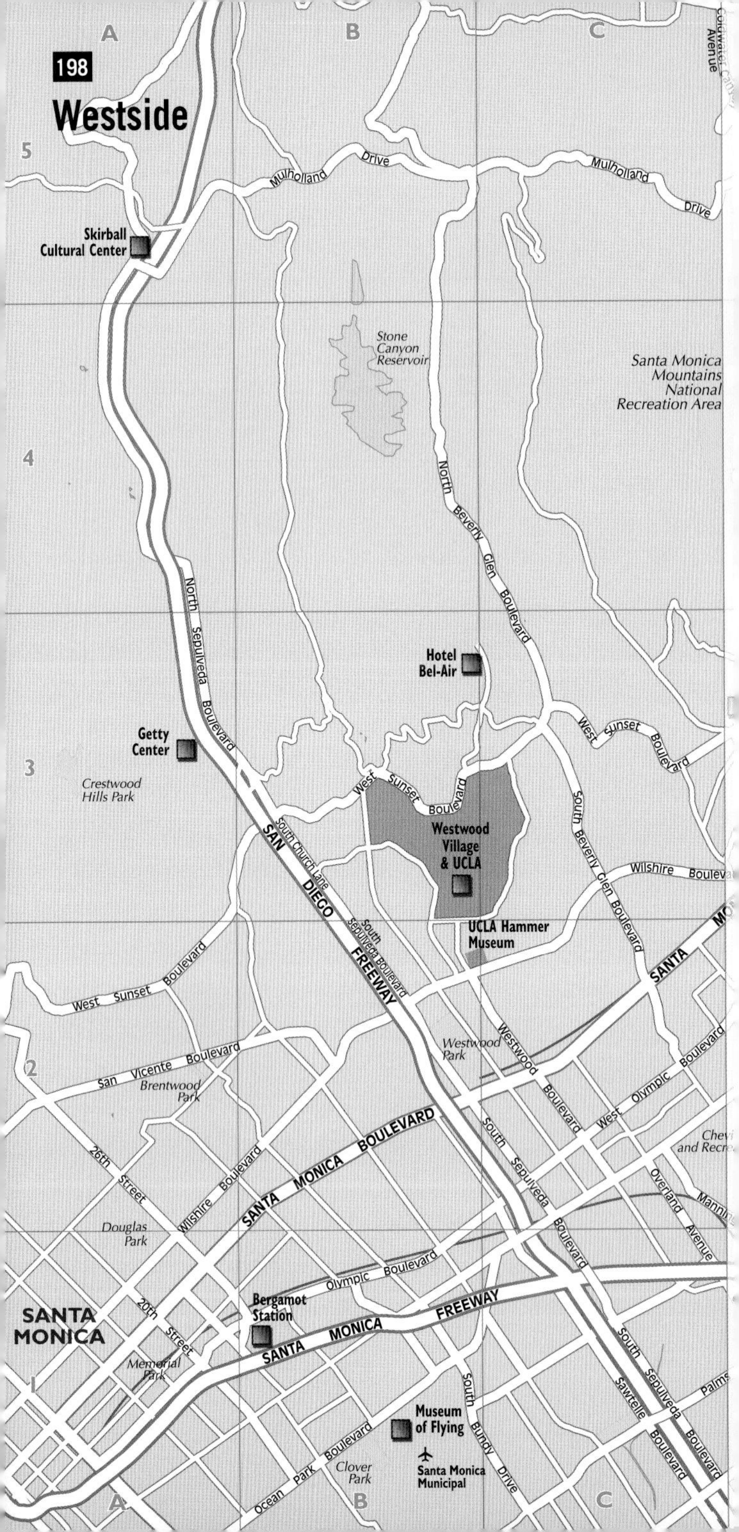
A
B
C
5
4
3
2
1
Coldwater Canyon Avenue
Mulholland Drive
Mulholland Drive
Skirball Cultural Center
Stone Canyon Reservoir
Santa Monica Mountains National Recreation Area
North Beverly Glen Boulevard
North Sepulveda Boulevard
Hotel Bel-Air
Getty Center
Crestwood Hills Park
West Sunset Boulevard
West Sunset Boulevard
Westwood Village & UCLA
SAN DIEGO FREEWAY
South Church Lane
South Beverly Glen Boulevard
Wilshire Boulevard
UCLA Hammer Museum
South Sepulveda Boulevard
West Sunset Boulevard
SANTA MONICA FREEWAY
Westwood Park
Westwood Boulevard
San Vicente Boulevard
Brentwood Park
West Olympic Boulevard
SANTA MONICA BOULEVARD
26th Street
Wilshire Boulevard
South Sepulveda Boulevard
Overland Avenue
Douglas Park
Olympic Boulevard
SANTA MONICA
Bergamot Station
20th Street
SANTA MONICA FREEWAY
Memorial Park
South Bundy Drive
Museum of Flying
Santa Monica Municipal
Ocean Park Boulevard
Clover Park
South Sawtelle Boulevard
South Sepulveda Boulevard
Palms

West Hollywood

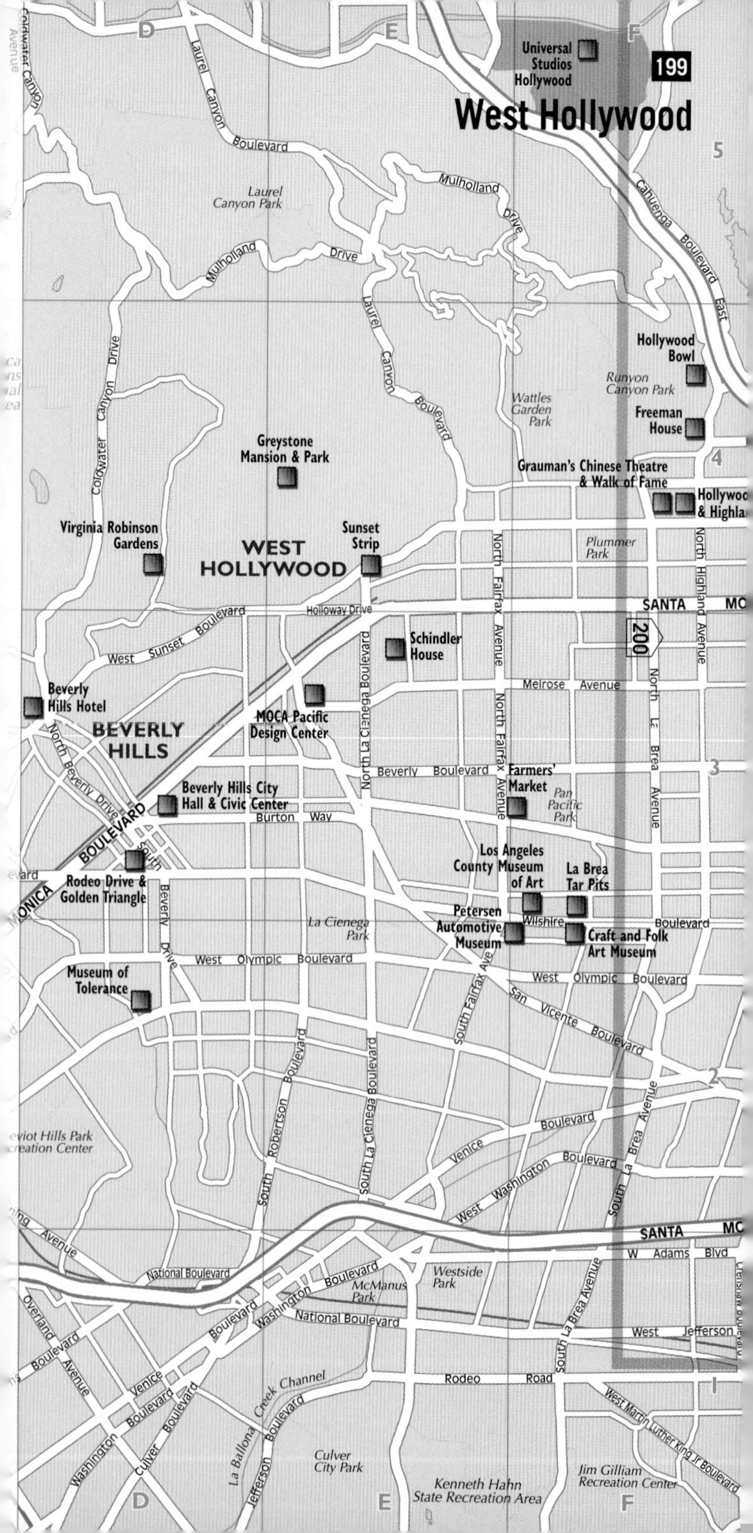

200
Griffith Park
A
B
C
5
4
3
2
1
Disney Studios
Johnny Carson Park
Forest Lawn Drive
Buena Vista Park
Toluca Lake
Autry Museum of Western Heritage
Los Angeles Zoo
Universal Studios Hollywood
Hollywood Sign
Griffith Park
Cahuenga Boulevard East
Hollywood Reservoir
Griffith Observatory
Drive
Hollywood Bowl
Runyon Canyon Park
Wattles Garden Park
Freeman House
Los Feliz Boulevard
Franklin Avenue
HOLLYWOOD FREEWAY
N Wilton Pl
Hollyhock House
Grauman's Chinese Theatre & Walk of Fame
Hollywood & Highland
Hollywood Boulevard
North Western Avenue
Barnsdall Park
North Vermont Avenue
Plummer Park
Vine Street
Fountain Avenue
North Highland Avenue
SANTA MONICA BOULEVARD
Santa Monica Boulevard
Hollywood Forever
North Rossmore Avenue
North Western Avenue
Melrose Avenue
Melrose Avenue
North La Brea Avenue
199
North Fairfax Avenue
North Normandie Avenue
Beverly Boulevard
Beverly
Farmers' Market
Pan Pacific Park
South Rossmore Avenue
South Wilton Place
South Western Avenue
West 3rd Street
Angeles Museum of Art
La Brea Tar Pits
Lafayette Park
Wilshire Boulevard
Wilshire Boulevard
196
Craft and Folk Art Museum
Southwestern University
West Olympic Boulevard
San Vicente Boulevard
West Olympic Boulevard
Crenshaw Boulevard
Arlington Avenue
South Normandie Avenue
South Vermont Avenue
West Pico Boulevard
Boulevard
Venice Boulevard
South La Brea Avenue
Washington Boulevard
West Washington Boulevard
SANTA MONICA FREEWAY
W Adams Blvd
Crenshaw Boulevard
South Hoover Street
South Normandie Avenue
West Jefferson Boulevard
West Jefferson Boulevard
University of Southern California

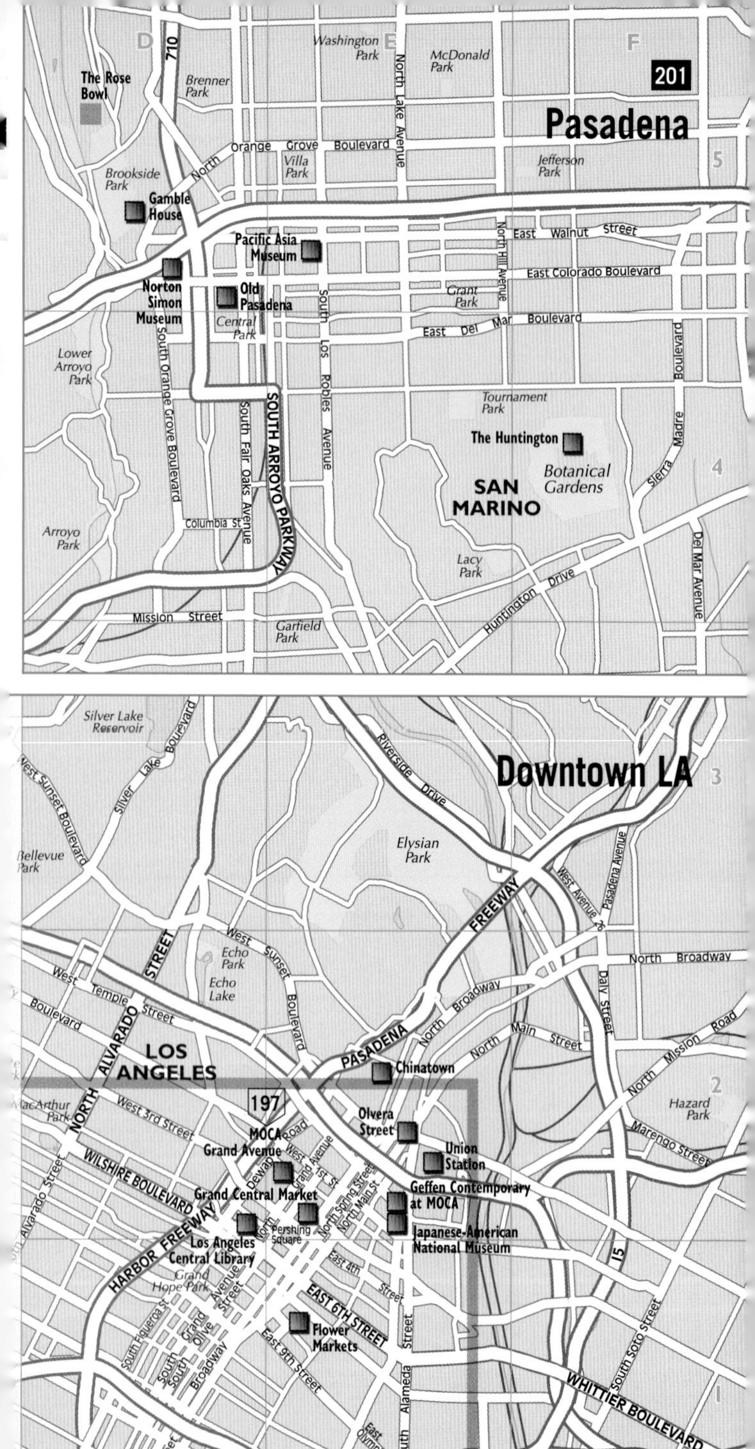

201
Pasadena
The Rose Bowl
Gamble House
Norton Simon Museum
Pacific Asia Museum
Old Pasadena
The Huntington
Botanical Gardens
SAN MARINO
Washington Park
McDonald Park
Brenner Park
Villa Park
Jefferson Park
Brookside Park
Central Park
Grant Park
Lower Arroyo Park
Tournament Park
Arroyo Park
Lacy Park
Garfield Park
North Orange Grove Boulevard
North Lake Avenue
East Walnut Street
North Hill Avenue
East Colorado Boulevard
East Del Mar Boulevard
South Los Robles Avenue
South Orange Grove Boulevard
South Fair Oaks Avenue
SOUTH ARROYO PARKWAY
Columbia St
Mission Street
Huntington Drive
Sierra Madre Boulevard
Del Mar Avenue
Downtown LA
Silver Lake Reservoir
Silver Lake Boulevard
West Sunset Boulevard
Bellevue Park
Riverside Drive
Elysian Park
Echo Park
Echo Lake
West Temple Street
Boulevard
NORTH ALVARADO STREET
LOS ANGELES
MacArthur Park
West 3rd Street
WILSHIRE BOULEVARD
HARBOR FREEWAY
PASADENA FREEWAY
North Broadway
North Main Street
North Mission Road
West Avenue 26
Pasadena Avenue
Daly Street
Hazard Park
Marengo Street
Chinatown
Olvera Street
Union Station
MOCA Grand Avenue
Grand Central Market
Geffen Contemporary at MOCA
Japanese-American National Museum
Los Angeles Central Library
Pershing Square
Grand Hope Park
Flower Markets
Dewap Road
West 1st St
Grand Avenue
North Spring Street
North Main St.
East 4th Street
EAST 6TH STREET
East 9th Street
South Figueroa St
South Grand
South Olive
Broadway
South Alameda Street
East Olympic Boulevard
South Soto Street
WHITTIER BOULEVARD
SANTA MONICA FREEWAY
East Washington Bvd
Main Street
197
710
15

South Bay
A
B
C
D
E
3
2
1
202
198
Paramount Ranch
Malibu Creek State Park
Malibu Canyons
Malibu Creek
Santa Monica Mountains National Recreation Area
Topanga State Park
Topanga Canyon
Will Rogers State Historic Park
Self-Realization Fellowship Lake Shrine
Will Rogers State Beach
Skirball Cultural Center
Getty Center
Hotel Bel-Air
Virginia Robinson Gardens
Greystone Mansion & Park
Sunset Strip
Beverly Hills Hotel
Schindler House
Rodeo Drive & Golden Triangle
Westwood Village & UCLA
Museum of Tolerance
Uplifters Club & Rustic Canyon Recreation Center
Montana Avenue
Bergamot Station
Museum of Flying
Santa Monica Beach & Pier
Main Street
California Heritage Museum
Marina del Rey
Venice Beach & Boardwalk
SANTA MONICA
SANTA MONICA FWY
CULVER CITY
Los Angeles International Airport
S SEPULVEDA BLVD
SAN DIEGO FWY
EL SEGUNDO
MANHATTAN BEACH
South Bay
Yerba Buena Beach
North Beach
Leo Carrillo State Beach
South Beach
Nicholas Canyon
El Pescador & La Piedra
Encinal Beach
El Matador
Trancas Beach
Zuma Beach
Westward Beach
Point Dume State Beach
Paradise Cove
Escondido Beach
Dan Blocker State Beach
PACIFIC COAST HIGHWAY
Malibu
Costa Beach
Big Rock Beach
Santa Monica Bay
1
10
23
27
42
105
405